The Hadassah Jewish Holiday Cookbook

Traditional Recipes from Contemporary Kosher Kitchens

The Hadassah Jewish Holiday Cookbook

Traditional Recipes from Contemporary Kosher Kitchens

EDITED BY JOAN SCHWARTZ MICHEL

INTRODUCTIONS BY *Rabbi Robert Sternberg, Claudia Roden, Steven Raichlen, Edda Servi Machlin, Susan R. Friedland, and Joan Nathan*

PHOTOGRAPHS BY LOUIS WALLACH

UNIVERSE

Published by Universe Publishing
A Division of Rizzoli International Publications, Inc.
300 Park Avenue South
New York, NY 10010
www.rizzoliusa.com

© 2008 Universe Publishing
Food photography © 2002 Louis Wallach

Photo and Project Editor: Ellin Yassky
Book Design: Lori S. Malkin
Photo Styling: Nir Adar

PHOTOGRAPHY CREDITS

©The Jewish Museum of New York/Art Resource, NY. The Jewish
Museum, New York, N.Y., U.S.A.: p. 55 (Accession #1984-71) (Coxe-
Goldberg Photography, Inc.); p. 111; p. 112 (Accession #1993-248)
(Joseph Parenell); p. 128 (Accession # JM19-64); p. 185 (Accession #
1999-85) (Richard Hori).

HUC Skirball Cultural Center, Museum Collection: pp. 13 (HUCSM
18.40), 14 (HUCSM 11.46a,b), 15 (HUCSM 33.19), 17 (HUCSM
73.10.4a–g) (Susan Einstein); pp. 56 (HUCSM 8.7), 134 (HUCSM
50.12), 135 (HUCSM 50.42), 196 (HUCSM 22.23) (John Reed
Forsman); p. 203 (HUCSM 23.41) (D. R. Guthrie); pp. 26 (HUCSM
33a.1), 237 (HUCSM 34.1) (Marvin Rand).

Institute of Contemporary History and Wiener Library, U.K.: p. 32.

2008 2009 2010 2011 / 10 9 8 7 6 5 4 3 2 1

ISBN-13: 978-0-7893-9991-5

Library of Congress Catalog Control Number: 2007932829

Printed in China

Acknowledgments

Many heartfelt thanks to everyone who made this happen.

To Hugh Lauter Levin, for wanting to do something special for Hadassah and coming up with the inspiration for this book; Alan M. Tigay, my fearless executive editor at *Hadassah Magazine*, for jump-starting the project and for his unwavering confidence and support; Deborah Meisels for everything including the bread; Zelda Shluker and David Shluker for their wonderful way with words; Alana Sher who should drop the law-school idea and become an editor; Libby Goldberg for her eagle eye and Daniel Kronengold for *his* eagle eye; Leah Finkelshteyn for her pats on the back; Dot Silfen for her suggestions and encouragement; to Jodie Berzin Rossi, and of course, to Bob DeBono.

This book would not have been possible without the wonderful movement called Hadassah, and I offer special thanks to three women who embody the larger organization—to Edith Zamost, former *Hadassah Magazine* chair, who had the faith; to Ruth B Hurwitz, chair of *Hadassah Magazine*, for her support and encouragement; and to Bonnie Lipton, Hadassah's national president, for her dedicated leadership and (not coincidentally) for her recipe for Hamantaschen.

Thanks also to Lori Malkin for her artistry and her in-a-pinch hand-holding. To recipe testers Helen Jones, Lori Shrager, Fran Sheff Mauer, and Penny Parkes, to Amy Freedman Gershberg, Stephen Perle, and Jane Yagoda Goodman. Many thanks to Louis Wallach and Nir Adar for their consummate skill in making everything look so great. And to Ellin Yassky for her guidance and good spirit, her warmth, knowledge, and understanding; a very patient person who made it all a lot of fun—and never lost her cool.

But most of all, thanks to my sweet mother, Ruthe Cohen Schwartz, whose magic way with food was an inspiration; and to my much-loved aunt, Henrietta Goldman, whose dedication to Hadassah is unbounded.

Table of Contents

SABBATH CHALLAH, recipe page 22.

PREFACE

by *Joan Schwartz Michel*

Joan Schwartz Michel is senior editor at Hadassah Magazine *and writes a food and recipes column for* The New York Jewish Week. *She has worked on a* Better Homes and Gardens *series,* Good Home Cooking, *and a Time-Life series,* Great Meals in Minutes, *and has numerous other cookbooks to her credit, including* The Foods of Israel Today, Good Enough to Eat *and* The Woman's Day Cookbook.

Hadassah's hallmark was always practical Zionism. While other organizations in the early Zionist movement engaged in debate, Hadassah built. By the time Israel was born, Hadassah had built much of the new state's medical and social welfare infrastructure.

Those early volunteers also recognized that any army—including an army of volunteers and their families—functioned best on a full stomach. So the Hadassah woman was always ready to roll up her sleeves not only to build but also to cook. It was in 1931 that the Hadassah women of Dorchester, Massachusetts, decided to put the activities together and produce the first fundraising cookbook. In 1948, the year of Israel's creation, came *Cook Book* from the Halifax chapter, and by 1966 it was *Edible Artistry,* by the women of the Lakeside, California, group.

Perhaps best known of all is the *Rochester Hadassah Cookbook* with its Ashkenazic and Sephardic components and extended Passover section. It has seen nine printings since 1972 and is still going strong. It has earned over $400,000 for Hadassah. That's a lot of cookies.

Once the women discovered this way to raise money for Hadassah they were on a roll. And they did it in all kinds of ways—from the spiral-bound *Eppes Essen* in 1978 from St. Petersburg, Florida, with its hand-sketched line drawings, to *Let's Eat* from Oklahoma City where women identified themselves as Mrs. Mendel and Mrs. Ben; from the stapled-together pages from Grand Rapids, Michigan, to the elegant productions from Chicago.

The books went through phases that reflected the changing American Jewish table. In the beginning, there were efforts to adapt all-American recipes to kashrut, passing through the jello-mold craze of the 40s to the frozen-food frenzy of the 50s. The 60s heralded the chicken chow mein era, and other friendly foods followed, such as Arroz Con Pollo, Brazilian Rice, Turkish White Bean Salad, an eclectic Bubbie's

Potato Lasagne, and the Peking Duck genre. And with an increasing health-food consciousness came turkey burgers, whole-wheat breads, brown rice, and all kinds of takes on veggies.

But did the chefs of Hadassah ever forget the old standby favorites, the latkes and bimuelos, kugels and adafinas that dreams are made of? Sure, sometimes they reduced the fat, and maybe the salt, but they never *ever* sacrificed the flavor.

These are foods that are our tradition, that constitute our history—and our future. Make no mistake about it; tradition survives only in the observance of it. The Jewish people have survived through faith, learning, dedication, education—and the special foods that mark our celebrations and our commemorations of the cycles of life.

All the recipes in this book have been checked and rechecked for adherence to kashrut, but if you have doubts about anything, please consult with your rabbi.

Our attention to detail in the Passover section was as scrupulous as possible. The most common forms of such products as mayonnaise, ketchup, anything made from soy, flavor extracts, vinegar, alcohol (anything made from grain, or anything that might have come in contact with it) are not kosher for Passover. Although we did not specify kosher-for-Passover versions of these products, we took the use of them for granted.

Also bear in mind that during Passover, Ashkenazim and Sephardim take different approaches to eating foods such as rice, peas, and legumes, while some Jews refrain from eating matza or matza products that have been soaked in any liquid. Again, when in doubt check with your rabbi.

Here are recipes, over 250 of the best, from Hadassah's great cooks around America and from Israel, and across generations. Hadassah women are as famous for their ways with glassfuls and pinches, with "till it feels right" and "you'll know when it's done" as they are for their building and support of hospitals and schools. This book is a tribute to the practical Zionism that connects nurturing a nation to nurturing a family.

Shabbat

SHABBAT HA-MALKAH

Introduction by Rabbi Robert Sternberg

Executive director of the Hatikvah
Holocaust Education Resource Center
in Springfield, Massachusetts, as well
as an outstanding cook and food
writer, Rabbi Robert Sternberg brings
a unique approach to Jewish cooking:
He treats it as gourmet cuisine.

A member of The International
Association of Culinary Professionals
and The James Beard Foundation,
Rabbi Sternberg is the author of
Yiddish Cuisine (Jason Aronson) and
The Sephardic Kitchen (Harper Collins).
In these books, besides wonderful tradi-
tional recipes, he offers rich cultural
histories, holiday traditions, and
charming folktales.

Page 10–11, top left: SHABBAT CHALLAH,
recipe page 22; *top right:* GEFILTE FISH,
recipe page 19; *right:* IRMA'S MATZA BALLS,
recipe page 29.

OPPOSITE: KIDDUSH CUP. *Hana Geber.
New York, 1982. Bronze, cast, and silver-
plated. HUC Skirball Cultural Center,
Museum Collection. Gift of the Artist.*

A GIFT FROM GOD

The Talmud (Shabbat 119a) calls Shabbat "Queen [ha-Malkah] of the Week." It is hard for me to describe the feeling that envelops me when I watch the sun sink beneath the horizon on Friday and I welcome in another Shabbat. No matter how rich or how colorful or how vivid an image I create, the awe I experience every time I visit Israel and climb the Mount of Olives to view the ancient walled city of Jerusalem as Shabbat approaches can never be fully conveyed in words. To really understand and appreciate Shabbat, it needs to be experienced, not only once, but over and over again.

Shabbat is the most important day in the religious life of a Jew. To understand Shabbat is to understand at a level beyond anything that words can express of our identity as Jews. Shabbat is our past, our present, and our future. Shabbat connects us with the creation of the world, with the Exodus of our people from slavery in Egypt, with our spiritual liberation at Sinai, and with our vision of the messianic era and the world to come.

As a concept, Shabbat actually existed before the Jewish people existed. There is even some debate in the Talmud about whether the first Jews (Abraham, Isaac, Jacob, Sarah, Rebecca, Rachel, and Leah) observed the Sabbath. But after we received the Torah, observance of Shabbat became a clear obligation for all Jews. The Fourth Commandment states, "In six days God created heaven and earth and sea and all that is in them . . . And God rested on the seventh day . . . Therefore God blessed the seventh day, Shabbat, and made it Holy . . ." (Exodus 20:11). We were commanded to remember how the world was created and how God rested on the seventh day after the work of creation was finished. By celebrating Shabbat every week we do the same as God did. We set aside the seventh day of the week every week to rest from our own creative endeavors. Shabbat was to be our most precious and special mitzvah. "It will be a sign for all time between Me and the people of Israel" (Exodus 31:17).

Shabbat is also directly linked to the Exodus from Egypt; the second time the Ten Commandments appear in the Torah, that link is emphasized: "Neither you, your children, your servants, your animals, or strangers within your gates shall do any creative work . . . You should remember that you were slaves in Egypt and that God brought you out . . . Therefore God commanded you to keep the Sabbath Day . . ." (Deuteronomy 5:14–15). We are commanded to remember the anguish of our experience as slaves to the Egyptians, who never allowed us a single day of rest. And in remembrance of this, the Torah tells us to extend the spirit of Shabbat to everyone and everything around us.

In the Midrash, *Olam HaBah* (the world to come) is described as a *Yom She-kuloh Shabbat*, one long, eternal Sabbath day. *Ye-mot HaMoshiach*, the messianic era, is described the same way. According to the Talmud, if every single Jew everywhere in the world was to celebrate Shabbat on the same Sabbath, the messianic era would begin immediately and the rest of life from this point forward would be experienced as one eternal Shabbat. It would also be an era of permanent peace in which war and conflict would no longer exist.

Shabbat is central to our spiritual fulfillment as a faith community. It is also central to our relationship with the entire human family. Everything a Jew does revolves around preparing for Shabbat.

SHABBAT IN THE HOME

From time immemorial, activity in the Jewish kitchen has revolved around preparation for Shabbat. The tastiest, most elaborate, and most beautiful meals have always been those made for Shabbat. In many Jewish homes, the Friday night dinner generally includes a fish course, a soup, and a meat course as well as a dessert, but what goes into the dishes can vary considerably within the ethnic communities of the Jewish world. All Jews bake a special kind of bread for Shabbat that is different from the bread eaten the rest of the week. The traditional lunch on Shabbat is an elaborate meal composed of many different cold dishes and one hot dish that has been set to cook on Friday before Shabbat begins. Once again, there are differences in these dishes that vary from Jewish community to community. A third meal, the *Seudah Sh'lishit*, is eaten before the conclusion of Shabbat on Saturday night. This is usually a meal of cold dishes. Challah is eaten both at Shabbat dinner and

Shabbat lunch and, while the *Seudah Sh'lishit* requirement can be fulfilled technically by eating a cake or some fruit or cookies, most traditionally observant Jews also eat bread at this meal.

A blessing over wine, the Kiddush, is made at both the Shabbat dinner and the Shabbat lunch. Candles are also lit at the start of Shabbat. Some Sephardic and Mizrachi (Middle Eastern) Jews also welcome Shabbat with a blessing over sweet-smelling spices. At the end of Shabbat, another ceremony, Havdalah, is made using wine, spices, and candles to bid goodbye to Shabbat and ask that the spirit of goodness that surrounds Shabbat be carried forward into the work week.

THE SPECIAL FOODS

Cuisine is a composite of three ingredients: the raw materials available to the cook in a particular climate and during a particular season, the cooking methods common to a particular region, and the artistry and creativity of the cook. These three elements were the basis of everything that gave cooking around the world regional differences. Jewish cooking, besides being influenced by regional cuisine, had to consider the laws of kashrut. Jews lived in almost every country in the world, and by applying kashrut to their regional cuisines, they created kosher versions of many local recipes. They also invented some that were uniquely Jewish. In addition, Jews made many contributions to the cuisines of the countries in which they lived. The laws of Shabbat, which prohibit cooking as a form of creative activity, have been responsible for many of these uniquely Jewish dishes.

For example, bread is the staple food of much of the world's people, and in most places it is baked every day. Daily bread is a simple dish, usually made only from flour, water, and yeast. It tastes best the day it is made. Day-old bread often needs to be refreshed by being warmed or toasted. The Jewish Sabbath breads all contain ingredients that increase the shelf life of the bread as well as enrich its flavor. Oil, eggs, and sugar are commonly added. These ingredients make the bread rich, extra moist, and flavorful, and they slow down the staling process so that the bread can still taste fresh the day after it is baked. It is no wonder that every recipe for challah, the most universal and best known of the Jewish Sabbath breads, always

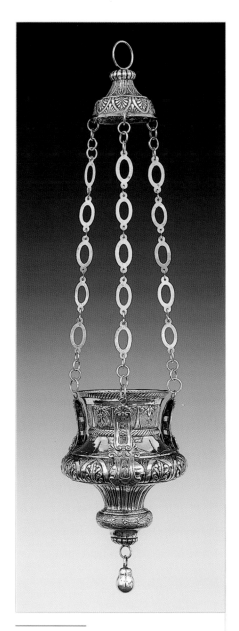

ABOVE: NER TAMID. *Naples, Italy. 1832-
1872. Silver, cast and repoussé. HUC Skirball
Cultural Center, Museum Collection. Gift of
Mr. and Mrs. Isadore Schagrin, Wilmington,
Delaware, in memory of their fathers, Mr.
Charles W. Schagrin and Mr. Isaac Starr.*

OPPOSITE: CANDLESTICKS. *Warsaw, early
20th century. Silverplate. HUC Skirball
Cultural Center, Museum Collection. Gift of
Dr. Eugene I. Majerowicz.*

contains oil, eggs, and sugar. In some countries, spices such as anise seeds
are also added to Shabbat challahs to give them extra flavor.

Fish dishes are important on Shabbat because fish are linked with
the messianic era. They are also associated with purity in Jewish tradition.
During the Great Flood in the time of Noah, the fish were the only animals
that weren't destroyed because, according to the Midrash, "they were without sin." In Ashkenazic countries, where fresh fish was expensive and hard
to come by, gefilte fish was invented by Jewish cooks as a kind of fish
stretcher. Freshwater fish like carp, pike, and whitefish were mixed with
other ingredients (onions, eggs, matza meal, carrots, and seasonings), and
every portion of the finished gefilte fish contained at least "a taste" of fish. In
Mediterranean countries fresh fish were much more available and many
interesting fish dishes were prepared using exotic herbs and spices, vegetables, nuts, and even fruits like plums or dates. Most of the fish dishes
served by Jews on Shabbat are eaten cold as a first course for dinner. But
some Sephardic Jews traditionally eat fish as their main course on Friday
night, often served with agristada (an egg-lemon sauce), temino
(a spicy tomato sauce), or simply cooked with garlic and fresh herbs.

Foods stuffed with meat and vegetable mixtures are another cate-
gory of traditional Shabbat dishes. The custom of eating these kinds of
dishes on Shabbat evolved from the belief that the manna given to the
Hebrews by God when they wandered in the Sinai wilderness was given
as a double portion on Shabbat. Because manna was believed to acquire
the taste of anything a person desired, the double portion of manna could
offer two different taste experiences, one stuffed inside the other. The
oldest known dish of this kind is pashtida, a kind of meat pie mentioned
many times in the Talmud. The word pashtida also appears in medieval
Spanish manuscripts, indicating that this type of food was part of the
culinary repertoire of the Jews in Spain. Impanadas, buleymas, borekas,
boyos, cigaras, hishak, rodanchas, pasteles, pastelikos, knishes, pireshkes,
tapads, sambousah, and pittas are all forms of savory stuffed pastries.
They are made with meat, fish, vegetables, herbs, cheese, and grain fillings
(i.e., kasha knishes). In Morocco, pastilla, one of the most elaborate savory
pastries, is made with three different fillings. Jews in Arab countries made
kibbeh, a stuffed savory pie with a shell of bulgur wheat filled with a spicy
ground meat mixture. Ashkenazic Jews also make kreplach, a type of
stuffed pasta. Jews from Kurdistan, Iraq, and Syria make kooba, a type
of meat-filled dumpling served in a soup on Shabbat. Stuffed cabbages,

grape leaves, zucchini, tomatoes, peppers, eggplants, artichokes, fennel bulbs, potatoes, quinces, and even rice cakes filled with meat called kobeba are traditional Shabbat dishes in different parts of the Jewish world. In Middle Eastern countries, dried fruits like apricots, prunes, and dates are stuffed with marzipan-like mixtures made of almonds, walnuts, or pistachios and served as part of dessert.

Hamin, a dish made of meat and other ingredients and cooked overnight in a very slow oven, is the first name given to that great variety of dishes made for Shabbat lunch throughout the Jewish world. This term comes from the Talmud but is still used by Sephardic and Middle Eastern Jews whose cooking was influenced by the cuisine developed in Babel (Babylonia). Other names for this type of dish are cholent, adafina, s'cheena, chalebibi, and loubi. Iraqi Jews made a hamin-type dish called tabeet, which is a combination of chicken and rice. In some communities, Ashkenazic and Sephardic, pots of the hamin or cholent were put into a communal oven, usually in the bakery, by each family and then brought home on Saturday after synagogue services. Hamin recipes vary from region to region but usually follow a similar prototype—a combination of meat, beans, root vegetables, and grains seasoned according to regional preference. Some Jews also put eggs into the hamin or add kneidlach or derma (dumplings), which absorb the flavors of everything in the pot as they expand. The long, slow cooking draws out sumptuous flavors. Hamin is believed to be the origin of many of Europe's favorite winter stews including French cassoulet, Spanish cocida, and Polish bigos.

SHABBAT GOES INTERNATIONAL

With globalization, economic interdependence, and the mass migrations of people from various countries throughout the world, regionality in cooking has become more of a historical memory than a living reality. Most countries today are diverse and multicultural. Israel is one of the most diverse and multiethnic countries of all. Jewish communities in other parts of the world are no different. Most Jews cook and eat eclectically and dishes from many types of cuisines often appear side by side in the same meal. While it still makes sense from a nutritional, economic, and culinary standpoint to live within the rhythm of the seasons, it is possible to make interesting and tasty meals by combining complementary dishes from a variety of ethnic cuisines in one meal. Shabbat becomes even more interesting and enjoyable

OPPOSITE: KIDDUSH SET FROM TREE OF LIFE SHTENDER. *Noah Greenberg and David Moss. © 2002 Bezalel Editions Limited, Sarasota, Florida. Design: Israel, 1990s. Walnut, silver. HUC Skirball Cultural Center, Museum Collection. Gift of Lee and Irving Kalsman in honor of their daughter Peachy Levy.*

when the challah is made with a variety of whole grains in addition to white flour, when the stuffed vegetable is a type of tropical fruit or vegetable like chayote or plantain, or when the Shabbat hamin is a Mexican chili con carne or a Creole gumbo with kosher ingredients.

One of my most memorable Shabbat dinners was one I prepared for some of my university students. I served them what I thought was a fairly simple meal—a variety of appetizers (chopped liver, hummus, kibbutz salad, and eggplant salad) followed by a chicken roasted with garlic and herbs, a rice pilav, and my grandmother's carrot and parsnip tzimmes. My guests were familiar with many of these foods but some of them were still surprised by how "different" they thought the food tasted that night. One of them asked me jokingly if I had added some secret ingredient to make everything taste so good.

"Shabbat is the only thing that is different here tonight," I explained. "This night itself is what is special to me—being here together, sharing a meal, having fun, getting to know each other better, and deepening our relationship because we are experiencing Shabbat together. This is something beautiful that all of us who are here tonight can carry away with them. The memory of this evening. I think that this is the only real secret ingredient in my recipes."

The time we spent together was a precious gift to all of us—a gift that was ours only because God gave us for one night in the week the chance to share Shabbat.

Shabbat Shalom!

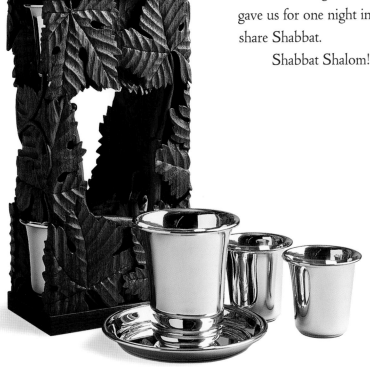

Chopped Liver

TIP
Consult your rabbinical authority
about how to kasher liver.

4 large onions, chopped
Olive oil as needed
Chicken broth as needed
1 pound chicken livers

6 hard-cooked eggs, cooled, cut
in quarters
Salt and freshly ground pepper
to taste

1. Preheat broiler. Sauté onions in 1 tablespoon olive oil and enough chicken broth to cover bottom of pan. Cook until translucent, adding more broth as needed.

2. Prepare livers, removing connecting and fatty tissue. Broil until kashered and tender. Let cool, cutting and discarding any crisp parts.

3. Combine onions in broth, the eggs, and livers in food processor; process until smooth. If necessary, add small amount of oil for desired consistency. Season with salt and pepper.

Makes about 3 cups

•§ MARY WAISLER, DIX HILLS HADASSAH, NEW YORK

Henrietta Szold's Stewed Fish with Lemon Velouté

1 medium onion, sliced
2 carrots, sliced
2 celery stalks with leaves, sliced
6 sprigs parsley
1 teaspoon white peppercorns
1 teaspoon ground ginger
Salt and freshly ground
   pepper to taste
4 pounds salmon, halibut, striped bass,
   sea trout, or rockfish, cut in steaks

VELOUTÉ
2 tablespoons unsalted butter
2 tablespoons all-purpose flour
2 egg yolks, well beaten
Juice of 1 lemon

Lemon slices for garnish
Chopped parsley for garnish

1. Put 2 quarts water in a flat, wide pan or fish poacher; add onion, carrots, celery, parsley, peppercorns, ginger, and salt and pepper. Bring to a boil, lower heat, and simmer, covered, 20 minutes to make a vegetable bouillon.

2. Put fish in bouillon. Bring to a boil, reduce heat, and simmer, covered,

The taste for sugar, acquired early on by the Hasidim, was eagerly promoted among their followers who settled in the areas of Volhynia and Podolia in Poland in the 1700s. It became widely cultivated in these provinces, where its pleasing taste enhanced traditional foods such as gefilte fish (elsewhere it was prepared with pepper) and became associated with the joy and sweetness of religious celebration.

By the early nineteenth century, the sugar beet was grown extensively in the south of Poland, where Hasidism was dominant, and by 1914 it appears that two-thirds of the industry was in Jewish hands.

10 minutes for each inch of thickness, until fish flakes easily with a fork. Remove fish, skin and bone it, and set aside. Strain liquid and reserve 2 cups.

3. Make velouté: In another pan, melt butter and stir in flour. Cook 2 minutes, stirring, and pour in the 2 cups fish bouillon, stirring until smooth. Add some sauce to well-beaten egg yolks, and pour the mixture back into the sauce, beating thoroughly. Add lemon juice to make the sauce creamy but don't let it boil again. Pour over fish. Garnish with lemon slices and parsley.

Serves 6 to 8

◆§ ILANIT GROUP OF HEWLETT HADASSAH, NEW YORK

Gefilte Fish

4 onions, diced	Salt and freshly ground pepper
Vegetable oil	to taste
3 pounds skinned and boned fish	1/4 cup bread crumbs or
(1-1/2 pounds salmon,	matza meal
1-1/2 pounds white fish),	2 carrots, grated
bones reserved	3 eggs, lightly beaten
2 teaspoons sugar	Horseradish for serving

1. Steam and sauté onions in a small amount of oil until golden. Grind fish, then grind in half the browned onions, the sugar, salt, and pepper, bread crumbs or matza meal, and 1 cup water (it will probably take another cup of water before finished). Chop in large chopping bowl, or beat in electric mixer, and add carrots. After fish has been chopped or beaten for a while, add eggs and continue chopping, adding more water in the process.

2. Place into a large kettle fish bones, remainder of browned onions, and water to fill about one third of the pot. Add salt and pepper and bring to a boil.

3. Keeping hands moistened with water, form fish mix into desired sized balls and drop into boiling water. Reduce heat to a simmer and cook, covered, at least 3-1/2 hours. Let cool in liquid. Serve with horseradish.

Serves about 6 to 8

◆§ PORTLAND HADASSAH, OREGON

Sweet and Sour Fish

3 pounds cleaned whitefish, cut in serving-size pieces	2 large onions, sliced
1 cup cider vinegar	2 teaspoons salt, approximately
Juice of 1 lemon	1 cup packed dark brown sugar
2 tablespoons mixed pickling spices, tied in cheesecloth	1/4 cup golden raisins
	6 gingersnaps, crumbled

1. Use a large heavy pan so there will be only one layer of fish. Bring to a boil cider vinegar, 2 cups water, the lemon juice, pickling spices, onions, salt, brown sugar, and raisins. Simmer, covered, 15 minutes.

2. Place fish in stock; cook uncovered over medium heat 20 to 30 minutes, until tender. Shake pan several times to keep fish from sticking.

3. Make paste of ginger snaps and 1/4 cup hot stock; pour over fish toward end of cooking. Let fish cool in liquid. Remove from pan; spoon stock around fish; chill. Prepare a day or two in advance. Refrigerate until ready to serve.

Serves 6

◆§ CANTON HADASSAH, OHIO

Herring Salad

TIP
This would be a nice dish for Seudah Sh'lishit.

8-ounce jar herring in cream sauce	Half a sour pickle, diced
2 cold cooked potatoes, diced	3 tablespoons beet juice
2 apples, peeled, seeded, and diced	1/4 cup walnuts, chopped
1/4 cup diced cooked beets	Mayonnaise to bind
	Rye bread for serving

1. Drain herring; reserve cream sauce, and slice herring.

2. In large bowl, combine herring, potatoes, apples, beets, and pickle. Stir in reserved cream sauce, beet juice, and walnuts. Add 1 to 2 tablespoons mayonnaise to bind. Chill, covered, 2 hours or overnight. Serve with sliced rye bread.

Serves 4 to 6

◆§ LIL SCHULMAN, ROCHESTER HADASSAH, NEW YORK

HERRING SALAD, recipe, right.

Chopped Eggs and Onions

1/4 cup oil	4 tablespoons mayonnaise
2 onions, coarsely chopped	1-1/2 teaspoons salt
8 hard-cooked eggs	1/4 teaspoon freshly ground pepper

1. Heat oil in skillet over medium heat. Add onions and sauté about 10 minutes, or until translucent; set aside to cool.

2. In medium bowl, chop hard-cooked eggs; stir in mayonnaise, sautéed onions, salt, and pepper. Chill thoroughly.

Makes about 1-1/2 cups

◄§ ADDY ADLER, AVIVA-OAKLAND HADASSAH, FLORIDA

Shabbat Challah

TIP
A 5-pound bag of flour contains about 16-1/4 cups.

Three (1/4-ounce) packages active dry yeast	2 tablespoons salt
2 teaspoons plus 1-1/2 cups sugar	1 tablespoon vanilla extract
4 cups warm water, divided	15 cups (about) unbleached all-purpose or bread flour
6 eggs plus 1 egg beaten for glaze	Poppy seeds
3/4 cup oil	

1. Dissolve yeast and 2 teaspoons sugar in 2 cups warm water. Set aside until bubbly. Grease 2 large baking sheets.

2. Blend into yeast mixture remaining 2 cups water, the 1-1/2 cups sugar, 6 eggs, the oil, salt, and vanilla extract.

3. Gradually combine flour with yeast-sugar mixture. Mix well and knead until dough is elastic. Try not to add more flour, but if dough is sticky, add only what is necessary.

4. Place in 2 large oiled bowls; turn to coat tops, and cover with a cloth. Set in warm place and let rise 2 hours.

5. Punch down dough and divide in 4 sections. Divide each section into 3 pieces. Roll out pieces of each section and braid. Place on prepared baking sheets. Cover and let rise again 1 hour. Meanwhile, preheat oven to 350 degrees.

6. Brush loaves with beaten egg and sprinkle with poppy seeds. Bake 30 to 35 minutes, or until golden.

Makes 4 loaves

◄§ PEGGY SAMET FINE, STEPHEN S. WISE HADASSAH, HOUSTON, TEXAS

Cinnamon Challah

Two (1/4-ounce) packages active	2 eggs, well beaten
dry yeast	7 to 7-1/2 cups unbleached
2 teaspoons plus 1 cup sugar	all-purpose or bread flour
1/4 cup warm water	Ground cinnamon
2 teaspoons salt	3 egg yolks mixed with
1/2 cup shortening	2 tablespoons honey
2 cups boiling water	

1. Dissolve yeast and 2 teaspoons sugar in warm water. In large bowl, combine remaining 1 cup sugar, the salt, shortening, and boiling water to melt together. After mixture cools, mix in beaten eggs and the yeast. Add flour to make dough (it should be slightly sticky to the touch).

2. Turn out onto floured surface and knead until smooth, about 10 minutes. Set dough in oiled bowl, turning to coat entire surface. Cover with dampened cloth and let rise in warm spot 1-1/2 to 2 hours. Meanwhile, grease three 8 x 4 inch loaf pans.

3. Turn dough onto floured surface. Divide in 3 equal parts for 3 loaves. Divide each part in 3 for braiding. Cover work surface with cinnamon and roll in it each rope for braiding. Braid into loaves and place in prepared pans. Cover, and let rise another hour. Meanwhile, preheat oven to 300 degrees.

4. Brush tops of loaves with yolk-and-honey mixture. Bake 15 minutes, then increase heat to 325 degrees and bake 15 to 20 minutes longer. Turn out onto wire racks and let cool.

Makes 3 loaves

◄§ AUDREY EDIDIN, NORTH BOUNDARY HADASSAH, CHICAGO, ILLINOIS

No-Knead
Food Processor Challah

TIP
If you like, sprinkle loaves with sesame or poppy seeds after brushing with egg wash.

One (1/4-ounce) package active dry yeast

1 teaspoon sugar

1/4 cup warm water

4-1/2 cups unbleached all-purpose flour, or bread flour

2 teaspoons salt

3 egg yolks, plus 1 egg yolk beaten with 2 teaspoons water

1 cup hot water

1/3 cup honey

2 tablespoons oil

1. Dissolve yeast and sugar in warm water. Set aside until bubbly. With metal blade in place add flour and salt to processor; pulse 4 times. Add 3 egg yolks, the hot water, honey, and oil. Pulse 4 times. Add yeast. Process until ball forms. If too sticky, add flour by the tablespoon. Process 1 minute more.

2. Place dough in greased bowl; turn to grease top. Cover with a towel and let rise in warm place until doubled, 1 to 2 hours. Meanwhile, lightly grease two 8 x 4 inch loaf pans

3. Punch down dough. Divide in half. Divide one half into 3 balls. Roll each ball into a rope with palms of hands. Braid 3 ropes to form challah. Repeat with second half of dough. Place loaves in prepared pans and cover with a towel. Let rise in warm spot until doubled, 1 to 1-1/2 hours. Preheat oven to 375 degrees.

4. Brush egg yolk and water onto challah. Bake 25 to 30 minutes, until nicely browned and bottom of challah sounds hollow when tapped. Let cool on wire rack.

Makes 2 loaves

◆§ Arlene S. Levin, North Boundary Hadassah, Chicago, Illinois

No-Knead Food Processor Challah, recipe above.

Challah

The word challah refers to the small portion of unbaked dough given by the Jews of the Temple period to the Kohanim as a Sabbath offering; when the Temple was destroyed this bread offering ceased. In commemoration, Jews today separate a small portion of unbaked dough which they bless (see prayer below) and burn. The rite conforms to the ancient biblical law, though its observance outside Israel is rabbinic in origin.

BARUCH ATAH ADONAI ELOHENU MELECH HA-OLAM ASHER KIDSHANU B'MITZVOTAV V'TZIVANU L'HAFRISH CHALLAH.

Blessed are You oh Lord our God, King of the universe, Who has sanctified us with His commandments and commanded us to separate challah.

Why do we use two loaves? Because two loaves remind us of the double portion of manna the Jews received each Friday during the time they wandered in the desert.

It is said that when the manna fell to the ground, it was protected by a layer of dew below and a layer of dew above, which is one reason the challah rests on a tablecloth and is covered by a special cloth. The challah is also often shaped into six-stranded braids so the total number of strands is 12, in honor of the 12 loaves of "showbread" placed in the Temple.

CHALLAH COVER. *Marianna Kirschstein. Germany. Late 19th century. Silk, silk and wool embroidery, silk chenille. Kirschstein Collection. Skirball Cultural Center, Museum Collection. Gift of the Artist.*

Grandma's Borscht

12 beets

2 medium onions

1-1/2 teaspoons salt, divided

1/2 teaspoon garlic salt

1/8 teaspoon freshly ground
 pepper

3/4 cup sugar, divided

Two (28-ounce) cans plum
 tomatoes

Fresh lemon juice, to taste

About 4 cups beet leaves

Sour cream

1. Remove leaves from beets, set aside. Cut tops and roots from beets, and scrub beets clean. Place in large pot with whole onions, 1 teaspoon salt, the garlic salt, pepper, and 1/2 cup sugar. Add water to cover tops of beets. Add tomatoes. Bring to boil and simmer, uncovered, 30 minutes.

2. Remove beets to cool. Remove onions and discard.

3. Peel beets and grate in food processor or by hand. Add to pot along with remaining 1/4 cup sugar, lemon juice, and remaining 1/2 teaspoon salt.

4. Cut out middle vein from beet leaves and slice leaves in thin strips. Stir into pot and simmer, uncovered, 30 minutes.

5. Adjust seasoning. Let cool and serve with dollop of sour cream for a dairy meal. Can be frozen. If thinner borscht is desired, add 1 quart water before seasoning is adjusted.

Serves 6

◈ RONNIE SIMON,
 ANN ARBOR HADASSAH,
 MICHIGAN

Cabbage and Tomato Chicken Soup

4- to 5-pound chicken
Half small green cabbage, shredded
1 large onion, sliced
2 tomatoes, peeled and coarsely chopped

3 carrots, sliced
3 cloves garlic, minced
1 tablespoon dried chives
1 teaspoon dried basil
Salt and freshly ground pepper to taste

1. Place chicken in a large pot and add enough water to cover. Cook 1 hour and remove chicken. Add remaining ingredients to pot and cook 1 hour. Preheat oven to 350 degrees.

2. Place chicken in baking dish and bake about 30 minutes. Remove from oven; set aside about 10 minutes to cool.

3. Remove chicken meat from carcass and return to soup pot. Cook until heated through.

Serves 6 to 8

❧ LORI NEWBERG, BUFFALO HADASSAH, NEW YORK

Bertha's Chicken Soup

4- to 5-pound stewing chicken, quartered
3 carrots, sliced
3 stalks celery with tops, sliced
1 medium onion, coarsely chopped
4 sprigs parsley
1 medium parsnip, peeled and cut into chunks (optional)

1 sweet potato, peeled
Salt and freshly ground pepper to taste
3 sprigs dill weed
2 tablespoons kosher instant soup mix

1. Place cleaned hen in a 6 quart kettle. Add enough water to cover and bring to a boil. Skim scum as it comes to the top.

2. Add carrots, celery, onion, parsley, parsnip, and sweet potato. Season with salt and pepper. Cover and simmer about 1 to 1-1/2 hours, until vegetables and chicken are cooked.

3. Add dill and some soup mix. Take out sweet potato, purée it and mix into soup.

Serves 6 to 8

◄ BERTHA FINK, READING HADASSAH, PENNSYLVANIA

Irma's Matza Balls

2 tablespoons chicken fat	*3 to 4 tablespoons matza meal*
1 onion, finely chopped	*1 egg, lightly beaten*
4 matzas	*Salt and freshly ground pepper to taste*

1. Melt chicken fat in large skillet over medium-high heat. Add onion and sauté until golden.

2. In large bowl, break matza into small pieces and soak in cold water. When matza is softened, squeeze out excess water.

3. Combine matza with matza meal and sautéed onions. Stir in beaten egg, salt, and pepper. Chill 1 hour.

4. Bring large pot of salted water to a boil. Using about 2 tablespoons mixture for each, shape with dampened hands into balls. Drop into boiling water and cook, uncovered, 15 to 20 minutes. Drain and transfer to soup.

Makes about 20

◄ IRMGARD LEFEBRE, OAKLAND HADASSAH, CALIFORNIA

Marrow Bone Matza Balls

2 large marrow bones, cut into
1-1/2 inch pieces
1 cup matza meal
Salt to taste

1/8 teaspoon nutmeg
1 cup boiling water
2 eggs

1. Dig out marrow from the bones with a sharp, pointed knife; there should be about 1/2 cup. Place marrow in small skillet and heat gently until melted. Meanwhile, bring large pot of salted water to a boil.

2. Remove skillet from heat and stir in matza meal until completely coated with fat. Add salt and nutmeg. Add boiling water and beat until mixture leaves side of skillet. Beat in eggs one at a time.

3. With wet hands, form mixture into small balls. Drop into boiling water and boil 30 minutes. Drain and transfer to soup.

Makes 12 to 15

ROSANN PECK, RICHMOND HADASSAH, VIRGINIA

Galushka
(Spaetzel)

1 egg, lightly beaten
1 teaspoon melted unsalted
margarine, or oil

1 teaspoon salt
2 cups all-purpose flour
1 tablespoon oil

1. In large pot, bring about 3 quarts salted water to a boil.

2. Mix egg with margarine in a deep bowl. Add 2/3 cup water and the salt. With a wooden spoon, beat in flour until a soft but resilient dough forms, about 3 to 4 minutes.

3. Place dough on a board. With a teaspoon, scoop dough into boiling water (or use spaetzel machine). Boil 12 to 15 minutes, or until cooked through.

4. Remove with slotted spoon to colander. Rinse quickly with cold water, then with slotted spoon spoon into an ovenproof serving dish. Sprinkle with oil, cover, and keep warm in a low oven.

5. Repeat until all dough is cooked. Transfer to soup.

Serves 4

SUSIE N. GUIORA, ANN ARBOR HADASSAH, MICHIGAN

Farfel
(Egg Barley)

1 egg, lightly beaten	Pinch of salt
1-1/2 cup all-purpose flour	

Knead all ingredients into a hard firm ball of dough. Grate on medium-fine grater. Spread on a board to dry thoroughly before storing away in jars. When needed, cook in boiling salted water 30 minutes. Drain and serve in chicken soup, or as a side dish with fat and gravy. The farfel may be boiled directly in the soup if preferred.

Makes 2 cups

◦§ ANN ARBOR HADASSAH, MICHIGAN

Mandlen
(Soup Nuts)

3 eggs	1-3/4 cups all-purpose flour,
1-1/2 tablespoons oil	approximately
1 teaspoon salt	1 teaspoon baking powder

1. Preheat oven to 375. Grease large baking sheet with sides.

2. In large bowl beat eggs, oil, and salt. Add flour and baking powder to form workable dough, adding flour as needed.

3. Divide dough into several pieces and roll into ropes 3/8-inch thick. Cut into 1/2-inch pieces.

4. Place on prepared baking sheet and bake until golden, 20 minutes. Shake pan occasionally, or turn nuts so they brown evenly on all sides.

Makes about 5-1/2 dozen

◦§ ANN ARBOR HADASSAH, MICHIGAN

Cholent: The Sabbath Stew

This is a food that is intrinsically Jewish, absolutely our own, not something we borrowed from the Hungarians or the Turks. The Torah commands that "You shall not burn a fire in your dwellings on the Sabbath." According to oral law, this means one should not ignite a fire on the Sabbath; one already lit was permitted to remain. And *tomnin et ha-hamin* (cover the hot foods) is included in the Sabbath liturgy as one of the things a person must do on Friday before nightfall.

There are many versions of these slow-simmering Sabbath stews called variously hammin (from the Hebrew for hot) or dafina (from the Arabic for covered); schalet in Western Yiddish, cholent in the East (from chaud lent, Old French for warm and slow).

The standard Ashkenazic cholent in America is primarily Polish-inspired: barley, beans, onion, potato, meat, and spices. The Sephardic Saturday meal-in-a-pot may include prunes and chickpeas, or rice and chicken, and be slightly sweetened with dates, while a German cholent would be more soup than stew. The custom of putting in unshelled eggs to become brown and creamy inside, known as huevos haminados, is popular among Sephardim.

So the cholent simmers through the night, and the smell rises from the pots, and even though it has no bodily substance or hands, it grabs you by the nose and drags you after it.

Families with their cholent pots, Bialystok, Poland.

1 cup dried chickpeas

MEATBALLS
1 pound ground beef
1/4 cup chopped raisins
1/4 cup finely chopped almonds
Pinch each ground cinnamon, mace, nutmeg
1/2 teaspoon each salt and sugar
1/2 cup dry breadcrumbs

SAUCE
1 tablespoon honey
1 teaspoon cumin
Pinch each of curry powder, turmeric, ginger, salt, freshly ground black pepper
1 bay leaf

CHOLENT
1 pound brisket or flanken, and/or soup bones
1 pound whole-wheat grains
1/4 cup oil
6 cloves garlic
1 teaspoon paprika
1 teaspoon salt
4 whole or halved potatoes, peeled
4 uncooked eggs, or more

1. The day before, place chickpeas in large bowl and cover with cold water. Set aside to soak overnight. Drain beans and rinse.

2. Prepare meatballs by combining ground beef with raisins, almonds, cinnamon, mace, nutmeg, salt, and sugar. Roll in breadcrumbs to seal and set aside.

3. Prepare sauce: Combine 1 cup water with honey, cumin, curry powder, turmeric, ginger, salt, pepper, and bay leaf. Bring to a boil; reduce heat. Simmer 10 minutes.

4. Place drained chickpeas and the brisket in a crockpot. In separate heat-resistant glass bowl combine grains with oil, garlic, paprika, and salt. Add enough water to cover, and place in crockpot. Add potatoes, uncooked eggs, and meatballs. Pour sauce into pot and bring to a boil. Reduce heat to low and cook 24 hours, checking water just before Shabbat.

5. To serve, place potatoes, eggs, sliced brisket, and beef balls on a platter. Serve chickpeas, grains, and sauce in separate containers.

Serves 8

◆ *BINGHAMTON HADASSAH, NEW YORK*

Crockpot Cholent

2 cups dried lima beans
1/4 cup lentils
3 large russet potatoes, peeled
  and quartered
1/4 cup barley
3 pounds flanken, cubed

1 large onion, cut up
6 cloves garlic
3 tablespoons kosher salt
1/2 teaspoon freshly ground
  pepper

1. The day before, place lima beans and lentils in large bowl and cover with cold water. Set aside to soak overnight. Drain beans and lentils and rinse.

2. Put potatoes on bottom of crockpot and add lima beans and the lentils. Add barley and flanken.

3. Add onion, garlic, salt, pepper, and enough water to cover, plus 1/2 cup more. Cook overnight on low.

Serves 8

◂§ *Amy Herman, Dix Hills Hadassah, New York*

TIP
Add a Sephardic touch by tucking in a few eggs to simmer along with the beans and the potatoes.

Cholent

1/4 cup dried kidney beans
1/4 cup dried lima beans
1/4 cup dried navy beans
1 pound stew meat, cut in cubes
3 potatoes, peeled and cut in half
1/4 cup barley

1-ounce package onion-soup mix
2 tablespoons ketchup
1/2 teaspoon salt
1/2 teaspoon freshly ground
  pepper
1 teaspoon hot pepper sauce

1. Place kidney, lima, and navy beans in large bowl and cover with cold water. Set aside to soak overnight. Drain beans and rinse.

2. In 6-quart crockpot, place beans, meat, potatoes, barley, onion-soup mix, ketchup, salt, pepper, and hot pepper sauce with enough cold water to cover.

3. Before Shabbat, set crockpot to low and cholent will cook overnight and be ready for Shabbat lunch.

Serves 4

◂§ *Sally Rosen-Lefkofksy, Raritan Valley Chapter of Dorot Group Hadassah, New Brunswick, New Jersey*

TIP
You cannot do anything about cooking once it's Shabbat, so the cholent has to be edible by the time Shabbat begins.

Crockpot Cholent, recipe above, right.

Best Cholent Ever

1 tablespoon olive oil

1 onion, diced

2 potatoes, cut up

1 sweet potato, cut up

Salt and freshly ground pepper to taste

Garlic powder to taste

1 to 2 pounds flanken or chuck, cut up

1-1/2 cups barley

4 cups boiling water

1/3 cup ketchup

1/3 cup honey

Half (of a 1-ounce) packet
    onion-soup mix

1 small prebaked potato kugel

1. Put olive oil in the bottom of a slow-cooking crockpot. Place all ingredients into the pot in the order given. Place kugel on top.

2. Cover, and cook on low heat 20 to 24 hours. Serve for Shabbat lunch.

Serves 8

❧ MILWAUKEE HADASSAH, WISCONSIN

Vegetarian Cholent

2 cups semolina

3 eggs

2 tablespoons sautéed onion

Salt and freshly ground pepper
    to taste

1 teaspoon baking soda

Oil for frying

6 russet potatoes, peeled and
    cut in half

6 eggs, uncooked

1 cup dried beans or chickpeas,
    soaked and drained

1. Make dough of semolina, the eggs, 1/2 cup water, the sautéed onion, salt, pepper, and baking soda. Form into small balls.

2. Heat oil in pan and fry semolina balls. Put semolina balls, the potatoes, the eggs, and chickpeas in large Dutch oven. Cover with water. Add salt and pepper and bring to a boil. Put in low oven overnight.

Serves 6

❧ HADASSAH ISRAEL

Semolina is durum wheat more coarsely ground than normal wheat flour. Most good pasta is made from semolina.

Mock Kishka

2/3 cup snack crackers
1/2 cup (1 stick) unsalted
   margarine, or oil
1 egg
1 carrot, grated

1 onion, grated
2 stalks celery, chopped
Pinch of garlic powder
Pinch of freshly ground
   pepper

1. Preheat oven to 400 degrees. Crush crackers in large bowl. Add melted margarine or oil, the egg, grated carrot, onion, the chopped celery, and seasonings.

2. Mix well with hands. Form into 2 logs. Wrap in lightly greased foil and freeze until needed.

3. Bake, wrapped in foil, 30 minutes, then open foil to brown 10 minutes.

Makes 10 to 12 servings

◄§ CHARLOTTE REITZES, RICHMOND HADASSAH, VIRGINIA

Stuffing Like Derma

19-ounce box toasted
   rice cereal
3 eggs
1/2 pound chicken fat
3 tablespoons matza meal

3 tablespoons all-purpose flour
1 carrot, grated
2 onions, grated
Salt, freshly ground pepper,
   paprika, garlic to taste

1. Preheat oven to 350 degrees. Place toasted rice cereal into a large plastic food storage bag and roll with rolling pin until crumbs form. Transfer to large bowl.

2. Beat in eggs. Cut chicken fat into small chunks and add to cereal mixture. Add 1/2 cup water, the matza meal, flour, carrot, onions, salt, pepper, paprika, and garlic. Roll up in oiled foil or put in casserole and bake 1-1/2 hours.

Serves 12

◄§ FAIR LAWN HADASSAH, NEW JERSEY

Yerushalmi Kugel

10 ounces angel hair pasta,
   cooked and drained
1/2 cup oil, divided
1/2 to 1 cup sugar

3 eggs, lightly beaten
1 to 1-1/2 teaspoons freshly
   ground pepper
Salt to taste

TIP
This kugel may also be baked uncovered in a 350 degree oven 45 to 60 minutes, until golden.

1. Preheat oven to 175 degrees or lowest oven temperature. Grease 10-inch tube pan or 13 x 9 inch baking pan. Add 1/4 cup oil to pasta and mix thoroughly; set aside.

2. Heat remaining 1/4 cup oil in medium saucepan and add sugar. Cook over low heat, stirring, about 5 minutes, until sugar dissolves and caramelizes. If sugar hardens, put back on low heat and stir until sugar dissolves.

3. Add pasta to hot oil-and-sugar mixture and mix well. Let cool a bit, and add eggs, pepper, and salt. Stir well and taste to see if more pepper and salt are needed.

4. Place pasta mixture in prepared pan. Put pan on cookie sheet and bake, uncovered, overnight.

Serves 16

◆ *Milwaukee Hadassah, Wisconsin*

Ed's Favorite Potato Kugel

6 eggs, lightly beaten
1/2 cup melted chicken fat, or
   more to taste
8 to 9 cups cubed peeled potatoes
   (about 5 pounds), in cold
   water to cover

2 very large onions, cut up
2/3 cup matza meal
1 tablespoon salt
1/2 teaspoon freshly ground
   pepper
1 teaspoon baking powder

1. Preheat oven to 350 degrees. Grease 13 x 9 inch baking pan. Combine eggs with chicken fat in one bowl, potatoes in another; onions in another; and matza meal, salt, pepper, and baking powder in another.

2. Put some egg mixture in blender. Add some potatoes and onions, and blend to grate. Pour into large bowl and repeat process with remaining egg

In Yiddish schmaltz means fat. No, not just fat, but flavorful fat. In America schmaltz has come to signify excessive sentimentality—sentimentality underlined, over-wrought, and overlaid. To the Jews of Europe, there was absolutely nothing like it.

HOW DO YOU MAKE SCHMALTZ?

• Remove fat from a large chicken or hen. Cut in pieces, put in a pot with a cut-up onion, and cover it with water.

• Simmer slowly until the water has cooked out and the onion has browned. (For a fine result, add some sliced apple when rendering the fat.) When cooled, strain into a container with a cover and refrigerate—it will keep for months.

What you're left with, those little bits of crisp fat and onion, are gribenes. They are great in chopped liver, chopped egg and onion, a meat kugel, knishes, or mashed potatoes.

mixture, potatoes, and onions. Stir in matza meal mixture and mix well. Pour into prepared baking pan.

3. Bake about 1 hour, until brown.

Serves at least 10

◆ DOT SILFEN, SHELANU HADASSAH, NEW YORK, NEW YORK

Mock Schmaltz

1 large onion, diced	*1 cup vegetable oil*

Cook onion in oil in saucepan over medium heat until golden. Strain and use as schmaltz.

Makes about 1 cup

◆ ROSALYN KARAS, B & P HADASSAH GROUP OF ILLIANA TIKVAH CHAPTER, MUNSTER, INDIANA

Pickled Beets

4 pounds beets	*2 teaspoons dry mustard*
2 cups sugar	*1/4 teaspoon powdered cloves*
2 cups vinegar	*(optional)*
1 teaspoon salt	

1. Scrub beets, leaving about 1/2-inch tail and 1-inch stem. Cook in boiling water until fork tender (time will vary from 30 to 45 minutes depending on size of beets).

2. When beets are just cool enough to handle, peel and slice.

3. In large saucepan, combine sugar, vinegar, 1/2 cup water, the salt, mustard, and cloves. Bring to a boil, stirring. Reduce heat and simmer until sugar is dissolved.

4. Add sliced beets and cook about 5 minutes. Transfer to sterilized screw-top jars and keep refrigerated.

Makes about 3 pints

◆ ROSE LYNN, B & P HADASSAH GROUP OF ILLIANA TIKVAH CHAPTER, MUNSTER, INDIANA

Continental
Cauliflower Salad

TIP

Far superior in flavor to the canned mission olive are the Greek kalamata, the French niçoise, and the Italian gaeta itri.

4 cups thinly sliced cauliflower	1/2 cup vegetable oil
1/2 cup pitted ripe olives, coarsely chopped	3 tablespoons fresh lemon juice
	3 tablespoons red wine vinegar
1 green bell pepper, seeded and chopped	1 teaspoon salt
	1 teaspoon sugar
1/2 cup chopped onion	1/4 teaspoon freshly ground pepper
1/4 cup chopped pimiento	

1. Combine cauliflower, olives, green bell pepper, onion, and pimiento in a large salad bowl.

2. Combine oil, lemon juice, wine vinegar, salt, sugar, and pepper in small bowl and mix well. Pour dressing over vegetables and toss to combine. Cover and refrigerate 4 hours to overnight.

Serves 4 to 6

◀ Mindy Ross, Chaverot Hadassah, Suffern, New York

Israeli Eggplant Salad
Marinated Style

TIP

This is also good stuffed into pitas with chopped green salad and hummus.

For a nice presentation, serve chilled with ripe tomato wedges, Greek or Israeli olives, cucumber spears, and scallions or sweet red onion slices.

2 to 3 firm medium eggplants, unblemished, about 8 ounces each	1 to 1-1/2 cups fresh lemon juice
Coarse salt	Freshly ground pepper to taste
Oil for frying (can be flavorless vegetable oil with a dash of olive oil for extra taste)	

1. Cut off eggplant stems and slice eggplant horizontally into 1/8-inch thick slices. Layer in shallow baking dish, and sprinkle with salt. Add cold water to cover and soak 1 hour. Drain, rinse, and pat dry on paper towels.

2. Heat some oil in large frying pan over medium high heat. Add single layer of eggplant slices and fry until golden; turn and brown other side.

Remove to plate. Add more oil to skillet if needed and continue frying eggplant until all slices are cooked.

3. Layer slices in glass or ceramic bowl or dish, sprinkling them with lemon juice and some pepper as you go. Pour any additional lemon juice over top. Cover dish with plastic wrap and let sit in refrigerator at least 3 days.

4. On second day, invert slices so top slices will be on bottom and vice versa, and baste with juices.

Serves about 6 to 8

◆§ PAULA HESSE, BIRMINGHAM HADASSAH, ALABAMA

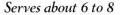

Glazed Roasted Chicken

6- to 7-pound chicken	**GLAZE**
Salt to taste	3 tablespoons unsalted
1 orange	margarine
1 small onion, quartered	3 tablespoons Dijon mustard
Freshly ground pepper	2 tablespoons honey
1 teaspoon dried thyme	1 tablespoon apricot preserves
1 teaspoon dried rosemary	
1/2 cup white wine	

1. Preheat oven to 350 degrees. Wash chicken and pat dry; salt the cavity.

2. Quarter orange and squeeze all the juice over the chicken. Put rinds and quartered onion inside the cavity. Tie legs together. Sprinkle chicken with salt, pepper, thyme, and rosemary. Place in roasting pan with wine and roast 40 minutes.

3. Combine glaze ingredients and pour over entire chicken. Roast 1 hour longer, basting often, or until chicken is done.

Serves 8 to 10

◆§ JOANN KUZON MULLANEY, GREATER SPRINGFIELD HADASSAH,
LONGMEADOW, MASSACHUSETTS

Chicken in Wine

2-1/2 to 3-pound chicken, cut in
   8 pieces
1 cup thinly sliced onion
2 cloves garlic, minced
2 cups sliced mushrooms
2 medium tomatoes, chopped

1/3 cup dry white wine
2 tablespoons balsamic vinegar
1 teaspoon crumbled dried thyme
1/2 teaspoon salt
1/2 teaspoon freshly ground black
   pepper

1. Spray large nonstick skillet with nonstick cooking spray; add chicken pieces and cook over medium heat until browned on both sides, about 6 to 8 minutes. Transfer to 13 x 9 inch baking pan.

2. Preheat oven to 350 degrees. Place onion and garlic in same skillet and cook, stirring occasionally, until onion is translucent, about 2 minutes. Add mushrooms; cook 1 minute longer. Stir in remaining ingredients and cook 1 minute more. Pour vegetable mixture evenly over chicken. Cover with aluminum foil and bake 25 minutes. Remove foil and bake 15 minutes longer, or until chicken is cooked through.

3. For Friday night, brown chicken, then cover and bake skin-side up 40 minutes. Fold back foil, turn off oven, and let chicken sit partly covered until ready to serve.

Serves 4 to 6

◆§ BARRY MINOWITZ, DIX HILLS HADASSAH, NEW YORK

CHICKEN IN WINE, recipe above.

Shabbat Chicken

2 tablespoons vegetable oil
1 small onion, sliced
2 whole cloves
1 stick cinnamon
1/2 teaspoon salt, or to taste

1 teaspoon turmeric
1 teaspoon grated gingerroot
1 clove garlic, minced
3- to 4-pound roasting chicken,
   cut in sixths

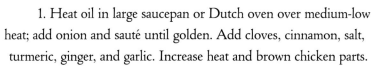

1. Heat oil in large saucepan or Dutch oven over medium-low heat; add onion and sauté until golden. Add cloves, cinnamon, salt, turmeric, ginger, and garlic. Increase heat and brown chicken parts.

2. Reduce heat, cover, and cook until tender, about 25 minutes. Check frequently and stir to minimize sticking.

3. Turn off heat; leave the top on the pan, and let it wait while the blessings are said.

Serves 4

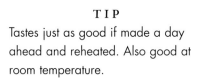

➳ Joyce Gropper, New York Hadassah, New York

Baked Breast of Chicken

4 boneless, skinless chicken
   breasts
1 cup soup-nut crumbs
1 teaspoon ground ginger
1 teaspoon garlic powder
1/2 teaspoon salt

1/4 teaspoon freshly ground
   white pepper
2 eggs, well beaten
1 cup apricot preserves
1/2 cup white wine
2 tablespoons margarine

1. Preheat oven to 350 degrees. Cut chicken breasts in half. Rinse with cold water and dry well with paper towels.

2. Combine soup-nut crumbs, the ginger, garlic powder, salt, and pepper in shallow dish. Dip each half chicken breast in beaten egg, then in crumb mixture. Arrange in single layer in 13 x 9 inch baking pan.

3. Combine preserves, wine and margarine. Microwave on high 2 to 3 minutes, or until mixture comes to a boil. Pour over chicken breasts and bake about 45 minutes, or until chicken is cooked through.

Serves 8

➳ Chaverot Hadassah, Suffern, New York

TIP
Tastes just as good if made a day ahead and reheated. Also good at room temperature.

Cherry Orange Roast Duck

Two 5-1/2 pound ducks
1/4 cup salad oil

ORANGE SAUCE
1 orange, pulp and grated zest
1 cup sugar
4 ounces red currant jelly
28-ounce can pitted Bing cherries

1. Preheat oven to 325 degrees.

2. Wipe ducks with damp cloth and brush with salad oil. Bake 1 hour. Pour off fat. Increase oven temperature to 400 degrees and bake 1 hour longer.

3. Meanwhile, prepare sauce. In medium saucepan, combine orange pulp, zest, sugar, red currant jelly, and 2 cups water. Bring to a boil, stirring, over medium heat. Reduce heat and simmer about 15 minutes, or until sauce is thick and syrupy. Stir in cherries.

4. Remove ducks from oven and reduce oven temperature to 250 degrees.

5. Cut ducks in quarters, arrange in shallow casserole. Cover with sauce and place in oven for at least an hour, or until heated through.

Serves 6 to 8

◄ SARA BELKOV, READING HADASSAH, PENNSYLVANIA

KASHA

Kasha is toasted buckwheat groats. Although usually regarded as a grain, in reality these stubby seeds come from an herb plant. Of Russian descent, the kernels are prepared in many ways; ground and used as flour, simmered and served as a porridge, or made into the famous Russian blini. Buckwheat is not a true cereal; it is not a grass. Its kernels are actually achenes, dry fruits similar to the "seeds" of the strawberry.

Kasha
(Buckwheat Groats)

2-1/2 cups buckwheat groats
1 teaspoon salt
1 teaspoon paprika
1 egg, lightly beaten

3 cups boiling water
2 tablespoons chicken fat
2 cups chopped onions, sautéed
(optional)

1. Preheat oven to 350 degrees. Grease 2-quart baking pan.

2. Mix buckwheat groats with salt, paprika, and egg. Put in prepared baking pan and place in oven. Cook about 10 minutes, or until browned.

3. Add boiling water and chicken fat and mix thoroughly. Add onions, if desired. Return to oven. Cook, covered, 20 minutes, or until tender. Use as a stuffing, or stir into gravy and serve with roasted meat.

Serves 6

◄ MRS. SAM WASSERMAN, OKLAHOMA CITY HADASSAH, OKLAHOMA

Beer Brisket

5- to 6-pound brisket of beef
1-ounce package onion-soup mix
2 to 3 cloves minced garlic
1 bay leaf
12-ounce bottle beer
6 tablespoons dark brown sugar
1/4 cup honey
2 tablespoons orange marmalade
Zest and juice of 1 lemon

1 tablespoon fruit brandy
1/2 tablespoon Worcestershire
sauce
1/2 teaspoon ground cinnamon
1/2 teaspoon ground ginger
Freshly ground black pepper
2 cups dried apricots
2 cups pitted prunes

1. Preheat oven to 325 degrees. Place a large sheet of heavy duty aluminum foil in large roasting pan. Place brisket on foil and sprinkle with soup mix over both sides of meat. Rub minced garlic over brisket. Add bay leaf, cover brisket with foil, and seal tightly. Cook 4 to 5 hours, or until fork tender.

2. Meanwhile, in large bowl combine beer, brown sugar, honey, marmalade, lemon zest and juice, the fruit brandy, Worcestershire sauce, cinnamon, ginger, and black pepper. Add apricots and prunes. Place mixture in saucepan. Cook over medium heat about 30 to 40 minutes, until fruits are tender. Set aside.

3. Remove cooked brisket from foil; let cool. Slice meat. Add skimmed pan juices and water to dried fruit mixture to make 4 cups liquid.

4. Place sliced brisket in large shallow dish and pour fruit mixture over meat. Cover and refrigerate 2 days.

5. Bake at 350 degrees 45 minutes to 1 hour, until heated through.

Serves 10 to 12

◆ COLETTE LOPATA, DEBORAH-ZAHAVA HADASSAH, CHICAGO, ILLINOIS

Poppy Seed Mandelbrot

1 cup plus 2 tablespoons sugar
Grated zest of 1 lemon or orange
1 cup oil
4 eggs
1 teaspoon vanilla extract
1/3 cup poppy seeds

4 cups all-purpose flour
1 teaspoon salt
1 teaspoons baking powder
1-1/2 teaspoons ground cinnamon,
divided

Pomegranates had been culti-vated in Egypt since before the time of Moses. The Jews wandering through the wilderness were heart-ened when the scouts they sent to Canaan brought some back from that "land of wheat, and barley, and vines, and fig trees, and pomegranates."

Because of the number of its seeds—some say 613, the number of mitzvot—the pomegranate repre-sented fertility and abundance in ancient times. Even today Sephardim set bowls of them on the table at Rosh Hashanah.

When the fruit is eaten raw, it is broken open, the kernels dislodged, and the flesh is sucked from the pits. From the rind comes an ink that one writer described as "unfading till the world's end." And pomegranates are proving to be the most powerful antioxidant available, better than red wine, tomatoes, Vitamin E, and a variety of other head-line-makers.

1. Preheat oven to 325 degrees. Grease baking sheet.

2. Blend 1 cup sugar with lemon or orange zest. In large mixing bowl beat oil with sugar mixture until combined. Add eggs, vanilla extract, and poppy seeds and blend thoroughly. Combine flour, salt, baking powder, and 1 teaspoon cinnamon. Beat into egg mixture until smooth.

3. Divide dough into 4 equal parts. Shape each piece into oval loaf about 1-1/2 to 2 inches wide and place 2 inches apart on prepared baking sheet.

4. Combine remaining 2 tablespoons sugar with 1/2 teaspoon cinnamon and sprinkle on top of loaves. Bake 35 to 45 minutes, until golden.

5. Remove from oven; transfer to wooden board, and cut into 1/2-inch-thick slices. Place cut side down on baking sheet and return to oven. Turn off oven and leave mandelbrot in 10 minutes longer, or until crisp.

Makes about 4 dozen

◆ RUTH BIERMAN, CHICAGO HADASSAH, ILLINOIS

Biblical Kugel

1/2 cup sugar	1/2 teaspoon ground ginger
2 teaspoons ground cinnamon	1 cup all-purpose flour
1/2 teaspoon ground cloves	1/2 teaspoon baking powder
1/2 cup oil	1 cup cooked barley
Salt	2 cups raisins
1 cup honey	2 cups cut-up dates
3 eggs	1/2 cup cut-up figs
1 cup pomegranate or other juice	1/2 cup candied fruits
Brandy, to taste (optional)	1/2 cup chopped almonds

1. Preheat oven to 350 degrees. Grease 10-inch tube pan.

2. Mix together sugar, cinnamon, cloves, oil, salt, honey, eggs, juice, brandy, and ginger. Add the flour, baking powder, barley, raisins, dates, figs, candied fruit, and nuts. Pour into prepared pan.

3. Bake 1 hour, or until nicely browned.

4. Excellent at room temperature. Serve with lemon sauce (page 174) or ignite brandy poured over top.

Serves 12 or more

◆ HADASSAH ISRAEL

Cocoa-Cinnamon Babka

TIP

This freezes well; save 2 loaves for another Shabbat.

2 (1/4-ounce) packages active
dry yeast

1/2 teaspoon plus 1-1/2 cups
sugar

1/4 cup warm water

1 cup non-dairy creamer

1/2 cup (1 stick) unsalted
margarine, softened

1 teaspoon salt

3 eggs, lightly beaten

Grated zest of half a lemon

4 to 5 cups all-purpose flour

6 tablespoons unsalted
margarine, melted

1 cup finely chopped nuts

1/2 cup raisins

2 tablespoon unsweetened
cocoa powder

1 tablespoon ground cinnamon

1 egg white, lightly beaten

1. Sprinkle yeast and 1/2 teaspoon sugar into warm water. Stir and set aside until frothy. Grease and flour three 9 x 5 inch loaf pans.

2. Heat non-dairy creamer to scalding and pour into large mixing bowl. Add margarine and stir to melt. Add 1/2 cup sugar, the salt, yeast mixture, the eggs, and lemon zest. Gradually add enough flour to make a soft dough. Knead on floured surface 10 minutes, until shiny and elastic. Place in a greased bowl, turning to coat entire surface. Cover and let rise until doubled, about 1-1/2 hours. Meanwhile, in small bowl combine remaining cup sugar with the nuts, raisins, cocoa powder, and cinnamon.

3. Divide dough in 6 parts. Working with one part at a time and refrigerating the rest covered, roll out to 1/8-inch thickness. Brush some melted margarine over dough. Sprinkle with nut mixture to cover three quarters of the dough. Roll up, tuck in ends, and place in a prepared loaf pan, seam side down. Repeat with a second part of dough and nut mixture, and tuck in alongside first roll.

4. Brush tops with egg white and sprinkle with some nut mixture. Repeat for remaining dough. Cover lightly with plastic wrap and set aside to rise until doubled, about 30 minutes. Meanwhile, preheat oven to 350 degrees.

5. Bake babka 40 to 50 minutes, until golden.

Makes 3 loaves

⇥ Janette Greenwood, Shelanu Hadassah, New York, New York

Cocoa-Cinnamon Babka, recipe above

Cocoa Honey Cake

1-1/2 cups all-purpose flour
  less 1 tablespoon
3 tablespoons unsweetened cocoa
  powder
1 teaspoon baking powder
1/2 teaspoon baking soda
Scant 1/2 teaspoon ground cinnamon
Scant 1/2 teaspoon ground ginger

Good hefty pinch of nutmeg
1/2 cup sugar
2/3 cup honey
2 eggs, lightly beaten
1/4 cup vegetable oil
1/4 cup apple juice, orange
  juice, or water
1 tablespoon sliced almonds

1. Preheat oven to 325. Lightly grease 8 x 4 inch loaf pan. Line bottom of pan with greased baking parchment.

2. Whisk to combine flour with cocoa, baking powder, baking soda, cinnamon, ginger, and nutmeg. In another bowl, add sugar and honey to beaten eggs and beat until very smooth and lightened in color. Gradually beat in oil until blended. Stir in flour mixture alternately with apple juice, orange juice, or water.

3. Pour batter into prepared pan and top with sliced almonds. Bake about 50 minutes, until tester comes out clean when inserted in center of cake. Let cool in pan 15 minutes, then turn out onto rack and carefully peel off paper.

4. When completely cool, wrap in plastic, then in foil.

Serves 6 to 8

◆§ ANNE SCHWARTZ, NEW HAVEN HADASSAH, CONNECTICUT

Carrot Cake

2 cups sugar
1-1/2 cups vegetable oil
4 eggs
2 teaspoons vanilla extract
3 cups all-purpose flour
2 teaspoons baking powder
2 teaspoons baking soda

2 teaspoons ground cinnamon
1 teaspoon salt
3 cups (about 8) grated carrots
1 cup drained crushed pineapple
  (almost all of a 20-ounce can)
1 cup chopped walnuts
1 cup golden raisins

1. Preheat oven to 350 degrees. Grease and flour two 8-inch round or square pans.

2. Beat sugar with oil; add eggs, one at a time, beating well after each. Beat in vanilla extract.

3. Whisk to combine flour with baking powder, baking soda, cinnamon,

and salt; beat into sugar mixture. Stir in carrots, pineapple, walnuts, and raisins. Pour batter evenly into prepared pans.

4. Bake 35 to 45 minutes, until a tester inserted in the center comes out clean. Let cool 10 minutes in pans, then turn out onto wire racks to cool completely. Freeze 1 cake, if desired, or frost with Orange Cream Cheese Frosting if serving cake with a milk meal.

Orange Cream Cheese Frosting

8-ounce package cream cheese, at room temperature

1/4 cup (half stick) unsalted butter, at room temperature

1 cup confectioners' sugar, or to taste

1 tablespoon grated orange zest

1 teaspoon vanilla extract

Beat cream cheese with butter until fluffy. Add sugar and beat well. Beat in orange zest and vanilla extract. Spread between layers and on outside of cake.

Makes enough frosting for 1 cake

◆§ TOBY SPITZER, CHARLOTTE HADASSAH, NORTH CAROLINA

Peach Torte

1-1/2 cups sugar

1/2 cup oil

3 eggs

Juice of half a lemon plus juice of 1 orange to make 1/2 cup

1 teaspoon vanilla extract

2 cups sifted all-purpose flour

2 teaspoons baking powder

1/2 teaspoon salt

3 or 4 fresh peaches, blanched, peeled, and thinly sliced

1. Preheat oven to 350 degrees. Grease 13 x 9 inch pan. Beat sugar with oil until well incorporated. Beat in eggs one at a time, beating well after each addition. Add juice and vanilla extract. Combine flour with baking powder and salt and stir into sugar mixture.

2. Pour into prepared pan. Press peaches gently into batter in 3 neat rows, about 12 slices each. Bake about 45 minutes, until cake tests done.

Serves about 16 to 18

◆§ SHIRLEY POLLOCK, LAUDERHILL HADASSAH, FLORIDA

Fall

HIGH HOLIDAYS BY THE NILE

Introduction by Claudia Roden

Author Claudia Roden travels extensively as a food writer. Her six books include A Book of Middle Eastern Food *and* The Book of Jewish Food, An Odyssey from Samarkand to New York *(Knopf). In this collection that took her 16 years to complete, she tells the stories of Jews through their food, her way of keeping alive the traditions and memories of the many communities whose worlds have vanished. It was for this stunning effort, published in 1996, that she was honored with The James Beard Award for The Best Cookbook of the Year, and The National Jewish Book Award for Sephardic and Ashkenazic Culture.*

Page 52–53, top left: ROUND RAISIN CHALLAH, *recipe page 58; lower right:* HONEY FISH, *recipe page 65.*

OPPOSITE: JEWISH NEW YEAR'S GREETING. *Happy Jack. Nome, Alaska, 1910. Engraved walrus tusk with gold inset. The Jewish Museum, New York, New York. Gift of the Kanofsky family in memory of Minnie Kanofsky.*

*I*n Cairo to give a seminar for the Association of Egyptian Chefs, I wandered around the city where I was born, looking for bits of my past. The temple in Sharia Adli was closed and guarded by soldiers with guns. It is something of a museum now but for me it holds many childhood memories that are still very much alive. I was a bridesmaid there at weddings of aunts and cousins, and that is where we celebrated my brother's bar mitzvah. On High Holidays I sat upstairs in the women's gallery with my mother. We looked down with pride at the men in their top hats and prayer shawls swaying from side to side, singing plaintive chants. As a community, we were on the whole lax in our religious observance, but the celebration of Jewish holidays was all-important.

Feasting was a major element of the holidays and each holiday had its own special foods that played a symbolic role in the rituals and celebrations. The choice of foods reflected the backgrounds of the families in our mixed community.

My own family had come from Syria and Turkey at the turn of the century. As children we were given little tasks when our mothers got together to prepare the special delicacies. We made little snakes of dough, turned them into bracelets, brushed them with egg yolk, and covered them with sesame seeds. We rolled almond paste into little balls and pressed pistachio nuts on the top. On the great day itself we helped to lay the lengthened table (several tables were put together). The embroidered white tablecloth, sparkling crystal glasses, silver goblets, candlesticks, and platters gave an air of enchantment to the room. We painted little cards with place names and different images—a flower, a boat, an egg—for each person. The seating was in order of age. The children were together at the end of the table.

In her book about Algerian Jewish traditions, *Le Culte de la Table Dressée—Rites et traditions de la table juive algerienne* (*The Cult of the Set Table—Rites and Traditions of the Algerian Jewish Table*), social anthropologist Joelle Bahloul describes the festive table as a place of cult, and the unfolding of the meal as a liturgical reenactment of what goes on in the temple. She writes that the ritualization of gastronomic acts transforms the kitchen into a sanctuary; the dining room into a miniature temple; the table into an altar; the convivial gatherings into a commune of the faithful, and the wife-cook into a high priestess. The lighting of candles by the woman of the house, the ritual washing of hands, the reciting of Kiddush (the prayer of sanctification of the day) over wine by the head of the family; the breaking of bread and passing of pieces with a sprinkling of salt—all these actions accompanied by blessings, hymns, and special prayers contribute to giving the meal a sacred character.

Our festive meals, shared by our extended family and friends, had that sacred character and were enthrallingly joyous occasions. Festivities went on for days. Weeks before Rosh Hashanah, Iro the dressmaker came to our house to sew our new dresses. My mother did the cutting from a French paper pattern and I unpicked the pins and pulled out the tacking threads. The Grand Temple was aflame with glittering chandeliers and golden embroideries and vibrated with the sobbing, wailing notes and long piercing sound of the shofar. After the celebratory dinners every member of the family was visited, the eldest first, in order of age, and in every home we were offered little delicacies.

Since my family settled in Britain we adopted the Ashkenazic custom of eating a piece of apple dipped in honey while a prayer is said asking God for a sweet year. In Egypt we dipped the apple slices in sugar, having dropped them first in water with a little lemon juice and orange blossom essence so that they shouldn't darken.

Traditional Ashkenazic New Year foods include a round challah with raisins because it looks like a crown and symbolizes continuity and the hope that the year will be rounded like a circle. The same bread is also baked in the shape of a ladder representing the ladder of life, which is in the hands of God, and in the shape of a bird following the words in Isaiah: "As hovering birds, so will the Lord protect Jerusalem." Chicken soup is eaten with round pasta—farfel or mandlen. A fish, symbol of fertility, is cooked with the head on to express the hope of being at the head of nations. In Yiddish folklore, carrots are associated with gold coins, and

carrot tzimmes is eaten as a symbol of prosperity and good fortune or, according to another interpretation, to increase merits over shortcomings. Honey cake, teiglach (honey pastries), and apple strudel are New Year sweets. A new fruit of the season is eaten—usually pomegranate, because of its regular appearance in the Torah with regard to the Land of Israel, and because it is said to have 613 seeds, the same number as the mitzvot.

The Sephardim used to eat a sheep's head baked in the oven so "that we may always be at the head and not at the tail and hold our heads up high." This very ancient tradition, which appears in writings in the early Middle Ages, also recalls the sacrifice of Isaac by his father Abraham. God, who had demanded the act, stopped it in time. At that moment Abraham saw a ram and sacrificed it to God instead. But in my time the sheep's head was generally substituted by brains, cooked as fritters or in an egg-and-lemon or tomato sauce or baked with eggs; by boiled tongue; or by fish with the head left on. We ate fresh or dried black-eyed beans as a symbol of abundance and fecundity. Other Sephardim ate chickpeas, rice, couscous, and sesame seed for the same reason. All kinds of dishes included pilafs, omelettes, gratins, salads, stuffed vegetables. Vegetable fritters and pies were made with green vegetables such as chard, spinach, broad beans, green peas, green beans, zucchini, and okra to symbolize a new beginning. Round foods such as meatballs, green peas, chickpeas, and round or ring-shaped breads and pastries embodied the aspiration that the year be full and rounded.

The New Year is a time for sweet things. Potatoes were replaced by sweet potatoes, onions were caramelized, and meats were cooked with apricots, cherries, quinces, prunes, dates, and raisins. Our meals ended with fresh dates, figs, and pomegranates—all of which are mentioned in the Bible. In Egypt we thought pomegranates would lead to our family bearing many children. We ate the seeds sprinkled with orange-blossom water and sugar. Pastries were made with sesame seeds and anise seed or stuffed with nuts or dates and soaked in syrup. Jams were made with quinces, figs, dates, and apples. White things—coconut jam and the sharope blanco (an almost all-sugar jam)—evoked purity while golden pumpkin jam, like other saffron-colored foods, evoked joy and happiness.

Yom Kippur was also a time for top hats and tails and finery at the temple. The evening service was dramatic and emotive, with the chanting of the Kol Nidre accompanied by heart-rendingly sad music and the Vidui or "confessions," when sins are enumerated while the heart is beaten with the right hand and the shofar is blown. The meal before the fast, eaten in the afternoon before sunset, was plain and simple—egg-and-lemon soup, boiled chicken with rice—with no sweets at the end. The fast was broken with a cold drink—lemonade or apricot juice, almond milk, orange or sour cherry syrup—followed by little savories and sweet pastries—borekas, cigars, cookies, pastries stuffed with nuts, buns with raisins and walnuts, sweet anise-flavored breads— served with tea. It was a dairy meal. In London my mother made sambousak with cheese, spinach phyllo, kahk, taramasalata, a cream-cheese dip, an eggplant cream, salads, and various pastries. In Egypt we waited until it was possible to eat meat and had another full meal with chicken— usually stuffed with rice, minced meat, raisins, and pine nuts. Chicken is the traditional Yom Kippur food because of the custom of kapparot (an atonement ritual), by which a chicken is killed for every member of the family. Dishes were prepared the day before and simply reheated.

Sukkot was one of the happiest of holidays. Some families built huts on their terraces and rooftops and on their balconies. They lined them with cloth and decorated them with plants and branches, and spent time in them—eating, drinking, and receiving guests. The huts represent the temporary dwellings the Jews lived in during their time in the wilderness and symbolize God's protection. In the Talmud it was laid down that "branches of fig trees on which there are figs, vines with grapes, palm branches with dates, and wheat with ears" should be used for the sukkah and that pomegranates and phials of wine should decorate the table. Later, rabbinic authorities included various kinds of nuts. Four such symbolic plants are named in the Torah: the esrog, which looks like a large lemon and has a magnificent fragrance; the young shoot of a palm tree; the branch of a myrtle bush; and the branch of a willow are part of the rituals. Blessings are recited while they are held together and gently swayed as a symbol that Jews should complement each other and be together in harmony.

Sukkot is also a harvest festival celebrating farming, nature, and the ingathering of fruit. Vegetables and fruit are the theme of the meals that are eaten in the sukkah. In Egypt it was a pretext for continual entertaining. Relatives and friends, including Muslims and Copts, dropped in and were entertained with vegetable mezzes (little hors d'oeuvres) served with arak (a fiery liquor) and all kinds of fruit salads and compotes, dried fruits and nuts, and sweet jams and preserves.

OPPOSITE: YOM KIPPUR BELT BUCKLE. *Central Europe, 20th century. Silver, repoussé; and linen embroidered with metallic thread. Skirball Cultural Center, Museum Collection. Gift of the Jewish Cultural Reconstruction, Inc.*

Herring in Sour Cream "Divine"

2 large jars (32 ounces each) herring in wine sauce	2 tablespoons mayonnaise
	1/4 cup sugar
1 quart (two 16–ounce containers) sour cream	1 large Bermuda onion, thinly sliced
	3 lemons, thinly sliced

1. Remove herring from jar and drain; place in bowl.

2. Mix sour cream with mayonnaise; stir in sugar.

3. In a large, wide-mouth jar layer onion slices, herring, lemon slices, and sour cream mixture. Refrigerate 5 days.

Serves 8 to 10

ᴥ ᴇsᴛᴇʟʟᴇ Mᴀᴜʀᴇʀ, Iɴᴅɪᴀɴᴀᴘᴏʟɪs Hᴀᴅᴀssᴀʜ, Iɴᴅɪᴀɴᴀ

ᴥ *Great for the Break Fast*

Round Raisin Challah

2 (1/4-ounce each) packages active dry yeast	1/4 cup honey
	2 tablespoons salt
2 teaspoons plus 1/2 cup sugar	8 eggs
3/4 cup warm water	10 cups all-purpose flour
1/4 pound (1 stick) unsalted margarine	1 cup raisins
	1 egg yolk beaten with 1 teaspoon water
1 cup boiling water	
1/4 cup vegetable oil	1/4 cup poppy seeds

1. Use one-quart measuring cup and dissolve yeast and 2 teaspoons sugar in warm water; set aside until mixture rises to the top of the cup.

2. Combine margarine with boiling water. When margarine is melted, add oil, honey, salt, and remaining 1/2 cup sugar. Pour into a mixing bowl and add eggs one at a time, beating well after each addition.

3. Add yeast mixture. Gradually add 9 cups flour until dough is formed. Turn onto well floured board and knead, gradually working in remaining cup flour. Turn dough into clean mixing bowl and cover. Let stand in warm place about 1-1/2 hours, until doubled in bulk. Grease cookie sheets.

4. Turn dough out onto board and knead in raisins. Divide dough into four parts and roll each part into a long rope. Holding one end with the left hand, twist rope counterclockwise until a round spiral is formed. Place the four

The theme of the books of life and death features prominently in the liturgy of Rosh Hashanah; the essential ritual is the sounding of the shofar. The Mishna permits the use of the horn of any animal except the cow because of its reference to the golden calf. A ram's horn eventually gained preference because of its association with the binding of Isaac.

Although the Scriptures are silent as to why the horn is blown on this day, Maimonides writes: "Awake from your slumbers, ye who have fallen asleep in life, and reflect on your deeds. Be not of those who miss reality in the pursuit of shadows, and waste their years in seeking after vain things."

At the festive meal it is customary to dip a piece of round challah and a piece of apple into honey as a token of the sweet year it is hoped will come. In some communities the loaves are baked in the shape of a ladder to symbolize the fate that lies ahead: some ascending, others descending, life's ladder.

round challahs on prepared cookie sheets, cover, and let rise 1 hour. Meanwhile, preheat oven to 350 degrees.

5. Brush loaves with egg wash, sprinkle with poppy seeds, and bake 35 to 45 minutes.

Makes 4 loaves

BIRMINGHAM HADASSAH, ALABAMA

Fruited Challah

1 cup lukewarm water	3 tablespoons oil
1 (1/4-ounce) package active dry yeast	3-1/2 cups all-purpose flour
3 tablespoons sugar	1 cup dried fruit bits
1 teaspoon salt	1 egg yolk, beaten with
2 eggs	1 tablespoon water

1. Pour lukewarm water into mixing bowl. Sprinkle in yeast and stir until dissolved. Add sugar and salt. Stir well and set aside until frothy.

2. Add eggs and beat with beater. Add oil and beat slightly. Gradually stir in 3 cups flour and the fruit bits. Knead 3 to 4 minutes on floured board, adding more flour if necessary (dough should feel smooth, not sticky). Place in lightly oiled bowl and brush top of dough with oil. Cover with warm, damp cloth and let rise 2 to 3 hours, until doubled in bulk. Grease cookie sheet.

3. Place dough on floured board and pound out air with fists. Divide into 4 equal parts. Stretch and roll three of them into 1-1/2-inch-thick ropes, twist into braid, and pinch ends to secure. Place on prepared cookie sheet.

4. Preheat oven to 350 degrees. Divide remaining dough into 3 parts; roll 1/2-inch thick. Twist into braid, and place on top of other braid. Then brush with egg wash. Let rise 10 to 15 minutes.

5. Bake about 45 minutes, until browned.

Makes one 1-1/2 pound loaf

SHERRON GOLDSTEIN,
BIRMINGHAM HADASSAH, ALABAMA

Kreplach

DOUGH	CHICKEN FILLING
2 cups all-purpose flour	(recipe below)
1/2 teaspoon salt	MEAT FILLING
2 eggs	(recipe below)

1. Put flour in bowl and make a well in center. Add salt, eggs, and 1/4 cup water and knead until smooth and elastic.

2. Roll out thin and cut into 2-inch squares. Put small ball of chicken or meat mixture on each square.

3. Dampen edges of each square and fold over into triangle; with a fork press edges together to seal. Work quickly so dough doesn't dry.

4. Let stand 10 minutes. Bring a large pot of salted water to a boil and drop in kreplach. Cook 15 or 20 minutes.

5. Drain. Serve with soup, or brown and serve as side dish.

Makes about 2 dozen

Chicken Filling

1 cup shredded boiled chicken	1 egg, lightly beaten
1/2 cup chopped onion, sautéed	1 teaspoon garlic powder

1. Put chicken and onion through grinder or grind in processor.
2. Add egg and garlic powder.
3. Mix well and use as filling for kreplach.

Makes 1 cup

Meat Filling

1/2- to 3/4-pound cooked beef or cooked ground beef	1 egg, lightly beaten
1 medium onion, chopped and sautéed	1 teaspoon garlic powder

1. Put meat and onion through grinder or grind in processor.
2. Add egg and garlic powder.
3. Mix well and use as filling for kreplach.

Makes 1 cup

◄ MIFFIE NAGORSKY, NORTH BOUNDARY HADASSAH, CHICAGO, ILLINOIS

KREPLACH, recipe above.

Matza Balls
Like Mama Used to Make

4 eggs

1/4 cup club soda

1 teaspoon salt

Dash of freshly ground pepper

1 cup matza meal

1/4 cup oil or melted unsalted
   margarine

1 tablespoon chopped parsley
   (optional)

1/8 teaspoon ground ginger (optional)

1. Beat eggs lightly. Add club soda, salt, and pepper. Mix in remaining ingredients. Cover and refrigerate 1 hour.

2. Bring large pot of salted water to a boil. Mix again, moisten hands, and form mixture into balls. Drop into boiling water and cover. Lower heat and cook slowly 45 minutes.

3. Remove with slotted spoon to soup.

Makes 8 to 10, depending on size

◦§ HADASSAH ISRAEL

Traditional Chicken Soup

1 large stewing chicken,
   quartered

3 quarts water (enough to cover
   chicken in pot)

1 large onion, sliced

2 large carrots, sliced

2 stalks celery with leaves, sliced

1 parsnip, quartered

6 sprigs parsley

1/4 cup chopped fresh dill

Salt and freshly ground pepper
   to taste

1. Wash and pat chicken dry and place in large soup pot. Add water and bring to a boil.

2. Lower heat, skim fat. Cover pot and simmer 30 minutes.

3. Add onion, carrots, celery, and parsnip and continue to simmer about 1 hour.

4. Add parsley, dill, salt, and pepper. Cook 30 minutes, or until tender. Let cool. Strain vegetables. Remove chicken; shred, and return to pot.

Serves 6 to 8

◦§ ORA HADASSAH, DELRAY BEACH, FLORIDA

A HEN (also called a fowl or stewing chicken) is a female chicken from 10 to 18 months old usually weighing 3 to 6 pounds. Their age makes them more flavorful but also less tender, and they are best cooked with moist heat. A PULLET is a younger hen, usually less than a year old. The baby of the bunch, a BROILER-FRYER is usually about 2-1/2 months old and can weigh up to 3-1/2 pounds.

◆ *Great for the Break Fast*

Chicken Soup with a Tomato Twist

1 large chicken, quartered, cleaned, and skinned
1 leek, split, cleaned, and chopped
3 carrots, cut in chunks
1 bunch dill, chopped
2 stalks celery with leaves, diced
Salt and freshly ground pepper to taste
28-ounce can whole tomatoes
Noodles, rice, or matza balls

1. Combine all ingredients in soup pot with 4 cups water and cook over low heat, partially covered, 2 hours for hen, less for pullet.

2. Remove chicken from pot. Take meat off bones and return to soup.

3. To serve, reheat and add noodles, rice, or matza balls. Soup may be frozen.

Makes about 2 quarts

◆ KAREN WOHLSTADTER, HEWLETT HADASSAH, NEW YORK

Colonial Carrot Bisque

6 tablespoons (3/4 stick) unsalted margarine, or olive oil
2 pounds carrots, thinly sliced
2 large onions, chopped
1 tablespoon minced fresh gingerroot
Grated zest of 1 orange
1/4 teaspoon freshly ground pepper
5 cups chicken-soup stock, divided
Minced fresh parsley

1. Melt margarine and add carrots and onions. Cover pot and simmer about 5 minutes, stirring occasionally, until vegetables start to soften.

2. Add ginger, orange zest, pepper, and 2 cups chicken-soup stock, and continue to simmer until vegetables are very tender, about 10 minutes.

3. Transfer to blender and purée soup. Return to pot and add remaining 3 cups soup. Bring to a simmer. Sprinkle servings with minced parsley.

Serves 8

◆ SYLVIA D. WEISS, EAST WINDSOR HADASSAH, CRANBURY, NEW JERSEY

Cauliflower Pie

1 large white cauliflower
5 tablespoons olive oil
4 to 5 large cloves garlic,
    minced

Salt and freshly ground pepper
    to taste
2 eggs, lightly beaten
2 tablespoons flour

1. Preheat oven to 450 degrees. Oil 9-inch pie plate. Bring large pot of salted water to a boil. Separate florets and discard core of cauliflower. Boil florets about 15 minutes, just until fork tender. Drain and mash.

2. Heat 3 tablespoons oil in large skillet. Add garlic and cook over low heat about 1 minute; do not let garlic burn. Add mashed cauliflower, salt and pepper, and stir over high heat until excess moisture has evaporated. Remove from heat and let cool 10 or 15 minutes.

3. Stir in eggs and flour and pour into pan. Spread evenly and sprinkle with remaining oil. Bake 30 minutes, until top starts to brown.

Serves 4 to 6

◆ MARC SCHWARTZ, NEW HAVEN HADASSAH, CONNECTICUT

Aunt Irma's Noodle Pudding

8-ounce package cream cheese,
    softened
1 cup sour cream
5 eggs, well beaten
12-ounce jar apricot jam
1 cup apricot nectar
1/2 cup milk
1/4 cup sugar
8 tablespoons (1 stick) unsalted
    butter, melted

1/2 pound plus 2 handfuls
    egg noodles, cooked
1/2 cup raisins

TOPPING
2 cups crumbled frosted flakes cereal
1 teaspoon ground cinnamon
6 tablespoons (3/4 stick)
    unsalted butter, cut into
    small pieces

1. Preheat oven to 350 degrees. Grease 13 x 9 inch pan.

2. Combine cream cheese, sour cream, beaten eggs, apricot jam, apricot nectar, milk, sugar, and melted butter in large bowl. Stir until thoroughly blended and smooth.

3. Stir in cooked noodles and raisins until thoroughly coated. Spoon or pour into prepared pan.

4. Combine crumbled frosted flakes cereal with cinnamon; mix with butter. Crumble over top of noodles.

5. Bake about 1 hour, until pudding is set and top is golden.

Serves 10 to 12

ᴥ *Regina Levin, Westport Hadassah, Connecticut*

Honey Fish

1 pound red snapper fillets	*3 tablespoons red wine vinegar*
3/4 cup cold water	*1/8 teaspoon ground cumin*
1/4 cup dry sherry	*2 teaspoons dry mustard*
1/2 teaspoon powdered anise	*1/3 cup boiling water*
1 teaspoon grated lemon zest	*2 tablespoons honey*
1 teaspoon low-sodium vegetable bouillon powder	

1. Place fish in a nonreactive 13 x 9 inch ovenproof pan. Add cold water, sherry, anise, lemon zest, and the bouillon. Cover and refrigerate 30 minutes.

2. Add wine vinegar, cumin, and dry mustard. Let stand 20 minutes.

3. While fish is marinating, combine boiling water and honey. Let stand 20 minutes. Meanwhile, preheat oven to 325 degrees.

4. Pour honey mixture over fish. Cover and bake 20 minutes, or until fish flakes easily.

Serves 4

ᴥ *Kaz Tanaka, Shatil Group Hadassah, New York, New York*

NON-REACTIVE COOKWARE

Some metals interact chemically with foods containing acidic substances such as lemon juice and vinegar, and can form compounds that make you ill. You should use a nonreactive pan for preparations containing wine or other acid foods such as tomatoes.

Stuffed Breast of Veal

STUFFING

2 kosher knockwurst, cooked, and
   finely chopped in processor
2-1/2 to 3 cups fresh bread crumbs
3 scallions, finely sliced, and
   browned in 1 tablespoon oil
3 tablespoons finely chopped parsley
1 teaspoon dried thyme
1/2 teaspoon freshly grated
   nutmeg
1/2 teaspoon crumbled dried sage
1/2 teaspoon salt, or to taste
1 egg, lightly beaten
Freshly ground pepper to taste
1 veal breast (5 pounds), bone in,
   with pocket cut for stuffing

SAUCE

2 tablespoons oil
2 large onions, thinly sliced
2 green or red bell peppers,
   seeded and deveined, thinly
   sliced
2 carrots, cut in chunks
3 leeks, white part only, cut in
   chunks, washed thoroughly
2 stalks celery, cut in chunks
2 cloves garlic, thinly sliced
1 to 1-1/2 cups chicken or veal
   broth, or water

1. Preheat oven to 400 degrees. Combine stuffing ingredients, mix thoroughly, and pack lightly into veal pocket. Sew pocket closed with string or secure with skewers inserted horizontally into meat.

2. Heat 1 tablespoon oil in large roasting pan over medium heat. Brown veal lightly on both sides; remove from pan.

3. Add remaining tablespoon oil to pan and sauté onions, bell peppers carrots, leeks, celery, and garlic until garlic is wilted, about 5 to 7 minutes.

4. Remove half of vegetables from pan; spread remaining half in bottom of pan. Place meat on top of vegetables and spread removed vegetables over meat. Add 1 cup broth or water and cover tightly with lid or aluminum foil. Put pan on middle shelf of oven. Roast veal 30 minutes.

5. Reduce temperature to 350 degrees. Add 1/2 cup more broth or water, if needed, and braise 2 hours longer. Meat is done when juices run clear with no trace of pink, or internal temperature reads between 160 and 165 degrees.

6. Transfer veal to large heated platter. Tent loosely with aluminum foil. Remove skewers or trussing string. Let meat rest 10 minutes before carving.

7. Skim fat from juices in the pan. Season and serve with vegetables. For a thicker sauce, degreased juices and vegetables can be pureed in a food processor or blender.

Serves 6 to 8

◆ PAULA HESSE, BIRMINGHAM HADASSAH, ALABAMA

STUFFED BREAST OF VEAL, recipe at right.

Tzimmes

2 pounds carrots	1/2 cup packed brown sugar
3 pounds yams	1 teaspoon salt
12-ounce package pitted prunes	4 tablespoons unsalted butter
1/2 cup sugar	or margarine

1. Preheat oven to 450 degrees. Slice carrots 1/2 inch thick. Slice yams into 1-1/2 x 1/2-inch chunks.

2. Combine all ingredients in 4-quart casserole. Add 2 cups water, cover and bake 1 hour.

3. Uncover and bake 1 hour more, stirring occasionally, until ingredients are tender and water is absorbed.

Serves 8 to 10

Linda Steigman, Shelanu Hadassah, New York, New York

Yankee Tzimmes

1 pound Oregon prunes	1 stick cinnamon
1-1/2 pounds chestnuts	1 lemon, cut in quarters
1 cup sugar	

1. Soak prunes in cold water overnight.

2. In the morning, make crosscuts in raw chestnuts and soak in water several hours.

3. Add sugar, cinnamon, and lemon to prunes and liquid and stir over medium-low heat about 30 minutes.

4. Preheat oven to 350 degrees. Drain chestnuts and roast until skins start to peel back, about 20 minutes.

5. When chestnuts are all peeled, remove cinnamon from the prunes. Lemon wedges may be left in, if desired.

6. Add chestnuts to prunes and fold in to mix well, but try to do it gently so as not to break up the chestnuts.

7. Reheat and serve in any place that normal tzimmes would do. Excellent with turkey or with pot roast.

Serves 6

Ilanit Group Hadassah, Hewlett, New York

TIP

High in fiber, rich in vitamins and antioxidents (and they have no fat!), Oregon prunes are slower growing than California prunes and are more slowly cured, which results in a richer flavor and a good size prune that is deliciously sweet.

Tzimmes, recipe above.

Tzimmes
with Potato Kneidlach

TIPS

If thickening is needed, dissolve
1-1/2 teaspoons cornstarch or
1 tablespoon flour in 2 tablespoons
cold water and stir in for last half hour.

Brown some flour in a dry skillet over
medium-high heat, stirring constantly.
It keeps well and comes in handy to
thicken sauces without whitening them.

*1/2- to 3/4-pound fat meat, such
   as short ribs, flanken, or part
   of a roasting chicken*
2 pounds carrots, sliced
1 white potato, thinly sliced
1 yam, diced
1/2 cup sugar
*1 teaspoon plus 3/4 teaspoon
   salt*
*1 teaspoon minced crystallized
   ginger (optional)*

*1-1/2 pounds potatoes
   (5 or 6 medium), preferably
   a combination of baking
   and red*
*1-1/2 tablespoons chicken fat,
   melted*
1 egg, lightly beaten
1/2 teaspoon flour
*2 tablespoons breadcrumbs,
   approximately*

1. Preheat oven to 350 degrees. Arrange meat, carrots, sliced potato, and yam in roasting pan on top of stove. Add sugar, 1 teaspoon salt, the ginger, and water to cover and bring to a boil. Put in oven and bake, covered, 1 hour.

2. Meanwhile, grate 1-1/2 pounds potatoes and drain through a fine sieve, pressing lightly. Add chicken fat, egg, flour, 3/4 teaspoon salt, and the bread-crumbs. Mixture should be barely firm enough to shape into 2 soft balls.

3. Remove tzimmes from oven and increase heat to 450 degrees. Heap some carrot mixture toward edges so potato kneidlach can be placed in depression in liquid. Bake, covered, 1 hour. Reduce heat to 350 degrees and bake 1 hour longer; uncover to brown last 30 minutes.

Serves about 8

◀ CANTON HADASSAH, OHIO

Chicken Tzimmes

1 cooked oven-roasted chicken
(about 2-1/2 to 3 pounds),
skin removed, cut in 8 pieces
2 cups peeled baby carrots
1 cup pitted prunes

1/4 teaspoon freshly ground pepper
2 cans (15-1/2 ounces each)
candied yams, drained, syrup
reserved
1 small lemon, cut in thin slices

1. Put chicken, carrots, prunes, pepper, and syrup from yams in a 3-quart saucepan. Bring to boil and lower heat. Cover and simmer 20 minutes, stirring once or twice.

2. Add yams and lemon slices.

3. Cover and simmer 5 minutes longer, or until yams are hot.

Serves 4 to 6

◄§ MRS. CHARLES FREILICH, GATESVILLE HADASSAH, TEXAS

Sweet and Sour Chicken Fricassee

TIPS
Best if made the day before so that fat can be skimmed off and flavors have a chance to blend.

One 12-ounce bottle of ketchup is equal to 1 standard measuring cup.

SAUCE
12-ounce bottle ketchup
8-ounce can whole cranberry
sauce
3 tablespoons grape jelly
3 tablespoons brown sugar
3 tablespoons fresh lemon juice
Pinch **each** of garlic powder,
onion powder, and salt

1 chicken (3-1/2 to 4 pounds), cut
in pieces, and skinned if desired

MEATBALLS
1 pound lean ground beef
1 egg, lightly beaten
1 small onion, grated
2 tablespoons breadcrumbs
Pinch of salt

1. Combine ketchup, 1-1/2 cups water, the cranberry sauce, grape jelly, brown sugar, lemon juice, garlic powder, onion powder, and salt in large pot. Add chicken and cook over medium heat, stirring, until mixture boils.

2. Prepare meatballs. Combine ground beef, lightly beaten egg, the grated onion, bread crumbs, and salt. Form mixture into small meatballs and add to sauce. Simmer, partly covered, 1 hour.

Serves 6 to 8

◄§ RIVA RITTBERG, BINGHAMTON HADASSAH, NEW YORK

Sweet-Spiced Turkey Breast

SPICE PASTE

3 large cloves garlic, minced

2 large scallions, minced

1 tablespoon safflower oil

1-1/4 teaspoons salt

1 teaspoon each *cinnamon,
allspice, coarsely cracked
black pepper*

ONIONS AND RAISINS

2 large Spanish onions (about
1 pound total), thinly sliced

1/2 cup golden raisins

2 tablespoons cider vinegar

Salt to taste

1 tablespoon minced parsley

1 skinned and boned turkey
breast (about 2-1/4 pounds),
rolled and tied

1. Position oven rack in center of oven. Preheat oven to 500 degrees.
Have ready heavy-duty foil and baking sheet.

2. Make the spice paste: In small bowl, mix garlic, scallions, oil, salt,
cinnamon, allspice, and pepper. Rinse turkey breast and pat dry with paper
towels. Rub paste evenly into entire surface of turkey.

3. Separate onion slices into rings. Put onions and raisins in center of
heavy-duty aluminum foil large enough to enclose turkey. Sprinkle with
vinegar. Place turkey breast on top of onions and raisins.

4. Tent turkey in airtight foil package, leaving small amount of air space
between foil and breast. Place turkey on baking sheet.

5. Roast 30 to 35 minutes, until instant-read thermometer inserted halfway
through thickest portion registers 170 degrees. Don't open foil to test
temperature, just insert thermometer through foil.

6. Carefully open foil. Let rest 10 to 20 minutes before cutting into
thin diagonal slices.

7. Arrange slices on warm platter. Spoon juices and onions over roast.

8. Sprinkle lightly with salt and minced parsley. Serve hot. May
also be served at room temperature or chilled.

Serves 6 to 8

◆§ NAOMI JAFFE, NORTH BOUNDARY HADASSAH, CHICAGO, ILLINOIS

*T*oday's instructions for cooking a turkey are much more specific and safety-conscious than earlier in American history. In 1824 **The Virginia Housewife** *said that a turkey of middle size would take merely an hour and a quarter to roast. The original* **Boston School Cookbook** *of 1895 recommended a high-heat jump-start, then lowered heat for the rest of the three hours it would take to roast a 10-pound turkey.*

Modern-day concern about salmonella has the FDA issuing conservative safety guidelines: temperature of a constant 325 for 18 to 24 minutes a pound for stuffed turkeys, 15 to 20 minutes for unstuffed. Birds of more than 14 pounds require less time per pound.

A higher oven—450 degrees for the first half hour, then 325 or 350 degrees until the correct internal temperatures are reached—185 degrees for thigh meat, 170 degrees for breast meat—is also acceptable. Any temperature below 325 degrees—the overnight 250 of a few years ago, for instance—does not allow the meat to reach and maintain a high enough temperature to prevent bacteria growth.

Roast Turkey with Brown Rice–Nut Stuffing

12-pound turkey
Salt and freshly ground pepper
   to taste
Ground ginger, to taste
Paprika, to taste
2 cloves garlic, crushed
Half a lemon
1/2 cup oil or melted margarine

STUFFING
2 cups brown rice
8 cups boiling water
1/4 cup oil
1 large onion, chopped
1 clove garlic, crushed
3 ribs celery, chopped

1/2 pound mushrooms, sliced
2 cups unsalted cashew nuts,
   coarsely chopped
1/4 cup chopped parsley
1/4 teaspoon freshly ground
   pepper
1 teaspoon salt
1/2 teaspoon dried thyme
1/2 teaspoon dried rosemary
1/4 teaspoon ground ginger
1/4 cup dry white wine

GLAZE
1 cup apricot jam
2 tablespoons fresh lemon juice

1. Preheat oven to 350 degrees. Sprinkle turkey cavity with salt, pepper, ginger, and paprika.

2. Make stuffing: Wash rice thoroughly and add to boiling water. Reduce heat to medium, cover, and cook 30 minutes. Strain and rinse with cold water.

3. Heat oil; sauté onion and garlic 5 minutes. Add celery and mushrooms; sauté 5 minutes longer. Combine with nuts, parsley, seasonings, and wine. Stuff cavity and neck loosely and sew or fasten with skewers.

4. Sprinkle outer surface of turkey with salt, pepper, ginger, and paprika; rub with crushed garlic and cut lemon, squeezing the juice over turkey. Wrap in aluminum foil. Roast turkey breast-side down in shallow roasting pan.

5. After 1-1/2 to 2 hours, turn breast-side up and roast another 1-1/2 hours.

6. Meanwhile, make glaze. Mix apricot jam and lemon juice with 1 cup water. Bring to boil over medium heat; cook 5 minutes. Pour over cooked turkey.

Serves 16 to 18

◀ *HADASSAH ISRAEL*

Mandarin Orange Kasha Stuffing

1 egg

1 cup raw kasha

1/4 cup (1/2 stick) unsalted
  margarine

1 cup chopped onion

1 cup chopped celery

2 cups hot chicken broth

1/4 cup golden raisins

1/4 teaspoon ground ginger

1/4 teaspoon dry mustard

3/4 cup (16-ounce can) Mandarin
  orange segments, drained, liquid
  reserved for basting

1/8 teaspoon seasoned salt

1. Combine egg and kasha in a small bowl and set aside.

2. In a large skillet over medium heat, melt margarine. Sauté onion and celery in margarine until tender. Add kasha and stir until each grain is separate.

3. Add hot broth, the raisins, ginger, and dry mustard. Cover skillet and simmer 15 minutes, or until liquid is absorbed and grains are tender.

4. Cool slightly; mix in orange segments and seasoned salt.

5. Fill neck and cavities of chicken, duck, or turkey. Roast poultry about 30 minutes to the pound, basting frequently with Mandarin orange juice.

Makes 3 cups

◆ SARAH SOLOMON, HILLCREST-SABRA-SCOPUS HADASSAH, FLORIDA

Sweet and Sour Tongue

1 large onion

3 large tomatoes

1 fresh beef tongue (3 to 3-1/2
  pounds)

Juice of 1 lemon

2 tablespoons honey

2 tablespoons sugar

1 small clove garlic

2 teaspoons salt

2 teaspoons allspice

1 clove garlic

1 small bay leaf

Dash of ground cinnamon

3/4 cup raisins

1. Slice onion and tomatoes and place in a large, heavy kettle with tongue and 3 cups water. Add lemon juice and honey. Bring to a boil over medium heat; reduce heat to low and simmer, partly covered, about 1 hour.

2. Add sugar, garlic, salt, and spices; continue cooking 2 hours longer or until tongue is tender.

3. Remove tongue from sauce. When just cool enough to handle, carefully peel off tough skin.

4. Strain sauce, pressing through onion and tomatoes.

5. Wash raisins and cook in strained sauce until soft. Slice tongue and return to sauce. Add extra salt or sugar if needed. Heat thoroughly when ready to serve.

Serves 6 to 8

◆ₛ JOAN GROSSMAN, THEODOR HERZL HADASSAH, CHERRY HILL, NEW JERSEY

Tongue in Raisin Sauce

1 fresh beef tongue (3 to
   3-1/2 pounds)
1 tablespoon salt
2 bay leaves

SAUCE
1/2 cup packed brown sugar
1-1/2 tablespoons all-purpose flour
1 teaspoon dry mustard
2 tablespoons fresh lemon juice
2 tablespoons vinegar
1/4 teaspoon grated lemon zest
2/3 cup raisins

1. Wash tongue. Place in large, heavy pot with 2-1/2 quarts water, the salt, and bay leaves. Cover, bring to a boil, and skim froth from surface. Re-cover, and simmer about 3 hours, or until tongue is tender.

2. Cool tongue in broth until it is easy to handle; remove from broth and peel off skin. Remove any bones and gristle.

3. Cut tongue into thin slices and place in shallow ovenproof dish.

4. Preheat oven to 350 degrees. Prepare sauce: In medium saucepan, combine brown sugar, flour, and mustard; stir in 1 to 1-1/2 cups water, the lemon juice, vinegar, and lemon zest. Cook, stirring over medium heat, until sauce has thickened. Add raisins and pour sauce over sliced tongue.

5. Bake uncovered about 15 minutes, or until heated through.

Serves 6 to 8

◆ₛ MARY SAFER, JACKSONVILLE HADASSAH, FLORIDA

According to the Bible, the principal things necessary for life are water, fire and iron, salt, milk, bread of flour, honey, the clusters of the grape, oil, and clothing. It is with the sweetness of honey that we evoke the anticipated sweetness of the New Year.

In biblical times honey was the principal sweetener and almost the only one. There were some alternatives, but rather unsatisfactory ones. The Bible is full of references to honey, but there is no mention of beekeeping. Although bees had been domesticated in other areas since the Bronze Age, the ancient Hebrews' lifestyle was nomadic, incompatible with such sedentary occupations as raising bees.

The Hebrew word for bee is *dhure*, from the root *dbr*, meaning word, which implies the bee's mission to reveal the Divine Word.

Honey Teiglach

4 cups all-purpose flour
2 teaspoons baking powder
1/2 teaspoon salt
6 eggs, lightly beaten
1 cup chopped nuts
1/4 cup raisins (optional)

SYRUP
2 cups honey
1 cup packed brown sugar
2 teaspoons powdered ginger
1/2 teaspoon freshly grated
    nutmeg (optional)
1/4 teaspoon ground cinnamon

1. Preheat oven to 350 degrees. Lightly grease baking sheet.

2. Combine flour, baking powder, and salt. Add beaten eggs and mix well. Knead 3 to 5 minutes, until smooth; refrigerate 15 minutes.

3. Break off pieces of dough and roll into ropes 1/2-inch thick, then cut into 1/2-inch pieces. Place on prepared baking sheet and bake 5 to 7 minutes, until golden.

4. Combine syrup ingredients in pan. Bring to a boil, then simmer, covered, 10 minutes.

5. Drop in dough pieces, nuts, and raisins, if using, and simmer 5 minutes, stirring with wooden spoon until teiglach are coated and golden.

6. Moisten large wooden board with cold water. With slotted spoon transfer teiglach to board. Lightly oil hands, and shape teiglach into large cone-shaped mound.

Makes 1 cone

◄§ HADASSAH ISRAEL

HONEY TEIGLACH, Recipe above.

TIPS

When melting sugar, 260 degrees is the hard ball stage: When a small amount of sugar syrup is dropped into very cold water, it forms a rigid ball that is still somewhat pliable.

One 12-ounce jar of honey is equal to 1 standard measuring cup.

DOUGH	SYRUP
7 large eggs	2 cups honey
2/3 cup vegetable oil	2 cups sugar
1 tablespoon honey	1 cup candied fruit, minced
1 tablespoon sugar	4 ounces (3/4 cup) walnuts,
1/4 teaspoon salt	coarsely chopped
1/2 teaspoon ground ginger	4 ounces (3/4 cup) hazelnuts,
5 to 6 cups all-purpose flour	coarsely chopped

1. Preheat oven to 400 degrees. Grease cookie sheet.

2. Make dough: Beat eggs with an electric mixer in a bowl with oil, honey, sugar, salt, ginger, and 5 cups flour until flour is absorbed and mixture is smooth. Add enough additional flour to form a pliable dough that can be rolled.

3. Pinch off small portions of dough and roll into long ropes; cut into 1-inch pieces. Bake on prepared cookie sheet about 10 minutes. Let cool.

4. To prepare syrup, place honey and sugar in a large pot and stir until temperature reaches 260 degrees on a candy thermometer. Add fruit and nuts and stir thoroughly.

5. While syrup is hot, add pieces of baked dough and simmer 5 minutes. Remove small amounts at a time with a slotted spoon and place on a greased cookie sheet in a thin layer. Let cool to lukewarm. Shape teighlach on a serving plate into a large mound to resemble a cone.

Makes 1 cone

◦§ PATTI SHOSTECK, ROSLYN HEIGHTS HADASSAH, NEW YORK

Dutch Boterkoek

◦§ *Great for the Break Fast*

2 cups all-purpose flour	1 cup sugar
1 cup (2 sticks) unsalted butter,	1/2 teaspoon vanilla extract
at room temperature	Pinch of salt

1. Preheat oven to 375 degrees. Lightly butter 9-inch round or square cake pan.

2. Mix all ingredients into smooth dough and pat into prepared pan. Flatten with a fork.

3. Bake 20 minutes, until lightly browned. Cut into squares before completely cool.

Makes about 3 dozen

◆ *Hetty deLeeuwe, North Shore Hadassah, Highland Park, Illinois*

Lil's Babka

BATTER	FILLING
1 (1/4-ounce) package active dry yeast	3 egg whites, at room temperature
1 teaspoon plus 2 tablespoons sugar	1 cup sugar
2-1/2 cups sifted all-purpose flour	1 cup golden raisins
1/2 teaspoon salt	1 cup chopped nuts
1/2 pound (2 sticks) unsalted butter, at room temperature	2 teaspoons ground cinnamon
	Melted unsalted butter
1/4 cup milk	
3 egg yolks	CRUMB TOPPING
	5 tablespoons all-purpose flour
	5 tablespoons sugar
	2 tablespoon soft unsalted butter

1. Add yeast and 1 teaspoon sugar to 1/4-cup warm water to dissolve; let sit until foamy.

2. Combine flour with salt; cut butter into flour until it resembles small peas. Stir in milk, egg yolks, remaining 2 tablespoons sugar, and the yeast mixture. Knead dough until it forms a ball, adding more flour if needed. Cover with plastic wrap or place in zip-lock bag, and refrigerate overnight.

3. Grease 10-inch tube pan. Divide dough in 2 parts. Roll out each into a 16 x 10 inch oblong.

4. Make filling: Beat egg whites until stiff; gradually beat in sugar. Spread over each piece of dough and sprinkle each with raisins, nuts, and cinnamon. Roll up from short end jelly-roll style and place in prepared pan to form one ring. Brush with melted butter.

5. Make crumb topping. Combine flour, sugar, and softened butter. Stir with a fork until crumbly and sprinkle over dough in pan. Cover loosely with clean towel and set aside to rise in warm place until doubled in bulk, about 1 to 1-1/2 hours. Meanwhile, preheat oven to 350 degrees.

6. Bake 45 minutes to 1 hour, until well risen and golden.

Serves 14 to 16

◆ *Susan Lourie, Columbia Hadassah, South Carolina*

Chocolate Lover's Angel Food Cake

1/4 cup plus 1 tablespoon unsweetened Dutch process cocoa powder	1-3/4 cups sugar, divided
	1 cup sifted cake flour
2 teaspoons instant coffee granules	1/4 teaspoon salt
1/4 cup boiling water	Whites of 14 eggs
2 teaspoons vanilla extract	(approximately 2 cups)
	2 teaspoons cream of tartar

1. Preheat oven to 350 degrees. Have ready an ungreased 10-inch angel food pan. In medium bowl, whisk cocoa, coffee granules, and boiling water until smooth. Whisk in vanilla extract. Let cool.

2. In another medium bowl, combine 3/4 cup sugar, the flour, and salt and whisk to blend.

3. In large bowl, beat egg whites until frothy. Add cream of tartar and beat until soft peaks form when beater is raised. Gradually beat in remaining 1 cup sugar, beating until very stiff peaks form when beater is raised slowly.

4. Remove a heaping cup of egg whites and place on top of cooled cocoa mixture. Dust flour mixture over remaining whites 1/4 cup at a time, and with a large wire balloon whisk, fold in quickly but gently. It is not necessary to incorporate every speck into the last addition.

5. Whisk together the egg-white-and-cocoa mixture and fold into the batter until uniform. Pour into pan (batter will come to within 3/4 inch of the top). Run a small metal spatula or knife through the batter to prevent air pockets. Bake 40 minutes, or until a cake tester inserted into the center comes out clean and the cake springs back when lightly pressed. (The center will rise above the pan while baking and sink slightly when done. The surface will have deep cracks like a soufflé.)

6. Invert pan, placing the tube opening over the neck of a soda or wine bottle to suspend it well above the counter. Cool the cake completely in the pan, about 1-1/2 hours. Loosen sides with a long metal spatula and disconnect sides from the center of the pan. (To keep attractive, press spatula gently against sides of pan and avoid up-and-down motion.) Dislodge bottom and center with a metal spatula or thin, sharp knife (a wire cake tester works well around the core). Invert onto a serving plate. Wrap any leftovers securely in plastic wrap.

Serves 16

Edith Zamost, Monroe Township Hadassah, New Jersey

Sephardic Farina Cake

➤ Great for the Break Fast

TIP
Make ahead and serve warmed or at room temperature, accompanied by cut-up fruit of the season.

1/4 cup (1/2 stick) unsalted
   butter
1 quart milk
1 teaspoon salt
1 cup uncooked farina

6 eggs
1-1/2 cups sugar
Grated zest of 1 lemon
2 cups ricotta cheese
1 to 3 teaspoons vanilla extract

1. Preheat oven to 375 degrees. Grease 13 x 9 inch baking pan.

2. Melt butter in large saucepan. Add 2 cups water, the milk, and salt, and bring to a boil. Gradually add farina, stirring constantly until mixture thickens, about 3 minutes.

3. Beat eggs with sugar and lemon zest until light. Add farina to egg mixture a little at a time, until all is combined. Stir in ricotta and vanilla extract.

4. Pour into prepared pan. Bake 1 hour and 20 minutes, or until a knife inserted in the center comes out clean.

Serves 12 to 14

➤ MARGE SCALLO, AVIVA HADASSAH, MAPLEWOOD/SOUTH ORANGE, NEW JERSEY

Plum Kuchen

2 cups sifted all-purpose flour
1 teaspoon baking powder
1/2 teaspoon salt
1/2 cup sugar, divided
1/4 cup shortening
1 egg yolk, lightly beaten
3/4 cup milk

1 pound Italian blue plums,
   halved and pitted
2 tablespoon chopped nuts
1/2 teaspoon ground cinnamon
   (optional)
1 tablespoon unsalted butter

1. Preheat oven to 350 degrees. Grease 8-inch square pan.

2. Sift flour with baking powder, salt, and 1/4 cup sugar. Cut in shortening. Combine egg yolk with milk and stir into dry ingredients quickly to form a soft dough. Spread batter into pan.

3. Arrange plums cut-side down decoratively over top and sprinkle with remaining 1/4 cup sugar, the nuts, and the cinnamon, if desired. Dot with butter and bake 35 to 40 minutes, until done.

Serves 6 to 8

➤ JEANETTE JACOBY, DAYAN GROUP HADASSAH, BALTIMORE, MARYLAND

If the vegetable kingdom has a royal family, it is certainly the Rosaceae, which includes the queen of all flowers, the rose, and the king of all fruits, the apple.

The apple has played a part in religion, magic, superstition, folklore, history, and medicine as far back as we can go, but not in the story of Adam and Eve. There is no mention of the apple in Genesis. What they ate was the fruit of the tree of the knowledge of good and evil. We may assume that the ancient Hebrews purposefully refrained from representing it as any specific known fruit, lest the mystery of the image be dissipated by attaching it to a commonplace object.

Nobody knows how many different varieties exist today, except that the numbers run into the tens of thousands. Whatever variety you eat, though, make sure to buy only those picked by the light of the waning moon. This advice comes from Horace, a first century B.C.E. Roman poet.

Delectable Apple Cake

5 medium apples (about 2 pounds), peeled, cored, quartered, and sliced
5 tablespoons plus 2 cups sugar
2 teaspoons ground cinnamon
3 cups all-purpose flour
1 tablespoon baking powder
1 teaspoon salt
1 cup oil
1 teaspoon vanilla extract
1/4 cup fresh orange juice
4 eggs, lightly beaten

1. Preheat oven to 350 degrees. Grease 10-inch tube pan. Toss apples with 5 tablespoons sugar and the cinnamon and set aside.

2. Combine flour with baking powder and salt; set aside. In medium bowl beat the 2 cups sugar with the oil and vanilla extract until thoroughly mixed. Beat in dry ingredients alternately with orange juice and beaten eggs.

3. Spread half the batter into prepared tube pan. Spoon half the apple mixture over batter, then spread remaining batter on top. Finally, spoon over remaining apples.

4. Bake about 1 hour and 30 minutes, covering lightly with foil if browning too much. Cool thoroughly in pan on wire rack, then turn out of pan.

Serves 14 to 16

ARLENE KARP, SAN DIEGO HADASSAH, CALIFORNIA

Shoshana's Apple-Pie Cake

DOUGH
2 cups all-purpose flour
1 cup sugar
1/2 teaspoon baking powder
1 egg
1 egg yolk (save white for glaze)
1 cup (2 sticks) unsalted margarine
Pinch of salt

1 pound plus 1 apple Granny Smiths, peeled, cored, and quartered
1/3 cup sugar combined with 1 teaspoon ground cinnamon
1/4 cup (1/2 stick) unsalted margarine

FILLING
2 pounds plus 1 apple Braeburn, peeled, cored, and quartered

GLAZE
Reserved egg white lightly beaten with 2 tablespoons sugar

1. Line oven with foil to catch any drips, then preheat to 350 degrees. Grease

10-inch springform pan. In bowl of food processor, process dough ingredients.

2. Remove pan sides and pat a bit less than half the dough onto bottom of pan. If dough is too soft to handle, dip hands lightly in water or flour to spread evenly over the pan. Replace pan sides.

3. Slice Braeburns with medium blade of food processor and spoon evenly into pan. Sprinkle with half the cinnamon-sugar. Grate Grannies, spoon over the Braeburns, and sprinkle with remaining cinnamon-sugar. Cut the 1/4 cup margarine into small pieces and spread over apples. Pat on remaining half of dough to cover top. Bake 45 minutes, or until golden.

4. Remove cake from oven and paint glaze over the top. Continue baking another 10 minutes. Superb with ice cream for a dairy meal.

Serves 8 to 10

🍂 *Shoshana Michel, Lakewood Hadassah, New Jersey*

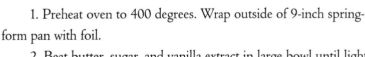

Bavarian Apple Torte

1/2 cup (1 stick) unsalted butter, softened
1/3 cup sugar
1/4 teaspoon vanilla extract
1 cup all-purpose flour
8-ounce package cream cheese, at room temperature
1/4 cup sugar

1 egg
1/2 teaspoon vanilla extract
4 cups (about 4 to 5) peeled, cored, and sliced apples
1/3 cup sugar
1/2 teaspoon ground cinnamon
Dash of freshly grated nutmeg

1. Preheat oven to 400 degrees. Wrap outside of 9-inch springform pan with foil.

2. Beat butter, sugar, and vanilla extract in large bowl until light and fluffy. Stir in flour. Press dough onto bottom and sides of springform pan. Bake until golden, 8 to 10 minutes. Let cool on wire rack.

3. In a medium bowl beat cream cheese, sugar, egg, and vanilla extract until smooth. Pour into crust.

4. Toss apple slices with sugar, cinnamon, and nutmeg. Spread over cheese layer. Bake 45 minutes, until edges are brown and cheese filling is set.

Serves 8

🍂 *Karen Berman, Rene Goodman, Sue Baer, Indianapolis Hadassah, Indiana*

Apple Strudel

10 apples (about 6 pounds),
    such as Empire or Rome,
    peeled cored, and sliced
2 tablespoons all-purpose
    flour
10 tablespoons (1 stick plus
    2 tablespoons) unsalted
    margarine or butter, melted,
    divided

2 tablespoons no-sugar-added
    strawberry or apricot jam
1 tablespoon ground cinnamon
1/2 cup raisins (optional)
1/2 cup chopped walnuts or
    pecans (optional)
Juice of 1 lime
Half of 16-ounce box frozen
    phyllo dough

1. Preheat oven to 350 degrees.

2. Toss apples with flour, 8 tablespoons margarine, the jam, cinnamon, raisins, and nuts, if using, and the lime juice in large bowl.

3. Grease 13 x 9 inch baking pan. Layer three sheets of phyllo lengthwise into left side of pan to cover most of the bottom and extend 2 to 3 inches over the side. Repeat for right side, overlapping phyllo on the bottom.

4. Place apple mixture on phyllo. Fold phyllo over apple mixture. Place 2 more sheets dough on top to cover apples, tucking edges into pan. Brush remaining 2 tablespoons margarine on top of dough and sprinkle lightly with cinnamon.

5. Cover and bake 50 minutes; uncover for 5 minutes to brown.

Serves 12

❧ Svetlana Waxman, Cascades Hadassah, Boynton Beach, Florida

Honey Cake

3-1/2 cups all-purpose flour
1 teaspoon baking powder
1 teaspoon baking soda
1 teaspoon ground cinnamon
1 teaspoon ground allspice
4 eggs, lightly beaten

1/2 cup warm coffee
1/2 cup oil
12 ounces strawberry preserves
1 pound honey
1/2 cup nuts (optional)

1. Preheat oven to 350 degrees. Grease 9 x 5 inch loaf pan and line with wax paper.

2. Combine flour with baking powder, baking soda, cinnamon, and allspice.

3. Combine beaten eggs, coffee, and oil. Beat in strawberry preserves. Beat in honey. Beat in flour mixture and add nuts, if using.

4. Pour into prepared pan and bake 1 hour, until done.

Serves 8 to 10

◆§ ELLEN MANDEL LEVINE, AMEET HADASSAH, TAMPA, FLORIDA

Honey Chiffon Cake

1 cup honey (1/2 cup buckwheat, 1/2 cup clover)

1 teaspoon baking soda

8 eggs, separated, at room temperature

1 cup sugar

3/4 cup oil

1 teaspoon vanilla extract

1-3/4 cups all-purpose flour

1 teaspoon salt

1/4 teaspoon ground cloves

1/4 teaspoon freshly grated nutmeg

1/2 teaspoon ground cinnamon

1/2 cup chopped walnuts

1. Preheat oven to 325 degrees. Have handy an ungreased 10-inch tube pan.

2. Bring honey to a boil. Add baking soda, stir, and let cool.

3. Beat egg whites until stiff, gradually beat in sugar. In separate bowl, beat egg yolks until frothy; gradually beat in oil and vanilla extract. Add cooled honey. Combine flour, salt, and spices and fold in. Add nuts.

4. Fold beaten egg whites into flour mixture. Pour into pan and bake 1 hour.

5. Touch lightly with finger; if it springs back, cake is done. Bake up to 15 minutes longer if needed. Remove from oven and invert pan until cool.

Serves 12

◆§ POLLY BAKER, HILLCREST-SABRA-SCOPUS HADASSAH, BROWARD, FLORIDA

Honey Cake Minis

1/2 cup (1 stick) unsalted
    margarine, at room
    temperature
1/2 cup firmly packed brown
    sugar
Grated zest of 1 orange
2 eggs
2/3 cup honey
2 cups all-purpose flour

1-1/2 teaspoons baking soda
1 teaspoon ground cinnamon
1 teaspoon freshly grated nutmeg
1/2 cup chopped or sliced
    almonds
1 cup chopped pitted dates, tossed
    with a little flour to coat
2/3 cup fresh orange juice

1. Preheat oven to 350 degrees. Grease and flour miniature muffin tins, or line with mini muffin papers.

2. Cream margarine and sugar until light and fluffy. Beat in orange zest. Beat in eggs one at a time, beating well after each. Beat in honey.

3. Whisk to mix flour with baking soda, cinnamon and nutmeg; add almonds and dates. Add to margarine mixture alternately with orange juice. Spoon 1 tablespoon batter into each cup.

4. Bake 15 minutes. Let cool in pan 5 minutes, then remove to wire rack to cool completely. Repeat with remaining batter.

Makes 5 dozen

⋅§ BERTHA LUKS, BIRMINGHAM HADASSAH, ALABAMA

Fasting on Yom Kippur

How many are aware that the mitzva of eating two full meals on eruv Yom Kippur is equal to the mitzva of the fast itself?

But that doesn't mean you have to stuff yourself. In fact, it's best to begin with small amounts of protein like fish or chicken, essential to maintaining stable blood sugar levels, as well as cooked vegetables and a salad with a light olive oil dressing. Skip thirst-inducing sweets for dessert and go with a piece of fruit. Drink hot decaffeinated tea at the end of the meal—hot foods will sustain you better. Don't use any spices which would create the need for drink, and nuts, too, can increase the flow of saliva and make it a tougher haul.

"The greatest part of the unpleasantness associated with fasting comes not from lack of food, but from dehydration," explains Mark Meskin, director of the nutrition education program at the University of Southern California School of Medicine in Los Angeles. "Make sure to take in lots of fluids the day before, maybe two quarts, but don't overdo the alcohol because it's diuretic." Much of the discomfort experienced by fasting coffee- and cola-drinkers is caused by caffeine deprivation, so taper off during the week or two before the holiday. "I'd be most concerned about those people taking drugs on a daily basis for heart disease, diabetes, high blood pressure, cancer—you could go on and on," adds Meskin. "With many of these drugs it's inappropriate to stop taking them for even a day. And if they must be taken with food or fluid, they really need to do that. They also need to eat and drink all during the day, because for these drugs to do their jobs one has to be consuming food regularly."

"The Torah indeed tells us people should not risk their lives to fast on Yom Kippur," says Rabbi Yitzchak Rosenbaum of the National Jewish Outreach Program. "We say there's a shiur [a minimum amount] you can eat before you violate the full prohibition." Rabbi Rosenbaum explains, "For food it's about the size of an olive, for water it's less than an ounce—about what you can fit into the side of your cheek—during any nine to 12 minute period." But always discuss the matter with both your doctor and your rabbi.

Hatima tovah. May you be written and sealed for a good year, and may you have an easy and meaningful fast.

Tante Manya's Honey Challah

2 (1/4-ounce) packages active
   dry yeast
3 tablespoons sugar
1/4 cup vegetable oil
2 tablespoons salt
1-1/2 cups honey

6 eggs, well beaten
14 cups all-purpose or bread flour
2 egg yolks beaten with
   4 teaspoons water
Poppy or sesame seeds (optional)

1. Grease 2 large cookie sheets. Mix yeast with 1/2 cup lukewarm water to dissolve. In large bowl, combine 2-1/2 cups water, the sugar, oil, salt, and honey, and stir until smooth. Mix in eggs; stir in yeast. Gradually add flour, mixing until dough is no longer too sticky and can be handled. Put into large greased bowl and turn to coat entire surface. Cover and let rise 2 hours, until doubled in bulk.

2. Punch down dough and let rise 2 hours longer.

3. Divide into 4 equal parts for 4 loaves. Divide each part in 3 for braiding. Braid, and place loaves well apart on prepared cookie sheets. Brush with yolk mixture and sprinkle with poppy or sesame seeds. Cover with towel and let rise 2 hours. Meanwhile, preheat oven to 350 degrees. 15 minutes before baking, brush again with yolk mixture and sprinkle with seeds.

4. Bake 30 to 40 minutes, until bread is a rich tawny color and sounds hollow when bottom is tapped.

Makes 4 loaves

◆ ANNA JACOBS, SCRANTON HADASSAH, PENNSYLVANIA

Egg Barley and Mushrooms (Farfel)

Half an 8-ounce box toasted
   egg barley
Half an 8-ounce box plain
   egg barley
1/4 cup oil

2 medium to large onions, cut up
4 to 8 ounces fresh mushrooms,
   sliced
Salt and freshly ground pepper
   to taste

1. Cook barley according to package directions.

2. Heat oil over medium-high heat and sauté onions and mushrooms until softened, about 10 to 12 minutes. Combine egg barley with onions and mushrooms. Season with salt and pepper.

Serves 4

◆ ROSELLE-CRANFORD HADASSAH, NEW JERSEY

BARLEY

*P*robably the world's oldest grain crop, barley is indigenous to Israel, one of the seven species with which the land was blessed. Abraham offered barley bread to the visiting angels; when Boaz first set eyes on Ruth she was gleaning barley.

For nutritive value barley is halfway between wheat and rye, with a higher protein content than rice. The most healthful form is the hulled, from which only the outer husk has been removed. Scottish barley has been husked and coarsely ground; pearl barley, also husked, has been steamed and polished.

Barley cooks up about triple in volume. Combined with water and lemon, it's used to make barley water, an old-time restorative. Belila, an excellent barley-based replacement for cake, is traditionally served by Sephardim to celebrate the occasion of a baby's new tooth.

Mushroom Barley Soup

2 to 3 pound flanken	10 ounces fresh mushrooms, sliced
Soup bones	3/4 cup barley, rinsed and
1 package fresh soup greens	drained
1/2 to 1 ounce dried	2 tablespoons light soy sauce
mushrooms	2 cloves garlic, minced
3 stalks celery, chopped	1 teaspoon dried thyme
2 onions, chopped	1 bay leaf
2 carrots, chopped	Salt and freshly ground pepper
1 tablespoon oil	to taste
1-ounce package mushroom-	Chopped fresh dill and parsley
soup mix	for garnish

1. Cover meat and bones with cold water. Bring to a boil and skim off foam. Add soup greens. Lower heat and simmer until meat is tender, about 2 hours. Strain stock; reserve meat, and discard soup greens. Chill stock and skim off fat. Meanwhile, cut dried mushrooms in pieces and wash well. Soak in water to cover.

2. Sauté celery, onions, and carrots in oil. Add to stock. Add dried mushrooms with soaking liquid, mushroom-soup mix, fresh mushrooms, barley, soy sauce, garlic, thyme, and bay leaf. Cook, partly covered, about 1-1/2 hours, until barley is soft, adding salt and pepper 15 minutes before cooking is done. Cut up meat, return to pot, and heat through. Remove bay leaf and adjust seasoning. Garnish each serving with dill and parsley.

Serves 8

◆ ROSELLE-CRANFORD HADASSAH, NEW JERSEY

Greek Lemon Soup

2 quarts chicken soup

1 cup matza meal

3 eggs, well beaten

Juice of 2 lemons

Salt to taste

Warm chicken soup. Add matza meal slowly, stirring constantly. Have ready 3 eggs, well beaten, and gradually beat in juice of 2 lemons. Add chicken broth slowly to egg mixture, mixing all the time. Be sure the soup is not hot so it will not curdle the eggs. Return to stove and heat very slowly, stirring constantly. Season with salt.

Serves 6 to 8

❧ *Dora Levy, Rochester Hadassah, New York*

TIPS

Rice, fine egg noodles, or egg farfel are good variations instead of matza meal.

This soup is better when prepared in the morning and reheated later. For a particularly delicious and gourmet touch, add 1/4 cup chopped walnuts when the egg mixture is added.

Pumpkin and Yellow Split Pea Soup

1-1/4 cups yellow split peas, rinsed and drained

1 large onion, minced

2-3/4 quarts chicken bouillon

Salt and freshly ground pepper to taste

4 tablespoons olive oil

1 teaspoon ground cinnamon

1/4 teaspoon ground ginger

1/4 teaspoon powdered saffron

1 pound fresh pumpkin meat, cubed

3 tablespoons minced Italian parsley

1. Put yellow peas, onion, and bouillon in medium-size saucepan. Bring to a boil, then lower heat and simmer, partly covered, 40 minutes, or until peas are tender.

2. Add salt and pepper, olive oil, cinnamon, ginger, saffron, and pumpkin. Simmer about 30 minutes, until pumpkin falls apart. Adjust seasoning and sprinkle with parsley.

Serves 6

❧ *Connie Michel, Westport Hadassah, Connecticut*

Top: PUMPKIN AND YELLOW SPLIT PEA SOUP, recipe right; Bottom: GREEK CASSEROLE, recipe page 101.

GARLIC

The aroma of garlic has permeated Jewish history. The Talmud says it satisfies and warms the body, makes the face shine, increases seminal fluid, and drives away enmity.

European Jews gave it the additional virtue of a curative. Mixed with salt and pepper it would banish tapeworm. A clove would ease the throb of an aching lower left incisor. If garlic was peeled, cut and left out overnight, turning black by morning, it was a sure sign that it had absorbed the demons from the air, protecting all from the evil eye—but it would also poison anyone who ate it.

During the Spanish Inquisition, many claimed the conversos could still be recognized as Jews from the garlic on their breath. Today, garlic has generally lost its reputation as an aphrodisiac, but modern scientific evidence strongly suggests that it may be able to disable a wide variety of infectious organisms, and aid digestion, circulation, and respiration. Garlic's main active component, allicin, gobbles up free radicals believed to be behind tumor growth, atherosclerosis and—the aging process!

Chicken Bouillabaisse with Garlic Mayonnaise

1/4 cup oil

1 roasting chicken (about 4 pounds), cut in 8 pieces

3 cups (about 3/4 pound) sliced onions

4 cups (about 1 pound) peeled and seeded tomatoes

1 clove garlic, crushed

3 cups sliced leeks (about 3/4 pound), washed thoroughly

1 cup tomato sauce

Grated zest of 1 orange

1/2 teaspoon fennel seed

1 teaspoon dried thyme

2 or 3 bay leaves

1/4 teaspoon saffron

Salt and freshly ground pepper to taste

2 cups dry white wine

Garlic Mayonnaise (recipe follows)

1. Heat oil in Dutch oven over medium-high heat. Add chicken pieces and sauté until lightly browned. Remove and set aside.

2. Add vegetables and sauté until softened, about 15 minutes.

3. Add tomato sauce, orange zest, fennel seed, thyme, bay leaves, and saffron, salt, and pepper to chicken and place on top of vegetables. Add white wine and simmer 30 minutes. Remove chicken and boil sauce until reduced and thickened. Return chicken to pan. Serve with Garlic Mayonnaise.

Garlic Mayonnaise

1 clove garlic, or more to taste

1 teaspoon kosher salt

1/3 cup bread crumbs

1 egg yolk

1/4 teaspoon dried oregano

Pimiento to taste

Hot pepper sauce to taste

Freshly ground pepper to taste

1 cup olive or salad oil

Pound the garlic and salt to a paste. Put into food processor or blender with remaining ingredients except oil. Blend until puréed. Add oil slowly while blending until consistency of mayonnaise.

Serves 6

✎ SHARYN COHEN, READING HADASSAH, PENNSYLVANIA

Chicken Swamp Soup

1 roasting chicken (about 4 pounds)

13-3/4 ounce can chicken broth, or more if needed

2 large onions, chopped

2 ribs celery and leafy ends, chopped

2 cloves garlic, crushed

3 tablespoons chopped fresh parsley

1 teaspoon chopped fresh dill, or more to taste

1 teaspoon paprika

1 tablespoon bottled steak sauce

1/2 teaspoon Worcestershire sauce

Salt and freshly ground pepper to taste

1/2 cup medium pearl barley, rinsed and drained

6 or 7 carrots, sliced into 1/4-inch pieces

2 parsnips, sliced

1 medium cabbage, shredded

1 cup frozen corn

1 cup frozen peas

1. Place chicken in large heavy pot. Add broth and enough cold water to cover chicken. Add onions, celery, garlic, parsley, dill, paprika, and steak sauce, Worcestershire sauce, and salt and pepper. Heat to boiling. Reduce heat, cover and simmer slowly 1 hour; remove chicken.

2. Add barley, carrots and parsnips and simmer 40 minutes.

3. Add cabbage, corn, and peas to pot. Correct seasonings and add more broth, if needed. Cook 20 minutes more. Meanwhile, cut chicken into bite-size pieces. When cabbage is tender, stir chicken into pot and simmer 5 minutes.

Serves 10 to 12

◄§ ST. PAUL HADASSAH, MINNESOTA

Ukrainian Borscht

3 pounds English short ribs
1 large onion, chopped
2 to 3 large beets, peeled, leaves and roots removed, beets diced
3 medium carrots, diced
3 celery stalks, diced
1 small head white cabbage, shredded
3 small potatoes, diced
2 tart apples, peeled, cored, and diced
28-ounce can crushed tomatoes
Three (8-ounce) cans tomato sauce
1 teaspoon salt
1/2 teaspoon freshly ground pepper
2 tablespoons chopped fresh parsley

1. Put short ribs in stock pot and cover with water by 3 inches. Add onion and bring to boil. Lower heat and simmer a few minutes while you skim off foam.

2. Add beets and simmer about 2 hours.

3. Add ingredients through tomato sauce. Bring to a boil, then lower heat and simmer about 1 hour. Remove meat, cut in bite-size pieces and return to pot. Add salt, pepper, and parsley.

Serves 8

ELENA BASKIN, SANTA CRUZ HADASSAH, CALIFORNIA

Black Bean Bisque

1 cup dried black beans, washed
4 cups vegetable stock or water
3-inch strip Kombu
1 onion, cut in chunks
2 large cloves garlic
1 large carrot, cut in chunks
1 bay leaf
1 teaspoon kosher salt, or to taste
3/4 teaspoon dried oregano
1/4 teaspoon dried savory
1/8 teaspoon grated gingerroot
Rice vinegar for topping
Olive oil for topping (optional)

1. Put beans in 3-quart saucepan with stock and Kombu. Bring to a boil, and skim foam. Lower heat, cover, and simmer 30 minutes.

2. Add ingredients through gingerroot and cook about 30 minutes, or until beans are soft. Remove bay leaf and purée soup. If too thick, add additional liquid. Heat 5 minutes more. Serve with 1 teaspoon each rice vinegar and oil per cup of soup.

Serves about 6

SANDY GOTTLIEB, COLUMBIA HADASSAH, SOUTH CAROLINA

Cabbage Soup

4 pounds flanken

2 onions, chopped

2 carrots, grated

2 fresh beets, grated

3- to 4-pound cabbage, grated
   or cut in eighths and thinly sliced

14- to 16-ounce can tomatoes with
   juice, tomatoes broken up

2 apples, peeled, cored, and
   grated

2 tablespoons salt

Freshly ground pepper to taste

1/2 cup packed brown sugar

1/2 cup fresh lemon juice

Boiled new potatoes

1. Bring 3 quarts water and the meat to a boil in large pot; skim off foam. Add onions, carrots, and beets. Lower heat and simmer partly covered 1 hour.

2. Add cabbage, tomatoes with juice, and apples, and cook partly covered 1 hour longer.

3. Add salt, pepper, brown sugar, and lemon juice and cook 15 minutes longer. Remove meat from pot; trim and cut in serving-size pieces and return to pot. Adjust seasoning and heat soup. Place a hot potato or two in warmed soup bowls and ladle soup and some meat over potatoes.

Serves about 14

❧ Ruthe Cohen Schwartz, Park Slope Hadassah, Brooklyn, New York

TIP

This is best made a day in advance and skimmed of excess fat. It also gives the flavors a chance to blend.

Traditional Stuffed Cabbage

1 large head cabbage (about
   3 pounds)

SAUCE

Two 28-ounce cans whole peeled
   tomatoes with juice

1 large onion, finely chopped

1 tart apple, peeled, cored, and
   coarsely grated

1/4 cup fresh lemon juice

1/4 cup granulated sugar

1/4 cup packed brown sugar

1 teaspoon sour salt

Full cup dark raisins

1 tablespoon kosher salt

1/4 teaspoon freshly ground pepper

FILLING

2 pounds lean ground beef

1 large onion, grated

2 eggs

2 tablespoons uncooked long-grain
   rice (omit if using for Passover)

1 tablespoon matza meal

2-1/2 teaspoons kosher salt

1/2 teaspoon freshly ground pepper

TIPS

Sour salt, or citric acid, is a white powder extracted from the juice of citrus and other acidic fruits. It is also produced by the fermentation of glucose. Found in the kosher food section of the supermarket, it is used to impart a tart flavor to traditional Jewish dishes.

For variety, you can add a handful or two of sliced mushrooms when making the sauce.

1. Prepare cabbage: Remove and discard any dark outside leaves. Bring a large covered pot of water to a boil. Add cabbage and cook about 10 minutes. Using a fork with a long handle, remove cabbage from pot, place it in a shallow pan, and remove as many leaves as possible, cutting them away from the core with a sharp knife. Shake excess water off the leaves and set aside.

2. Bring the water back to a boil, return cabbage to water and boil about 5 minutes. Using same procedure, remove as many leaves as possible. Repeat until you remove about 20 leaves. Pare raised portion of vein. Set leaves aside.

3. Prepare sauce: Place tomatoes with liquid in saucepan and crush tomatoes with wooden spoon. Bring to a boil over medium heat. Reduce heat and cook 15 minutes, or until slightly thickened. Stir in onion, apple, lemon juice, granulated sugar, brown sugar, sour salt, raisins, kosher salt, pepper, and cook 15 minutes longer.

4. Taste sauce; it should be well balanced between sweet and sour. If you like sweeter sauce, add a little more sugar. For a more tart sauce, add more lemon juice.

5. Prepare filling: Place all ingredients in large mixing bowl and mix thoroughly.

6. Assemble rolls: Place one cabbage leaf concave side up. Depending on size of the leaf, put 3 to 4 tablespoons filling in center of the leaf. Roll up tightly, tucking in ends. Repeat until all the filling has been used.

7. Spoon thin layer of sauce onto bottom of large covered saucepan or Dutch oven. Arrange stuffed cabbage rolls seam-side down in layers over the sauce. Pour remaining sauce over stuffed cabbage. Cook, covered, over low heat 1-1/2 to 2 hours.

Serves 8

◦§ *Beverly Friedman, Fair Lawn Hadassah, New Jersey*

Stuffed Cabbage Rolls
(Vegetarian Style)

FILLING

2 tablespoons minced onion

1 tablespoon oil

1 cup uncooked brown rice

1-1/2 cups vegetable stock

1/4 cup toasted slivered
   almonds or sunflower seeds

2 tablespoons raisins

1/2 teaspoon ground cinnamon

1/2 teaspoon salt

Dash of freshly ground pepper

SAUCE

1 onion, thinly sliced

2 tablespoons oil

1 tablespoon whole-wheat flour

2 cups fresh or canned tomatoes,
   chopped, and 1 cup tomato juice

1 cup mushrooms, sliced

1/8 teaspoon freshly ground pepper

1/2 teaspoon salt

1/4 teaspoon powdered cloves
   (optional)

1 large head cabbage

1/4 cup fresh lemon juice

2 tablespoons raisins

1. Make filling: Sauté onion in oil, then stir in rice and sauté a few minutes longer. Add vegetable stock, nuts, raisins, and seasonings. (Nuts may be replaced with any crunchy vegetable, like chopped carrot or celery.) Bring to a boil. Cover, lower heat, and simmer 45 minutes.

2. Make sauce: Sauté onion in oil until soft. Stir in whole-wheat flour and cook 2 to 3 minutes. Gradually add tomatoes and tomato juice, the sliced mushrooms, and seasonings, stirring constantly. Simmer 30 minutes.

3. Remove core from cabbage and steam over boiling water 5 minutes. Carefully peel off 18 or so outer leaves. Preheat oven to 350 degrees.

4. Place 2 tablespoons filling on each leaf, tuck in sides, and roll up. Lightly grease large baking dish. Spread sauce in bottom and place stuffed leaves seam-side down over sauce in several layers, if necessary. Cover with foil and bake 45 minutes.

5. Sprinkle lemon juice and raisins over cooked cabbage rolls.

Serves 8

◄§ ESTHER WEITZMAN, SANTA CRUZ HADASSAH, CALIFORNIA

TRADITIONAL STUFFED CABBAGE, recipe page 96.

Stuffed Peppers

6 bell peppers (2 green, 2 red, 2 yellow),
   1/2 inch of top cut off; pepper seeded

2 tablespoons oil

2 onions, sliced

3 cups canned tomatoes

2 teaspoons sugar

3 teaspoons salt, divided

1/2 teaspoon freshly ground pepper

1 pound ground beef

3/4 cup cooked rice

4 tablespoons grated onion

1 egg

3 tablespoons cold water

3 tablespoons honey

1/4 cup fresh lemon juice

1/4 cup seedless raisins

1. Pour boiling water over bell peppers to cover and let soak 15 minutes.

2. Heat oil an ovenproof casserole just large enough to hold the bell peppers snugly. Lightly brown sliced onions.

3. Add tomatoes, sugar, 1-1/2 teaspoons salt, and the ground pepper. Cook over low heat, covered, 30 minutes.

4. Mix beef with rice, remaining 1-1/2 teaspoons salt, the grated onion, the egg, and cold water. Place some meat mixture in each drained bell pepper and stand them in sauce. Cover and cook over low heat 45 minutes. Add honey, lemon juice and raisins and cook uncovered 30 minutes longer.

Serves 6

◄§ Jan Simons, Clifton Park Hadassah, New York

Stuffed Peppers, recipe above.

Greek Casserole

1-1/2 pounds ground lamb or
    beef, or mixture of both
1 cup chopped onion
l large clove garlic, minced
Salt and freshly ground pepper
    to taste
Grated lemon zest to taste

1 teaspoon dried mint leaves
1/4 cup uncooked long grain rice
1-1/2 cups zucchini slices
1 cup beef broth
1 cup plain dry browned bread
    crumbs

1. Preheat oven to 350 degrees.

2. Lightly brown meat, onion, garlic, and seasonings over medium heat. Spread raw rice on bottom of medium-size casserole.

3. Place half the zucchini slices on top; cover with browned meat mixture. Top with remaining zucchini slices.

4. Pour broth over entire casserole. Sprinkle bread crumbs on top, cover with foil, and bake about 45 minutes, until rice is done.

Serves 6

◄§ GERTRUDE UNGER, ELANA-ZEHAVA-LEORA HADASSAH, WHITE PLAINS, NEW YORK

Beef Short Ribs

3 to 4 pounds short ribs, cut in
    serving pieces
1-1/2 teaspoons salt
3-1/2 ounce can pineapple
    tidbits
1/4 cup water
1/4 cup chopped green bell pepper

1/2 teaspoon dry mustard
1/2 cup ketchup
1/4 cup apple cider vinegar
1/2 cup minced onion
3 heaping tablespoons sugar
Flour if needed for thickening
Hot cooked rice

1. Brown ribs in Dutch oven. Pour off drippings.

2. Sprinkle ribs with salt. Cover and cook slowly about 2 hours, until tender. Pour off drippings.

3. Combine remaining ingredients and pour over ribs; cook, covered, 30 minutes. Thicken gravy with flour if desired. Serve with rice.

Serves 4

◄§ MIRIAM BERGEN, SIOUX CITY HADASSAH, IOWA

Southern Mustard Short Ribs

2 tablespoons oil

4 pounds beef short ribs

2 medium onions, sliced

2 cloves garlic, crushed

3 tablespoons prepared mustard

2 teaspoons fresh lemon juice

1-1/2 teaspoons sugar

1 teaspoon salt

1/2 teaspoon freshly ground

   pepper

1. Preheat oven to 350 degrees. Heat oil in heavy skillet. Add ribs in batches and brown on all sides. Do not crowd skillet as the ribs will steam and not brown.

2. Remove ribs and place in baking dish with tight-fitting lid large enough for all the ribs. Pour off drippings and add sliced onions and crushed garlic to skillet. Cook over low heat until onions and garlic are softened, about 15 minutes. Spoon onions over browned ribs.

3. Combine 1/2 cup water with the mustard, the lemon juice, sugar, salt, and pepper; pour over ribs and onions. Cover tightly and cook until fork-tender, about 1-1/2 to 2 hours.

Serves 4

◆§ BESS ROTHSTEIN, JACKSONVILLE HADASSAH, FLORIDA

Corned Beef and Cabbage
(Romanian Style)

1 corned beef brisket, at least

   3 pounds

2 cloves garlic, chopped

2 small onions, chopped

Vegetable oil

16-ounce can whole or sliced

   tomatoes

2 celery stalks, cut in 1-inch

   pieces

2 carrots, cut in 1-inch pieces

2 small potatoes per person

Sour salt, if needed

1 small head cabbage, shredded

1/2 cup beef broth or consommé

1. Put corned beef in large pot with water to cover. Bring to a boil over medium-high heat, then lower heat to a simmer. Add garlic and cook, covered, 45 minutes to 1 hour per pound, or until meat is just fork-tender.

2. Meanwhile in large soup pot, sauté chopped onions in oil until translucent.

TIP

You can buy a plastic-wrapped corned beef brisket and prepare it according to package directions, adding garlic.

Add tomatoes, celery, carrots and potatoes. Taste for tomato flavor. If more is needed, add a small bit of sour salt.

3. Add cabbage together with 1/2 cup water and the broth.

4. After it has cooked about 1 hour and 30 minutes, remove corned beef from water and slice 3 pieces for each person. Place slices in the soup pot and cook all ingredients for an additional 45 minutes, or until fork-tender. Serve in a deep soup dish.

Serves 6 to 8

⋗ *Louis Fraiberg, Ann Arbor Hadassah, Michigan*

Baked Chicken with Cider and Apples

2 roasting chickens, quartered	Salt and freshly ground pepper
2 cups apple cider	to taste
1 cup unbleached all-purpose	3 tablespoons brown sugar
flour	1/3 cup applejack
1 tablespoon ground ginger	2 apples, cored and cut in thin
2 teaspoons ground cinnamon	wedges

1. The day before serving, put chicken pieces in a shallow pan. Pour cider over chicken and refrigerate covered overnight, turning pieces occasionally.

2. Preheat oven to 350 degrees. Grease large shallow baking pan. Remove chicken from cider and cook cider in a saucepan over low heat 5 minutes. Set aside.

3. Combine flour, ginger, cinnamon, salt, and pepper in paper or plastic zipper bag. Toss chicken pieces in flour mixture 1 at a time, and place skin-side up in prepared pan. Bake 40 minutes.

4. Meanwhile, combine cider, the brown sugar, applejack, and apple slices. Pour over chicken and bake 25 minutes more, basting occasionally with pan juices.

Serves 8

⋗ *Jodi B. Okun, Shatil Group Hadassah, New York, New York*

*T*he lemon usually enters cooking only through its separated juice or peel. Frozen juice is a passable substitute, but the bottled variety is not recommended. Though one lemon provides 40 to 70 percent of the minimum daily requirement of Vitamin C, it begins to lose its potency soon after it's squeezed—by 20 percent after only eight hours at room temperature or 24 hours in the refrigerator.

TIP

Lengthy beating is the secret of a good pound cake.

Double Lemon Pound Cake

1 cup (2 sticks) unsalted margarine, softened	1 teaspoon lemon extract
1/2 cup (4 ounces) vegetable shortening	2 teaspoons grated lemon zest
2 cups granulated sugar	3 cups sifted all-purpose flour
5 eggs	1-1/2 teaspoons baking powder
1/4 teaspoon salt	7 ounces lemon-lime soda
1 teaspoon vanilla extract	Confectioners' sugar for dusting (optional)

1. Preheat oven to 325 degrees. Grease well a 10-inch tube pan.

2. Cream margarine with vegetable shortening. Add sugar and beat until very light. Add eggs one at a time, beating well after each addition.

3. Add salt, vanilla extract, lemon extract, and lemon zest. Whisk to mix flour with baking powder and add alternately with lemon-lime soda to beaten mixture, beginning and ending with flour.

4. Spoon into prepared tube pan and bake 80 to 85 minutes until tester comes out clean when inserted in center of cake. Let cool in pan. Turn out onto wire rack and sprinkle with confectioners' sugar if desired.

Serves 12 to 16

❧ LIBBIE G. WEISMAN, SYRACUSE HADASSAH, NEW YORK

The Czar's Mandel Bread

6 eggs, at room temperature	2 cups all-purpose flour
2 cups sugar	1/2 to 1 cup mixture of sliced
1 cup vegetable oil	almonds and broken walnuts,
1 teaspoon vanilla extract	according to taste, tossed with
1 teaspoon ground cinnamon, plus additional to taste	1 teaspoon of the flour

1. Preheat oven to 325 degrees. Lightly oil and flour a 17 x 11 inch jelly-roll pan. Beat eggs until fluffy; gradually beat in sugar. Beat in oil, vanilla extract, and 1 teaspoon cinnamon, then fold in flour.

2. Mix in nuts and put on prepared jelly-roll pan, patting dough to the edges. Bake 35 minutes, until a toothpick inserted in the center comes out

clean and cake is dark golden around the edges. Raise oven temperatures to 350 degrees.

3. Remove cake from oven and cut into thin rectangular pieces. Sprinkle with more cinnamon and separate onto two cookie sheets. Put back in oven 10 minutes, or until lightly browned all over.

Makes about 6 dozen

⋗ ETHEL TIGAY YOLLICK, SHARON GROUP OF HADASSAH, WEST BLOOMFIELD, MICHIGAN

Esrog Cookies

3 cups all-purpose flour	1-1/4 cups flaked coconut
1-1/2 teaspoons baking soda	48 pitted prunes
1/4 teaspoon salt	1 pound confectioners' sugar
2 teaspoons ground cinnamon	Fresh lemon juice
3/4 cup (6 ounces) vegetable shortening	Lemon food coloring
1 cup packed light brown sugar	Washed and dried lemon leaves (optional)
1 egg	
1/3 cup light molasses	

1. Mix flour, baking soda, salt, and cinnamon. Cream shortening until fluffy, then beat in brown sugar, egg, and molasses. Beat in flour mixture and coconut. Cover and chill 1 hour.

2. Preheat oven to 375 degrees. Grease cookie sheets. Cut dough into 48 equal pieces. With floured hands, flatten each into a circle. Put a prune on top of each, then pinch dough to enclose prune completely; place seam-side down on cookie sheets. Smooth tops and pinch ends to resemble a lemon half. Bake 15 minutes, or until puffed and firm to the touch. Let cool on rack.

3. Mix confectioners' sugar with enough lemon juice to make it the consistency of heavy cream; add food coloring until lemon colored. Spread thick layer of frosting on flat side of 24 halves. Press remaining halves against frosting to make 24 whole lemon shapes. Use remaining frosting to coat the outsides and let stand at room temperature until frosting has dried well. Place on platter surrounded with washed and dried lemon leaves, if desired.

Makes 24

⋗ ROCHESTER HADASSAH, NEW YORK

One of the distinctions of Calabria, Italy, is its ability to produce what some consider the best esrogim in the world. The rough-skinned citrus fruit—which to grow in its purest form requires special care—is vital to Sukkot.

Early on the esrog attained Jewish significance as a motif on coins, synagogue walls, and mosaics. As Jewish law evolved, though, it became problematic: Grafting made cultivation easier, but to some impure.

Enter Calabria a half century ago, when it became apparent that the Riviera del Cedro (Citron Riviera), most specifically the town of Santa Maria del Cedro near Cosenza, had particularly good climactic conditions. Nowadays, from July to early September, rabbis arrive to make their selections.

In mishnaic and talmudic times when it was widely cultivated in Eretz Israel, the esrog was comparatively cheap. Today, an especially beautiful one can cost more than it costs to feed a family for a week.

ESROG MARMALADE, recipe right.

Grandma's Cinnamon-Sugar Cookies

2-1/2 cups all-purpose flour	1 cup plus 1/4 cup sugar
1/2 teaspoon baking powder	1 egg
1/4 teaspoon salt	1 teaspoon vanilla extract
1/2 pound (2 sticks) unsalted butter, softened	1 teaspoon ground cinnamon

1. Preheat oven to 400 degrees. Have ready ungreased cookie sheet.

2. Sift together flour, baking powder, and salt. Set aside.

3. In a large mixing bowl with an electric mixer, beat butter with 1 cup sugar until light and fluffy. Beat in egg and vanilla extract.

4. Slowly stir in flour mixture by hand, a little bit at a time, until well blended.

5. In a separate bowl, mix together remaining sugar and the ground cinnamon.

6. Using the palms of your hands, roll pieces of dough into 1-inch balls, roll in sugar-cinnamon mixture, and place on cookie sheet, leaving about 1 inch between each ball. Bake 10 to 12 minutes, until bottom of cookies are light brown. Transfer to wire racks to cool.

Makes about 4-1/2 dozen

◆§ JEAN JUDASHKO, WASHINGTON HEIGHTS HADASSAH, NEW YORK

Esrog Marmalade

1 esrog	Water
1 orange	Sugar

1. Slice esrog and orange very thinly; remove seeds. Place slices in bowl with water to cover overnight.

2. Drain fruit and put in saucepan. Add water to cover, and bring to a boil. Drain fruit again. Repeat process.

3. Spoon the drained fruit into measuring cup and combine in a saucepan with an equal amount of sugar. Cover and cook at medium to low heat 45 minutes. Remove from heat and let cool. Marmalade will still be thin, but it thickens as it cools.

Makes 1 pint

◆§ LESLIE HELEN BAYER, AVIVA HADASSAH, MAPLEWOOD/SOUTH ORANGE, NEW JERSEY

Winter

HANUKKAH—FRY, FRY AGAIN

Introduction by Steven Raichlen

What goes around comes around.

When I was young, we'd celebrate Hanukkah with my grandparents. Being the only grandchild, I got to light all the candles (a double treat, for boys love to play with matches). My efforts were rewarded with envelopes of Hanukkah gelt and heaping platters of deliciously greasy latkes (fried potato pancakes).

Now I'm the grown-up, the gelt-giver, and the maker of latkes, but I still look forward to the Festival of Lights. I love the glow of the candles—a symbol of light amid the darkness of winter.

I savor the fact that in our world of compulsive calorie-counting and nutritional correctness, this is the one time of the year when you can eat fried foods with impunity. The Festival of Lights brings special delight for children, of course, but it's enough to give a cardiologist nightmares. For Hanukkah is unique among holidays in that custom involves the consumption of fat.

Hanukkah usually plays second fiddle in the United States. After all, how can a menorah compete with Christmas trees or fat red-suited men driving reindeer? And when's the last time you heard any Hanukkah songs amid the endless Christmas music blared over shopping mall loudspeakers?

How different the holiday season is in Israel! Some years ago, I was lucky enough to be in the Promised Land during Hanukkah. When I touched down at Ben-Gurion Airport, there was nary a Santa Claus in sight. As our taxi sped to Tel Aviv, the overpasses were festooned with menorahs, not evergreens. In the busy Ben Yehudah shopping area, just as in the States, there was a public lighting each night—not of a Christmas tree, but of a giant candelabrum.

Hanukkah may not be the most sacred of the Jewish holidays, but it is certainly one of the most festive. The holiday commemorates the victory of a small band of Jewish patriots over a Syrian army in the second century B.C.E. Led by Antiochus IV, the Syrians occupied the Holy Land and outlawed the practice of Judaism. The crowning insult

Steven Raichlen is the author of the James Beard Award-winning cookbook, Healthy Jewish Cooking (Viking) and the best-selling Barbecue Bible and How to Grill (Workman Publishing). He cooks his latkes (by frying, not baking) in Coconut Grove, Florida.

Page 108–109, left to right: Sufganiyot, *recipe page 124;* Helen Levine's Hezenblosen, *recipe page 123; and* Hanukkah Gelt Chocolate Fudge Cake, *recipe page 126.*

Opposite: Hanukkah Lamp. *Johann Michael Schüler. Frankfurt am Main, Germany. 1st half 18th century. Embossed silver. Musée du Judaisme, Paris, France.*

came when Antiochus converted the great Temple of Jerusalem to the pagan gods of the Greeks.

Incensed by the religious persecutions, a Hebrew priest and his five sons organized an armed rebellion. They took the name Maccabee, meaning, "hammer," and an anagram formed from the first letters of the first four words of the daily prayer *Mi Kamocha Ba'Elim Adoshem*, "Who is like You, oh Lord." Using fighting techniques that would later be called guerrilla warfare, the Maccabees defeated Antiochus in 166 B.C.E.

Their first task was to rededicate the Temple (Hanukkah literally means "rededication"). But when they went to rekindle the Holy Light, they discovered they had only enough oil to burn for a single night. A messenger was dispatched to a distant city to fetch more holy oil, but he was not expected to return for a week.

It was then that the miracle of Hanukkah took place. The small supply of oil burned for 8 straight days, until the messenger returned. To celebrate, Jews light an eight-branched candelabrum, called a menorah—one candle for each night and one candle higher than the rest that's used to light the others. And appropriately from a foodie's point of view, we eat foods fried in oceans of oil.

Hanukkah is celebrated by Jews the world over. But as I learned during my stay in Israel, the festival foods vary from country to country. In America, Hanukkah centers around fried potato pancakes served with applesauce or sour cream. (Or if you're particularly gluttonous, as I am, you take both.) I couldn't imagine a Hanukkah party without latkes.

But that's exactly what awaited me at the Kibbutz Kfar Hanassi, where our son, Jake, spent the year after high school. We were greeted by great platters of sufganiyot—freshly fried doughnuts filled with bright red strawberry preserves. Indeed, throughout our travels in Israel, jelly doughnuts were far more common than latkes.

My Greek aunt, Rosa Miller, taught me about a different Hanukkah tradition. The Ladinos, Sephardic Jews of Greece, honor Hanukkah with fried desserts. One popular holiday dish is loukoumades, crisp round fritters drizzled with honey-scented syrup.

My strangest Hanukkah was a few years ago, while I was writing a book called *Healthy Jewish Cooking*. Alarmed by my cholesterol count, my doctor had urged me to go on a low-fat diet. I did fine until December rolled around, but I couldn't bear the thought of Hanukkah without latkes. Now I had already figured out how to make low-fat kreplach (using wonton wrappers instead of egg dough) and even how to slash the fat in chopped liver (by substituting roasted mushrooms for most of the liver). So I wasn't about to be deterred by a simple latke.

The solution lay in a technique I call "bake-frying." I "fried" the latkes in a light misting of oil on a non-stick baking sheet in a super hot oven. (The oil helped them crisp and brown.) In a further nod to health, I used olive oil, which boosts levels of HDL (high density lipoproteins—the "good" cholesterol), while lowering levels of LDL (the "bad" cholesterol). To give my low-fat latkes a richer, fattier taste, I used Yukon gold potatoes, which have a naturally buttery flavor. Bake-frying works better with smaller pieces of food, so I formed my latkes in 2-1/2 inch disks that could be dispatched in one or two bites.

I thought my low-fat latkes were pretty tasty, but my family almost booed me out of the house. The next year, I hauled out my skillet and took Lipitor.

I've been frying my latkes ever since.

I guess you can take the fat out of a latke, but you can't have Hanukkah without the fat.

Potato Latkes

4 large potatoes	Dash of freshly ground pepper
1 large onion	2 tablespoons all-purpose flour
2 eggs, lightly beaten	Oil for frying
1 teaspoon salt	

1. Grate potatoes and onion on fine grater and squeeze out about half the liquid.

2. Add remaining ingredients except oil to potato mixture.

3. Heat oil in medium skillet over medium heat. Put about 2 tablespoons batter for each latke into hot oil and fry until golden on both sides, turning once. Remove from skillet to paper towels to drain.

Serves 4

◆ JEAN GELFAND, SIOUX CITY HADASSAH, IOWA

ABOVE: EXECUTIVE DREIDL. *Michael Berkowicz and Bonnie Sroloivtz, 1993. Brass and silverplate and painted. The Jewish Museum, New York. Purchased with funds given by the Judaica Acquisitions Fund.*

Probably among the world's best foods, potatoes are one of the all-time great comfort foods, right up there with chicken soup. A nutritional treasure, a 6-ounce potato, for instance, has 110 calories (the same amount of rice or pasta has 400), 213 grams carbohydrate, 3 grams protein, and no fat or cholesterol. Rich in riboflavin, iron, and thiamin, it also yields an extraordinary amount of Vitamin C.

There are hundreds of varieties. Russet Burbank is ideal for baking, mashing, or frying; the medium-starch "all-purpose" is exactly that. Sometimes referred to as "waxy," firm-textured, low-starch varieties are ideal for steaming, roasting, and barbecuing.

A greenish tinge to the skin means the potato has been badly stored and can turn bitter. Cut out any sprouts before cooking—they're toxic. Keep at room temperature and use within 10 days (refrigeration turns the starch to sugar). To avoid rot, remove from plastic bags and store loosely in a vegetable bin or a brown bag.

Mixed Vegetable Latkes

1/2 cup shredded potato	*1/4 cup all-purpose flour*
1/2 cup shredded carrots	*Salt and freshly ground pepper to taste*
1/2 cup shredded zucchini	*2 eggs, lightly beaten*
1/2 cup shredded sweet potato	*Vegetable oil for frying*
1/4 cup chopped onion	*Sour cream or yogurt for serving*

1. Drain excess liquid from shredded vegetables.

2. Combine ingredients through eggs in large bowl.

3. Heat oil in medium skillet over medium heat. Put about 2 tablespoons batter for each latke into hot oil and fry until golden on both sides, turning once. Remove from skillet to paper towels to drain. Keep warm in 200 to 250 degree oven until all are cooked. Serve with sour cream or yogurt.

Serves 4

➺ SHIRA HADASSAH, PORT CHESTER, NEW YORK

Cheesy Zucchini Potato Latkes

4 large zucchini, about 2 pounds total	*1 teaspoon fresh lemon juice*
2 large potatoes, about 1 pound total	*2 cloves garlic, crushed (optional)*
1 medium onion, grated	
1 cup bread crumbs	*1 teaspoon each salt and freshly ground pepper*
1/2 cup all-purpose flour	
1/2 cup grated cheddar cheese	*1 tablespoon sugar (optional)*
1 egg, lightly beaten	*Oil for frying*

1. Wash zucchini, trim ends, and grate. Remove as much liquid as possible either in a salad spinner or strain and squeeze in a towel.

2. Peel potatoes and grate, or use food processor or blender. Follow instructions for zucchini.

3. Place zucchini and potatoes in large bowl and add remaining ingredients through sugar. Blend thoroughly.

4. Heat oil in medium skillet over medium heat. Put about 2 tablespoons batter for each latke into hot oil and fry until golden on both sides, turning once. Remove from skillet to paper towels to drain.

Serves 6 to 8

➺ HADASSAH ISRAEL

CARROT LATKES. recipe above, right.

Carrot Latkes

1 pound carrots
2 eggs
1 scallion, finely chopped
1/2 clove garlic, minced
Salt and freshly ground pepper
    to taste

1/2 to 3/4 cup matza meal
Oil for frying
Sour cream and chopped scallion
    greens for garnish

1. Clean carrots and grate finely. Transfer to a fine strainer or colander. Press carrots against sieve and allow liquid to drain 10 minutes.

2. Beat 2 eggs in a large bowl. Add drained carrots, the scallion, garlic, and salt and pepper. Add sufficient matza meal with frequent mixing until mixture is fairly firm and can hold the shape of a latke.

3. Heat oil in medium skillet over medium heat. Put about 2 tablespoons batter for each latke into hot oil and fry until golden on both sides, turning once. Remove from skillet to paper towels to drain. Garnish with sour cream and scallion greens.

Serves 4

~ *ABE KOBLIN, DAYAN GROUP, BALTIMORE HADASSAH, MARYLAND*

Elaine's Apple Cinnamon Latkes

1 egg
3 tablespoons sugar
1 teaspoon ground cinnamon
1 teaspoon salt

3 cups coarsely chopped apples
    (about 3 apples)
3/4 cup all-purpose flour
Oil for frying

1. Beat egg until foamy. Add sugar, cinnamon, and salt. Mix well.

2. Add chopped apples to egg mixture a few at a time. Add flour and blend mixture until smooth.

3. Heat oil in medium skillet over medium heat. Put about 2 tablespoons batter for each latke into hot oil and fry until golden on both sides, turning once. Remove from skillet to paper towels to drain.

4. Cover and keep latkes in 250 degree oven until all are made.

Serves 4 to 6

~ *ELAINE BINDER, CHAVEROT HADASSAH, SUFFERN, NEW YORK*

Apple Yogurt Pancakes

TIP

For a really low-calorie version, use low-fat yogurt, skim milk, and cook on a non-stick griddle sprayed with vegetable cooking spray.

1-1/4 cups sifted all-purpose flour
1/2 teaspoon salt
1 teaspoon baking soda
1/8 teaspoon baking powder
8 ounces plain yogurt

1/4 cup milk
1 egg yolk, lightly beaten
2 egg whites
1/2 cup thinly sliced apples
Oil for frying

1. Sift flour with salt, baking soda, and baking powder. Combine yogurt, milk, and egg yolk. Stir into flour mixture until ingredients are moistened (batter will be lumpy).

2. Heat oil in medium skillet over medium heat. Beat egg whites until stiff but not dry and fold into batter. Gently stir in apple slices. Put about 2 tablespoons batter for each latke into hot oil and fry until golden on both sides, turning once. Remove from skillet to paper towels to drain.

Makes about 12

⋙ *CLIFTON PARK HADASSAH, NEW YORK*

Oatmeal Yogurt Pancakes

1 egg or 2 egg whites
6 ounces peach or other lite
   fruit flavor yogurt
1/2 cup quick cooking rolled oats
1/2 cup all-purpose flour
2 tablespoons wheat germ

1/2 cup nonfat milk, or more
1 tablespoon sugar
1 tablespoon baking powder
2 teaspoons oil
1/2 teaspoon baking soda
Yogurt for serving

1. Preheat griddle over medium heat. Grease griddle.

2. Beat egg in large bowl. Carefully add remaining ingredients through baking soda.

3. For each pancake, pour about 2 tablespoons batter onto hot griddle. Cook 2 minutes, or until puffed and dry around edges. Turn and cook other side until golden. Serve with additional yogurt.

Serves 10

⋙ *ROSLYN SQUIRES, FLORIDA ATLANTIC REGION HADASSAH,*
   HENRIETTA SZOLD NURSES COUNCIL

Fred's Pancakes

1 cup cottage cheese

1 cup sour cream or yogurt

1 cup sifted all-purpose flour

4 eggs

1/2 teaspoon salt

2 tablespoons sugar, or to taste

1 teaspoon vanilla extract

Vegetable oil for frying

Syrup, jam, honey, or
    confectioners' sugar for serving

1. Blend all ingredients through vanilla extract in food processor until fairly smooth. Heat a non-stick skillet with a little vegetable oil over medium heat. Place ladle-loads of mixture in the skillet. When bubbles start popping on top, turn them over, and do other side. At the right temperature, it takes about 1 to 2 minutes per side.

2. Serve with your choice of syrup, jam, honey, confectioners' sugar, or just plain.

Makes about 16, depending on size

GRANDPA FRED D. ROSS, BALTIMORE HADASSAH, MARYLAND

Pompushkes

8-ounce container cottage cheese

1 cup grated peeled apples

2 eggs

1 cup sifted all-purpose flour

2 tablespoons sugar

1 teaspoon baking powder

1/4 teaspoon ground cinnamon

1/4 teaspoon salt

1/4 cup sour cream, plus
    additional for serving

1 cup vegetable shortening

1. Combine cottage cheese, apples, and eggs in mixing bowl; beat until well blended. Sift flour with sugar, baking powder, cinnamon, and salt. Stir into cheese mixture. Stir in 1/4 cup sour cream.

2. Heat shortening in skillet over medium heat. Put about 2 tablespoons batter for each latke into hot oil and fry until golden on both sides, turning once. Remove from skillet to paper towels to drain.

3. Serve hot with sour cream.

Makes 16

MRS. SAM SINGER, OKLAHOMA CITY HADASSAH, OKLAHOMA

TIP

Pompushkes is Yiddish for doughnuts, but these are more like pancakes. The recipe is probably of Czech origin.

Cheese Kreplach

DOUGH
1/2 pint sour cream
2 eggs, beaten
1/4 cup (1/2 stick) unsalted
  butter, melted
3 cups all-purpose flour
3 teaspoons baking powder
1 teaspoon salt

FILLING
1/4 pound (half an 8-ounce
  package) cream cheese
8-ounce container cottage cheese
1 egg, lightly beaten
2 tablespoon unsalted butter,
  melted

1. Preheat oven to 375 degrees. Lightly butter baking pan.

2. Make dough: Mix sour cream with eggs and 1/4 cup melted butter in large bowl. Sift flour with baking powder and salt and stir into sour-cream mixture. Knead about 10 minutes.

3. Make filling: Blend cream cheese with cottage cheese; add egg and melted butter and mix well.

4. Roll out dough 1/4-inch thick and cut into 3-inch squares.

5. Place 1 tablespoon cheese filling on each square. Fold dough over cheese to make triangle. Pinch edges firmly together to seal well.

6. Place in prepared pan and bake about 40 minutes, or until browned.

Makes about 1 dozen

◅ PORTLAND HADASSAH, OREGON

Potato Kugel

4 tablespoons oil
4 large potatoes, grated
2 heaping tablespoons
  all-purpose flour
1 tablespoon quick-cooking
  rolled oats

1/2 teaspoon baking powder
1 cup crushed cornflakes
1 cup chopped onion, sautéed
2 eggs, lightly beaten
Salt and freshly ground pepper
  to taste

1. Preheat oven to 350 degrees. Pour oil into 1-1/2 quart casserole or baking pan and place in oven for about 5 minutes, or until oil is hot.

2. Meanwhile, in large bowl combine grated potatoes, the flour, rolled oats, baking powder, crushed cornflakes, sautéed onion, eggs, and salt and pepper.

3. Remove pan from oven and carefully pour in potato mixture. Bake about 35 to 45 minutes, or until cooked through and golden on top.

Makes 6 servings

MIRIAM GOLDBERGER, NORTH BOUNDARY HADASSAH, CHICAGO, ILLINOIS

Rose's Best Kugel

1 pound medium egg noodles
6 eggs, lightly beaten
1/4 cup sugar
1-3/4 cups cottage cheese
1 cup sour cream
1 cup whole milk ricotta cheese
4 ounces (half an 8-ounce package)
*   cream cheese, softened*
2 cups milk

1 cup raisins
1 teaspoon salt
2/3 cup coarsely chopped
*   almonds*
2 tablespoons unsalted butter,
*   at room temperature*
1/4 cup firmly packed light
*   brown sugar*
1 cup apricot preserves

1. Preheat oven to 350 degrees. Place oven shelf in middle position. Lightly grease 13 x 9 inch baking pan.

2. Bring large pot of salted water to a boil. Add noodles and cook about 4 minutes, until barely tender and still firm. Drain and place in baking pan.

3. Mix together eggs, sugar, cottage cheese, sour cream, ricotta cheese, cream cheese, milk, raisins, and salt in large bowl. Pour over noodles and stir well. Bake 30 minutes and remove kugel from oven.

4. Meanwhile, combine almonds, butter, brown sugar, and preserves in medium saucepan over medium heat. Cook 3 to 4 minutes, stirring constantly, until well combined and bubbling. Drop mixture by spoonfuls over noodles and spread evenly.

5. Return kugel to oven for 50 to 60 minutes, or until top is browned and bubbly. Serve warm.

Serves 10 to 12

JIM SCHUMAN, SHIRA HADASSAH, PORT CHESTER, NEW YORK

Holiday Brisket Pot Roast

5-pound brisket

Salt and freshly ground pepper
    to taste

1 clove garlic, crushed

Meat tenderizer (if needed for
    second cut brisket)

3 tablespoons oil or shortening

1 cup chopped onion

2 stalks celery with tops, sliced

1/2 cup ketchup

1/2 cup Concord wine
    (Shabbat wine; sweet kosher
    wines are best)

3 carrots, sliced

12 ounces fresh mushrooms,
    sliced

1. Rub meat with salt and pepper. Rub with crushed garlic. Heat oil or shortening in Dutch oven or roasting pan. Sauté onions and celery in oil. When onions are translucent, push to side and brown meat on both sides for about 20 minutes. Meanwhile, preheat oven to 350 degrees.

2. Combine ketchup and wine in measuring cup and pour over meat. Add sliced carrots. Roast, covered, about 2 hours, basting occasionally with sauce.

3. When meat is almost tender and can be sliced, remove to cutting board and slice on an angle into thin slices; keeping shape of meat intact, return to roasting pan.

4. With large spoon, baste meat and vegetables, making sure that juice runs between each slice of meat, and vegetables remain on top of roast. Add mushrooms.

5. Return to oven and roast for another half hour. Carefully remove roast from pan onto heated serving dish and spoon sauce and vegetables on top of meat slices.

Serves 8 to 10

◄ MILDRED SILVERMAN, WEST ORANGE HADASSAH, NEW JERSEY

TIPS

Can be prepared in advance and frozen for yontif. Can be doubled and tripled.

Freshly steamed Brussels sprouts makes a simple and a good side dish for this brisket.

HOLIDAY BRISKET POT ROAST, recipe above.

Fried Chicken Cutlets
(Syrian Jewish Style)

TIP
For a slightly different version, try ground cumin instead of the cinnamon.

MARINADE
3 tablespoons fresh lemon juice
1 tablespoon olive oil
4 large garlic cloves, minced
1/4 teaspoon ground cinnamon
Salt and freshly ground pepper
   to taste
1-1/2 pounds skinless, boneless
   chicken cutlets

BATTER
1/2 cup all-purpose flour
1/4 cup cornstarch
1/2 teaspoon salt
2 teaspoons baking powder
2/3 cup cold water,
   approximately
Oil for frying

Lemon wedges and chopped
   parsley for garnish

1. In a large mixing bowl, whisk together lemon juice, olive oil, garlic, cinnamon, salt, and pepper. Add the chicken and toss to coat thoroughly. Cover and marinate 2 to 3 hours in the refrigerator, turning chicken occasionally.

2. Make batter: Whisk flour, cornstarch, salt, and baking powder to combine. Pour in water and whisk until smooth.

3. Heat about 1 cup oil in large heavy skillet over medium-high heat, until hot but not smoking. Remove 1 tablespoon warm oil from pan and whisk into batter.

4. Dip chicken in batter to coat and slip into hot oil. Carefully turn chicken when it is light golden, 2 to 3 minutes. Cook second side 2 to 3 minutes, until cooked through and golden. Do not crowd pan. Repeat with remaining chicken and batter.

5. Drain cutlets on paper towels. Transfer to an ovenproof platter and keep warm in 200-degree oven until remaining pieces are done. Serve immediately, garnished with lemon wedges and parsley.

Serves 4 to 6

⌒ JACKIE GOLDMAN, JACKSONVILLE HADASSAH, FLORIDA

Yosi's Israeli Salad

4 small plum tomatoes
2 kirby cucumbers, peeled
3 scallions (white and green parts)
1/2 cup flat leaf parsley
1/4 cup fresh mint leaves
   (optional)

1/4 cup chopped fresh dill
3 to 4 tablespoons olive oil
Juice of 1 lemon (a bit more
   to taste)
Salt and freshly ground black
   pepper to taste

Finely chop all vegetables. Dress with parsley, mint, dill, oil, lemon juice, salt, and pepper. Serve at room temperature.

Serves 6 to 7

◄ SUSAN CAZARY, FAIRFIELD HADASSAH, CONNECTICUT

Helen Levine's Hezenblosen

2 cups all-purpose flour,
   approximately
3 eggs
Pinch of salt

1/2 teaspoon orange or
   lemon extract
Confectioners' sugar
Oil for frying

1. Sift flour and mix with eggs, salt, and orange or lemon extract. Knead until soft but firm. If dough is sticky, add a little more flour. Let dough rest 10 to 15 minutes.

2. Roll out thin on floured board; cut into 2-inch squares. Make a slit in center and pull corners through slit. Other designs can also be cut from the dough. Heat oil in skillet.

3. Drop in Hezenblosen and fry until golden, turning from time to time. Drain on paper towels and sprinkle with confectioners' sugar.

Makes 3 dozen

◄ OAKLAND HADASSAH, CALIFORNIA

HEZENBLOSEN. Recipe above. Be creative with the presentation!

Bimuelos or Loukoumades
(Sephardic Fritters)

BATTER
2 (1/4-ounce) packages active
    dry yeast
1-1/3 cups warm water
1 egg
1/2 teaspoon salt
1/2 cup oil
3 cups all-purpose flour

Oil for frying

SYRUP
1 cup honey
1 tablespoon water

Ground cinnamon for
    sprinkling

1. In a large bowl, dissolve yeast in 1/3 cup warm water. Whisk in egg, salt, and oil. Let stand 5 minutes, until foamy.

2. Stir in flour all at once. Gradually stir in remaining cup water. Cover and let rise 1 hour in warm, draft-free place.

3. Combine honey and water for syrup and bring to boil.

4. Heat 2 to 3 inches oil to 375 degrees in large saucepan. Drop dough from tip of tablespoon (which has been dipped in hot oil) into hot oil. Cook until puffed and brown, then turn and brown other side. Drain on paper towels. Dip in warm syrup and sprinkle with cinnamon.

Makes about 36

LENA GLICK, MOTHER OF ISOBEL DVORSKY, OAKLAND HADASSAH, CALIFORNIA

Sufganiyot
(Israeli Jelly Doughnuts)

1 (1/4-ounce) package active
    dry yeast
1/2 cup sugar
1/4 cup lukewarm water
3-3/4 to 4 cups all-purpose flour
3/4 cup milk, approximately,
    at room temperature
1 egg
1 egg yolk

1/2 teaspoon salt
2 teaspoons grated lemon zest
4 tablespoons (1/2 stick) unsalted
    butter, at room temperature
Oil for frying
Jelly or jam
Confectioners' or granulated
    sugar

1. Dissolve yeast and a good pinch of the sugar in the water; let stand until foamy.

Try frying one doughnut to start. Once it seems done, take it out and cut it open to see if the inside is cooked.

Injectors are available at specialty stores. Or cut a slit in the doughnut; warm the jam, and with a dairy turkey baster squeeze in the jam.

2. Put 3-3/4 cups flour in work bowl of processor fitted with the steel blade. Add yeast, the milk, egg, egg yolk, salt, lemon zest, butter, and remaining sugar. Process until dough becomes sticky and elastic, gradually adding more milk or flour if needed. Remove dough to bowl, cover, and let rise in warm place until doubled in bulk, about 1 hour (or refrigerate up to 24 hours and let come to room temperature before proceeding).

3. Pinch off pieces of dough and form into small balls the size of golf balls. Cover and let rise 30 minutes.

4. Heat 4 inches oil to 360 degrees in deep fryer. Without crowding, add doughnuts and fry until undersides are deep brown, about 3 minutes. Turn and fry other side. Lift out with slotted spoon and drain on paper towels.

5. With an injector, insert a teaspoon jam into each doughnut. Roll in confectioners' or granulated sugar and serve immediately.

Makes about 2 dozen

◆§ *ZELDA BERNSTEIN PARNES, EAST GREENWICH HADASSAH, RHODE ISLAND*

Doughnuts

3/4 cup orange juice or water	2 eggs, lightly beaten
1/2 cup (1 stick) unsalted margarine	1/2 teaspoon salt
1/4 cup sugar	Vegetable oil for frying
2 (1/4-ounce) packages active dry yeast	Confectioners' sugar and ground cinnamon for dusting
4 to 4-1/2 cups all-purpose flour	

1. Combine orange juice, margarine, and sugar in medium saucepan; heat until margarine melts. Transfer to large bowl, let cool to lukewarm, and add yeast. Stir until dissolved.

2. Combine ingredients through salt and knead on floured surface until smooth (you may need to add more flour). Place dough in greased bowl, cover, and let rise in warm spot until doubled in bulk, about 1 hour.

3. Punch down and shape small pieces of dough into balls, rings, or braids. Cover and let rise 30 minutes.

4. Heat 3 inches vegetable oil to 375 degrees. Fry doughnuts until puffed and brown. Turn and brown other side. Drain on paper towels. Put a few teaspoons confectioners' sugar and a bit of cinnamon into a paper bag, add doughnuts, and shake.

Makes about 42

◆§ *BUFFALO HADASSAH, NEW YORK*

Baking Powder Doughnuts

2 eggs, well beaten
1 cup granulated sugar
2 tablespoons shortening
3-1/2 cups all-purpose flour
4 teaspoons baking powder
1/2 teaspoon salt

1/4 teaspoon freshly grated
  nutmeg
1/4 teaspoon ground cinnamon
3/4 cup milk
Oil for frying
Confectioners' sugar for dusting

1. Combine eggs, sugar, and shortening. Beat well.

2. With a whisk, combine flour with baking powder, salt, nutmeg, and cinnamon. Stir into egg mixture alternately with milk. Chill dough 2 hours.

3. Heat 1/2 inch oil in skillet to 375 degrees. Roll dough 1/3-inch thick on floured board and cut with doughnut cutter. Fry in hot oil, turning once. Drain on paper towels.

4. When cool, sugar doughnuts by placing one at a time in a bag with confectioners' sugar; shake well.

Makes 2 dozen

Aviva Hadassah, Maplewood/South Orange, New Jersey

MAKE HANUKKAH GELT AT HOME

Combine in top of a double boiler:
  1 pound confectioners' sugar
  1 pound semisweet chocolate
  1/2 cup unsweetened cocoa powder
  1/4 teaspoon salt
  6 tablespoons unsalted butter
  1/4 cup milk
  1 teaspoon vanilla extract

Place over simmering water and stir until smooth.

Quickly spread onto a wax paper-lined cookie sheet. Let cool, then cut into circles.

Wrap individually in foil and store in refrigerator.

Hanukkah Gelt Chocolate Fudge Cake

1-3/4 cups all-purpose flour
2 cups packed light brown sugar
3/4 cup unsweetened cocoa powder
2 teaspoons baking soda
1 teaspoon baking powder
Pinch of salt
2 eggs
1/2 cup vegetable oil
1 cup strong coffee
1 cup buttermilk or plain yogurt

FROSTING
1 cup (2 sticks) unsalted
  margarine or butter, softened
5 ounces unsweetened
  chocolate, melted and cooled
4 cups confectioners' sugar
1/4 cup whipping cream or
  milk
2 bags gold foil-covered
  chocolate coins (gelt)

1. Heat oven to 350 degrees. Grease 9-inch springform pan.

2. Stir together flour, brown sugar, cocoa, baking soda, baking powder, and salt in large bowl.

3. In another bowl, lightly whisk eggs. Add oil, coffee, and buttermilk; mix

HANUKKAH GELT CHOCOLATE FUDGE CAKE

well. Add this mixture to dry ingredients. Using large wire whisk or electric mixer, beat two minutes.

4. Pour into pan (batter will be thin). Bake 45 to 55 minutes, or until cake tests done. It should be slightly puffed up in center and spring back when touched. Let cool to room temperature.

5. Make frosting: Beat margarine or butter until smooth; add cooled melted chocolate. Slowly blend in confectioners' sugar. Add enough cream or milk to make a thick, spreadable frosting; beat until light and fluffy. Remove pan sides and frost cake; decorate with gelt.

Serves 12

◆ *ARLENE FREEDMAN, DEBORAH-ZAHAVA HADASSAH, CHICAGO, ILLINOIS*

Helene's Coffee Cake

2 cups all-purpose flour
1-1/2 teaspoons baking powder
1 teaspoon baking soda
1/2 cup (1 stick) unsalted butter, at room temperature
1 cup sugar
2 eggs

1 cup sour cream
1 teaspoon vanilla extract

FILLING AND TOPPING
1/2 cup nuts, coarsely chopped
1/4 cup sugar
1/2 teaspoon ground cinnamon

1. Preheat oven to 350 degrees. Grease 9- or 10-inch springform pan, or 10-inch tube pan.

2. Whisk to combine flour, baking powder, and baking soda. Cream butter, sugar, and eggs; add sour cream and vanilla extract. Add dry ingredients to creamed mixture and beat well.

3. For topping, in separate bowl, mix, nuts, sugar, and cinnamon. Pour half of batter into prepared pan and top with half of filling; repeat layering.

4. Bake about 60 minutes, until cake tests done.

Serves 20

◆ *HELENE SHEFFLER, RISHON GROUP HADASSAH, PITTSBURGH, PENNSYLVANIA*

Let's Play Dreidel!

The dreidel, or trendel, a spinning top, known in Hebrew as the s'vivon, is played on Hanukkah. Its four letters are nun (נ), gimel (ג), hay (ה), and shin (ש), standing for the Hebrew words nes gadol hayah sham—a great miracle happened there. In Israel the letter shin is replaced by the letter peh (פ), a great miracle happened here.

Each player receives an equal number of coins, nuts, raisins, candies or candles, and each puts one of them into the middle. One person at a time spins the dreidel. The Hebrew letter that it falls upon determines what should be done:

Nun—the player does nothing   Gimel—the player takes everything in the kitty
Hay—she takes half   Shin—he adds something to the kitty

When one person has won everything, the game is over. If you are using edible playing pieces, the fun continues as you eat your winnings!

HANUKKAH LAMP. *Johann Valentin Schüler. Frankfurt, c. 1680. Silver: repoussé, cast, chased, appliqué and parcel-gilt. The Jewish Museum, New York. Gift of Norman S. Goetz, Henry A. Loeb, Henry L. Marx, Ira A. Schur, Lawrence A. Wein, Leonard Block, Gustave L. Levy, and Robert I. Wischnick.*

Ricotta Cheese Cake

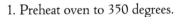

CRUST

5-1/2 tablespoons melted
  unsalted butter, divided

1-1/2 cups crushed lemon cookies
  or vanilla wafers

BATTER

3 eggs

1-1/2 pounds ricotta cheese

2/3 cup sugar

1/3 cup sour cream

1 teaspoon baking powder

1/3 cup cornstarch

1 teaspoon vanilla extract

2-1/2 teaspoons grated
  lemon zest

1/3 cup raisins (optional)

1. Preheat oven to 350 degrees.

2. Make crust: Add 2-1/2 tablespoons melted butter to crushed cookies. Press over bottom and up sides of 9-inch springform pan. Bake 6 minutes. Let cool. Meanwhile, lower oven temperature to 325 degrees.

3. Make batter: In food processor or mixer, blend eggs, ricotta cheese, sugar, and sour cream until smooth. Add baking powder to cornstarch then add to cheese mixture with vanilla extract, 3 tablespoons melted butter, and the zest. Process, stopping machine to scrape down sides. Add raisins, if desired. Pour into cooled crust and bake 60 minutes, or until set.

Serves 8 to 12

◄§ DORIS MILLER, ANN ARBOR HADASSAH, MICHIGAN

Dessert Ricotta Balls

1 pound ricotta cheese

2 eggs

3 tablespoons sugar

1 cup milk

1 teaspoon vanilla extract

3 cups self-rising cake flour

Oil for frying

Confectioners' sugar for dusting

1. Mix all ingredients except oil and confectioners' sugar in mixer. Heat oil in deep fryer.

2. When oil is hot, drop in mixture by tablespoons. When ricotta balls rise to the surface and are browned on both sides, remove with slotted spoon and drain on paper towels. Dust with confectioners' sugar.

Makes 3 dozen

◄§ MARY DRAGONE, HILLCREST-SABRA-SCOPUS HADASSAH, FLORIDA

Spring

PASSOVER

Introduction by Edda Servi Machlin

pring is the most beautiful time of the year with its rebirth of nature that covers branches and grounds with tender new greenery and an array of brilliant colors. If this beautiful season is the busiest time of the year for many, for Jews, who salute spring with the celebration of so important a holiday as Pesach, it is certainly even more so.

But let me tell you how busy spring was for my family at Passover time, as I was growing up in my native village in Italy.

To start, we had to make our own matza, having the wheat milled expressly for us into the finest flour, then separated from the bran so it would be free of even a speck of chametz (since bran facilitates the process of leavening), then to the baking of the prepared matzot. This preparation took place in our community kosher oven located in an underground cave, the accessibility to which was thrilling and dangerous at the same time. I both eagerly anticipated and dreaded the descent over those eternally humid and clammy steps that led to the working site. But once I had managed to arrive unscathed inside the bakery, I became enthralled by the bustling activities that were carried out in those two primitive chambers. In the first, preparing matzot and the Passover sweets took place. In the second was the oven for baking the matza.

First, flour was mixed with icy water in a huge copper tub, then quickly transferred to the marble kneading table above which, attached to the wall, was a hinged long, heavy shaft maneuvered up and down over this loose mass to achieve compactness. Small pieces of dough were cut off and brought to another marble surface where they were kneaded by hand and rolled into 1/4-inch-thick round cakes. Then dextrous fingers trimmed them all around the perimeter and pinched concentric rows of holes inside to make them look like doilies. A metal comb was used to

With The Classic Cuisine of the Italian Jews Volumes I and II *(Giro Press), Edda Servi Machlin singlehandedly rescued one of the world's finest tables from almost certain oblivion after the destruction of her native Italian community during World War II.*

Born in the ancient Tuscan ghetto of Pitigliano, one of the cultural centers of Jewish life going back 2,000 years, she is the author also of Child of the Ghetto. *Her two daughters now grown, she lives with her husband Gene in New York.*

Page 130–131, left to right:
GOLDEN CHICKEN BOUILLON, recipe page 144; SID'S MATZA BALLS, recipe page 144; and TZIMMES/KUGEL, recipe page 153.

OPPOSITE: MATZA. (Courtesy of Edda Servi Machlin).

prick the tops to prevent blisters and finally they were quickly taken to the second chamber to be baked in a very hot stone oven.

The whole operation, from start to finish, had to take no longer than 18 minutes, after which time the dough would begin the process of leavening, thus becoming chametz.

Whereas the making of the matzot and sweets was a relatively short-lived project, the preparations at home took a whole month. First came the thorough cleaning. (The custom of having a separate set of dishes and utensils to be used only at Passover is an Ashkenazic one.) Every dish, glass, or piece of flatware was first dipped in a mud-like mixture of boiling water and ashes from the stove, then washed in soap and water, and finally rinsed in clear running water. Drawers and cabinets were lined with new sheets of tissue, then the house painters would invade with paper bags full of powdered pigment of all colors. A smell of lime, varnish, and cleanliness filled the air as room after room was freshly whitewashed and given a new pastel shade.

This was the time of the year when the dressmaker was hired by the day to come to our home and alter our parents' outfits and recycle them into little dresses and suits for us.

The night before the Seder was *bedicat chametz*, the ritual searching for leavened bread. During the day with the help of our mother we placed a morsel of bread in one corner of every surface. At night our father lit a candle after reciting a brief prayer, then turned the lights off and we followed him as he went in the semidarkness in search of the chametz. Silently we took turns to indicate where he would find the pieces of bread, and silently he brushed each one and its crumbs into a large paper cone using a sturdy long feather. When the last piece of chametz was collected, the feather went into the cone and this was tightly closed. The next morning the *biur chametz*, the burning of the cone and its contents, took place. Now the house was purified and ready for the great night.

My childhood Seder was celebrated in our home for all the Jewish families or family representative right after the service at temple and before all went to consume their festive meals in the intimacy of their homes. The Haggadah and the blessings were read by my father in Hebrew and everyone knew what those words meant. At the signal *ya-dayim*, for instance, the women would go around with water pitchers, basins, and towels for the washing of the hands, once silently, and once with the blessing, which each individual recited also in Hebrew. For the enunciation of the ten plagues, the windows were thrown open. The glass from which a drop of wine was poured into a basin for each plague was thrown into the basin after the last plague was called out; it was eventually disposed of to ward off the possibility that the plagues might hit our homes. The door was kept open during the portion of the Haggadah that reads, "Let the hungry come and eat; let the thirsty come and drink." This practice inevitably attracted multitudes of Christian children begging for a piece of matza.

This tradition of celebrating the Seder in our home with the entire community went on even during the period of the fascist anti-Jewish laws of the late 30s and early 40s. Then came the ill-fated October 16, 1943, the first Nazi raid that cost the Jewish community of Rome over a thousand people.

We were no longer safe. Of our family of seven, four children, ranging from 21 to 13, were able to escape capture; the fifth, age nine, and our parents were taken to an Italian concentration camp. Even under these exceptional circumstances, the four of us who were free managed to celebrate the first night of Passover.

We had spent the winter months roaming the countryside in search of shelter from the cold and something to put in our mouths. Often people slammed their doors in our faces threatening to hand us over to the Germans. But by April 1944 we had found shelter, and we began to watch the sky carefully because we knew that when the moon would be as round as a cake of cheese it would be the fourteenth of Nissan, the first night of Passover. With excitement we began to make a few matzot with flour from the farmer who was sheltering us and baked them in the rustic outdoor stone oven between the farmhouse and the barn.

With the little money we had left, we bought a live kid goat from a peddler who was eager to sell it at any price. The night the full moon appeared we celebrated the first Seder by reciting excerpts of the Haggadah we knew by heart and having a full Passover meal interspersed with laughter and tears, for that—I still remember as if it were yesterday—was the night of Saturday, April 8, and the next day our little brother would mark his tenth birthday—in captivity. These memories of a lost and irreplaceable world will always remain dear to me.

PINE NUTS

Historically, pine nuts are seeds of the stone pine native to the Mediterranean region. They are labor intensive and extremely difficult to harvest, thus the high-end cost.

Every 100 grams of pine nuts contains 31 grams of protein, the highest found in nuts or seeds. But they can turn rancid easily, so must be stored airtight in the freezer or fridge.

Besides their obvious nutritional value, pine nuts appear to have had a reputation as an aphrodisiac. Galen, a Greek physician of the second century C.E., recommended having a glassful of thick honey, 20 almonds, and one hundred pine nuts before going to bed. Three nights of this potion would produce some desirable results.

North African Haroset

1/2 cup pine nuts, chopped
1 hard-cooked egg yolk, finely chopped
1 apple, peeled and grated
1/2 cup sugar
1/2 cup ground almonds

1/2 cup chopped walnuts
Zest and juice of 1 lemon
Ground cinnamon to taste
Ground ginger to taste
Sweet wine to bind

Mix all ingredients until mixture comes together. Refrigerate.

Makes about 2 cups

◆§ Miriam Ostrovitz, Swampscott/Marblehead Hadassah, Lynn, Massachusetts

Haroset from Suriname

2-2/3 cups (7-ounce package)
   unsweetened shredded coconut
2 cups chopped walnuts
1-1/2 cups raisins
1-1/2 cups dried apples
1-1/2 cups prunes

1-1/2 cups dried apricots
1-1/2 cups dried pears
1/4 cup sugar
1 tablespoon ground cinnamon
1/2 cup cherry jam
Sweet red wine

1. Combine in saucepan all ingredients except cherry jam and wine. Add enough cold water to just cover fruit. Bring to a boil, then reduce heat

The first words of the four questions asked at the beginning of the Haggadah, "What is different?" date back to Mishnaic times, originating in contemporary dining customs at festive meals. The four questions became part of the Seder celebration as a reminder to the father to fulfill the biblical injunction, "And thou shalt tell thy son in that day, saying It is because of that which the Lord did for me when I came forth out of Egypt."

The third of the four questions enumerated by the Mishna to be asked during the Seder—"Why do we eat only roasted meat [of the paschal sacrifice]?"—was omitted after the destruction of the Temple and the consequent cessation of sacrifices, and "Why do we recline?" was substituted. As late as Rashi and Maimonides, the Mah Nishtanah was probably recited by the person conducting the Seder rather than asked by the children, as is customary today.

and simmer about 1-1/2 hours, stirring occasionally, and adding more water if necessary.

2. Remove from heat; stir in cherry jam. Set aside to cool.

3. Add just enough sweet red wine to be absorbed by the fruit. Refrigerate until well chilled.

Makes about 9 cups

◆§ MONTCLAIR HADASSAH, NEW JERSEY

Yemenite Haroset

10 pitted dates, chopped	1 teaspoon ground ginger
10 figs, chopped	Red wine
1 tablespoon sesame seeds	Matza meal

Combine fruit, sesame seeds, and ginger. Add red wine and matza meal to bring it to the consistency you want.

Makes about 2-1/2 cups

◆§ RAQUEL SEGAL, DIX HILLS HADASSAH, NEW YORK

Israeli Haroset

15 pitted dates, chopped	1/2 cup red wine
3 bananas, mashed	1 teaspoon ground cinnamon
1 apple, peeled and chopped	Sugar or honey to taste
Juice and grated zest of 1 orange	(optional)
1 cup almonds, chopped	Matza meal, if needed

Combine fruits, nuts, wine, cinnamon, and sugar or honey. Add matza meal to get the consistency you want.

Makes about 6 cups

◆§ RAQUEL SEGAL, DIX HILLS HADASSAH, NEW YORK

Ashkenazic Harosis

3 tart apples, peeled, cored, and chopped

1 cup blanched almonds, coarsely ground or chopped

1-1/2 tablespoons honey

2 tablespoons ground or chopped pecans

1/2 teaspoon ground ginger

Grated zest of half a lemon or orange

Wine as needed

Mix ingredients through lemon or orange zest. Add wine to make the right consistency.

Serves 5 to 7

◦§ *Fran Bongarten, Fairfield Hadassah, Connecticut*

Persian Haroset

1 unpeeled pear, cored and finely chopped

1 unpeeled apple, cored and finely chopped

1 cup finely chopped walnuts

1 cup finely chopped almonds

1 cup finely chopped hazelnuts

1 cup finely chopped pistachio nuts

1 cup chopped pitted dates

1 cup chopped raisins

2 teaspoons ground cinnamon

2 teaspoons grated gingerroot

1 tablespoon apple cider vinegar

Sweet wine

1. Combine pear, apple, walnuts, almonds, hazelnuts, pistachio nuts, dates, and raisins in a large bowl, and blend well, being careful not to chop the mixture into a paste. Add cinnamon, gingerroot, cider vinegar, and enough wine to bind.

2. Place on a platter and shape into a pyramid. Cover and refrigerate.

Makes 5 cups

◦§ *Raquel Segal, Dix Hills Hadassah, New York*

Persian Haroset, recipe right.

Although the origin of the date palm is lost in antiquity, what is certain is that it grew about 5,000 years ago. It was said to have been fashioned from the earth left from the creation of Adam. It was also said that eating dates would ease the pain of childbirth.

An account in Exodus shows the people "under threescore of palm trees and camped there by the waters." The palm is thought to have been primarily ornamental in early biblical history; it appears as a major motif in King Solomon's Temple.

At 120 calories per five or six dates, this popular fruit is absolutely loaded with potassium and has no sodium, fat, or cholesterol.

Pressed dates are available in Middle Eastern markets.

Halek
(Iraqi Haroset)

5 pounds pressed, pitted dates

1. Soak dates overnight in just enough water to cover.
2. Mash the dates in the water by hand, or process in small batches in food processor.
3. Put a cheesecloth over a large bowl. Pour dates with liquid onto the cheesecloth. Close cheesecloth and squeeze dates gently so that date liquid gathers in the bowl. Continue until all liquid is squeezed out of cheesecloth.
4. Discard contents of cheesecloth. Pour date liquid into a pot (not teflon) and bring to a boil. When froth forms, remove with a spoon and discard. Lower heat to medium and continue cooking, stirring every 2 or 3 minutes, 2 to 3 hours, or until orange froth forms and liquid is the consistency of syrup.

Makes about 1 quart

◄ RAHEL MUSLEAH, GREAT NECK HADASSAH, NEW YORK

Potato, Egg and Onion Appetizer

3 or 4 russet potatoes
4 hard-cooked eggs
1 onion, grated
1/4 cup chopped green bell
   pepper (optional)

3 tablespoons chicken fat or unsalted
   margarine, melted
Salt and freshly ground pepper
   to taste

1. Boil potatoes in jackets until tender. Drain, let cool. Peel and chop with eggs until very fine.
2. Add remaining ingredients and mix well. Chill.

Serves 4

◄ ORA HADASSAH, DELRAY BEACH, FLORIDA

Kuftellis
(Romanian Passover Dish)

1-1/2 pounds chopmeat
Seasonings of choice
2 eggs, lightly beaten
Matza meal for rolling
Oil for browning

32-ounce jar borscht, beets
  removed and reserved for
  another use
Oregano or parsley sprigs for
  garnish

1. Season chopmeat to taste and roll into small meatballs. Dip each meatball into beaten egg, then matza meal, then egg again, and matza meal.

2. Spoon oil into skillet and heat. Brown meatballs in heated oil on all sides, then drain on paper towels.

3. Transfer meatballs to 3-quart pot and pour in borscht. Cover and simmer slowly about 1 hour.

4. Serve meatballs with pot juices, garnished with sprigs, as a delicious appetizer.

Serves 6 to 8

LESLEY GRANT, BINGHAMTON HADASSAH, NEW YORK

KUFTELLIS, recipe above, right.

Chopped Liver

1/2 pound chicken livers
2 hard-cooked eggs
1 tablespoon minced onion

1 onion, chopped and sautéed in
1/4 cup chicken fat or oil
Salt and freshly ground pepper
to taste

1. Broil chicken livers until well done. Drain and place in bowl with remaining ingredients.

2. Use a food chopper until well mashed. You can also use a good processor, pulsing 4 or 5 times. Do not pulverize. Should have a coarse texture.

Makes about 1-1/2 cups

❧ SHELANU HADASSAH, NEW YORK, NEW YORK

TIP

Salting is not sufficient to draw out the blood of liver. To kasher, it must be broiled. Consult with your rabbincal authority on how to kasher liver.

Vegetarian Chopped Liver

3 tablespoons unsalted margarine
1 cup sliced fresh mushrooms
1 cup chopped onions
3 hard-cooked eggs
1/4 pound walnuts

1 teaspoon salt
1/4 teaspoon freshly ground
white pepper
Lettuce leaves and tomato
wedges for garnish

1. In a large skillet, melt margarine over low heat. Add mushrooms and onions and sauté until onions are golden.

2. Pass mushrooms, onions, hard-cooked eggs, and walnuts through a grinder or chop very fine in a chopping bowl. Season with salt and pepper. Chill thoroughly. Serve on lettuce leaves and garnish with tomato wedges.

Serves 6

❧ ELLYN KESSLER, LYLAH HADASSAH,
PINELLAS COUNTY, FLORIDA

TIP

1 pound of walnuts equals 3-1/2 cups chopped.

My Cousin Ilene's Gefilte Fish Mold

Finely diced green bell pepper
 and carrots, to decorate mold
 (optional)

4 pounds whitefish
2 pounds pickerel or yellow pike
1/2 cup matza meal
3 tablespoons sugar

1 tablespoon salt
1/2 teaspoon freshly ground
 pepper
3 carrots, cut in chunks
3 large onions, cut in chunks
2 tablespoons oil
4 eggs

1. Have market clean and bone fish. You will end up with about 3-1/2 pounds usable fish.

2. Preheat oven to 325 degrees. Lightly oil 12-cup mold. Sprinkle sides of mold with green bell pepper and carrots if desired.

3. Place half the fish, matza meal, sugar, salt, and pepper in food processor and process until well ground. Put in large bowl. Place remaining fish, matza meal, sugar, salt, and pepper in processor and process until well ground. Add to fish mixture in bowl.

4. Put carrots, onions, oil, and eggs in processor. Process until smooth. Add to fish and stir until well incorporated. Spoon into mold and bake, uncovered, 1-1/4 hours. When done, most of the moisture is absorbed and rim browns and comes away from mold.

5. Unmold at once. Cover lightly and completely with wax paper and let cool. Refrigerate well covered.

Serves 16

◄§ Regina Levin, Westport Hadassah, Connecticut

Golden Chicken Bouillon

2 carrots, sliced	1 clove garlic, chopped
1 onion, sliced	4 peppercorns
1 teaspoon chicken fat	1/4 bay leaf
4-pound pullet	1 teaspoon salt
2 sprigs parsley	Minced parsley
1 leek, diced, washed thoroughly	

1. In large pot, brown carrots and onion lightly in the chicken fat.

2. Add 7 cups water, the pullet, parsley, leek, garlic, peppercorns, and bay leaf. Simmer gently, partly covered, about 1 hour. Add salt during last 15 minutes.

3. Remove chicken and strain soup. Let cool, then refrigerate overnight.

4. Reheat soup and serve sprinkled with parsley.

Serves 6 to 8

◦ ALICE WEINSTOCK, ROSLYN HEIGHTS HADASSAH, NEW YORK

TIP

Browning the onions and carrots gives a lovely rich color to the broth. Serve it with matza balls and carrot slices, if desired. Reserve the chicken for salad.

Sid's Matza Balls

2 eggs, lightly beaten	1/8 teaspoon freshly ground
2 tablespoons vegetable oil	black pepper
2 tablespoons chicken stock	Pinch of ground nutmeg
or water	Pinch of dried marjoram
1 teaspoon salt	Scant 1/2 cup matza meal

1. In medium bowl, mix together eggs, oil, chicken stock or water, the salt, pepper, nutmeg, and marjoram. Add matza meal and mix well. If necessary, add a little extra water or some matza meal to make a batter that is not stiff or loose but holds together without movement when the bowl is shaken. Cover and refrigerate at least 1 hour.

2. Bring 2 quarts salted water to a rolling boil. Roll 8 to 10 matza balls between dampened palms and drop into boiling water. Cook, covered, 40 minutes. With a slotted spoon, transfer matza balls to hot soup with which they will be served.

Makes 8 to 10

◦ SID HACK, COLUMBIA HADASSAH, SOUTH CAROLINA

Matza Kugel

3 cups crumbled matza
6 eggs
1 cup sugar, divided
1/2 teaspoon salt
1/2 teaspoon ground cinnamon, divided

1/2 cup raisins
1/2 cup slivered almonds
4 apples, peeled, seeded, and grated
1 teaspoon grated orange zest
1/4 cup (4 tablespoons) unsalted margarine, melted

1. Preheat oven to 350 degrees. Grease 1-1/2 quart casserole. Soak matza in water until soft; squeeze dry.

2. Beat eggs; beat in 1/2 cup sugar, the salt, and 1/4 teaspoon cinnamon until blended.

3. Stir matza, raisins, almonds, apples, and orange zest into egg mixture. Place in prepared casserole.

4. Combine remaining 1/2 cup sugar with remaining 1/4 teaspoon cinnamon and sprinkle over kugel. Pour melted margarine over all.

5. Bake 45 minutes, until browned.

Serves 8

➡ HELEN WEINSTOCK, FLORIDA-BROWARD HADASSAH, COCONUT CREEK, FLORIDA

Egg-Rich Onion Kugel

6 eggs, separated, at room temperature
2 cups finely chopped onions
1/3 cup oil

1/3 cup matza meal
1-1/2 teaspoons salt
1/4 teaspoon freshly ground pepper

1. Preheat oven to 350 degrees. Grease 2-quart casserole.

2. Beat egg yolks until thick and creamy. Add onions, oil, matza meal, salt, and pepper. Mix thoroughly. Beat egg whites until stiff but not dry and fold into onion mixture.

3. Pour into prepared casserole. Bake about 30 minutes, or until knife inserted in center comes out clean.

Serves 6

➡ RAY GREENBERG, WEST ORANGE HADASSAH, NEW JERSEY

Dried Fruit Kugel

4-1/2 cups broken matza

3 eggs, lightly beaten

1/2 cup sugar

1/4 cup (4 tablespoons) melted
 unsalted butter or margarine

2 tablespoons orange juice or water

1/4 teaspoon salt

1/4 teaspoon ground ginger

1/3 cup slivered almonds, toasted

1/2 cup chopped dried apple

1/2 cup chopped dried peaches
 or apricots

1/3 cup raisins

2 tablespoons unsalted butter
 or margarine

Light cream

1. Preheat oven to 350 degrees. Lightly grease 1-1/2 quart baking dish.

2. Combine matza with enough water to cover. Let stand 5 minutes; drain any excess liquid.

3. Beat eggs with sugar, melted butter or margarine, the orange juice, salt, and ginger. Add matza with almonds and dried fruit. Transfer to prepared baking dish. Dot top with 2 tablespoons butter or margarine.

4. Bake 35 to 40 minutes, until light brown. Serve warm with cream.

Serves 6 to 8

◄ ROSEANNE LEVINE, HANNAH LEVINE HADASSAH, LEOMINSTER, MASSACHUSETTS

Shabbat Carrot-Apple Kugel

8 carrots, peeled and grated

3 apples, peeled, cored, and grated

1 cup dried cherries

1/2 cup pistachio nuts

1/4 cup grated orange zest

4 eggs, lightly beaten

1 cup matza cake meal

1/2 cup oil

1/4 cup fresh lemon juice

1 teaspoon ground cinnamon

1 teaspoon salt

1/2 teaspoon ground ginger

1/2 teaspoon ground allspice

1. Preheat oven to 425 degrees. Grease two 8 x 4 inch loaf pans.

2. Combine all ingredients and divide evenly between the pans. Cover tightly with foil and bake 20 minutes, then reduce heat to lowest and bake overnight, or at least 8 hours.

Serves 10 to 12

◄ RUTH SHERMAN, BOCA RATON HADASSAH, FLORIDA

SHABBAT CARROT-APPLE KUGEL, recipe, right.

Peta-de-Spinoche
(Matza Spinach Pie)

Two (10-ounce) packages fresh
   spinach
4 eggs, lightly beaten

1 teaspoon salt
5 ounces walnuts, chopped
10-ounce box matza

1. Preheat oven to 400 degrees. Grease 13 x 9 inch baking pan.

2. Wash spinach, cut off stems, let drain. Chop spinach in small pieces into large bowl; add beaten eggs, the salt and chopped nuts (save some of nuts to put on top of the Peta).

3. Soak matza until pliable and drain. Line prepared pan with half of matza; spread with spinach mixture; cover with balance of matza. Sprinkle top with remainder of chopped walnuts and bake 1 hour.

Serves 8

BETTY HURVITZ, ROCHESTER HADASSAH, NEW YORK

Whitefish Loaf

2 pounds firm-fleshed whitefish
2 medium onions, cut in
   chunks
1 whole egg
2 egg whites
1 large carrot, grated

Scant 1/2 cup matza meal
1 teaspoon vegetable oil
1 teaspoon sugar
1/2 teaspoon salt
Freshly ground white pepper to taste
1/2 teaspoon freshly grated nutmeg

1. Preheat oven to 350 degrees. Grease 9 x 5 inch loaf pan or 8-cup decorative fish mold.

2. Combine fish and onions in bowl of food processor fitted with steel blade and process until almost smooth. Place in large mixing bowl and stir in 1/2 cup cold water, the whole egg and egg whites, the grated carrot, matza meal, oil, sugar, salt, pepper, and nutmeg. Stir to mix thoroughly.

3. Spoon mixture into prepared pan and bake about 1 hour, or until set. Let cool in pan.

4. Turn fish loaf out of pan. Cover and refrigerate.

Serves 8

LAURIE STERLING, DUPAGE/WILL HADASSAH, NAPERVILLE, ILLINOIS

Celery Root with Carrots

2 cups 1/4-inch-thick slices celery
    root (about 1 pound)
1 cup 1/4-inch-thick slices carrots
    (about 1/2 pound)
1 tablespoon oil

Juice of 2 lemons
1 teaspoon salt
1 tablespoon potato starch
1 tablespoon sugar

TIP
This dish is a Sephardic specialty
served at the Seder.

1. Put vegetables in pot with enough water to cover. Add oil, lemon juice, and salt. Cook, covered, until vegetables are tender, about 20 minutes.

2. Mix potato starch, sugar, and 1/4 cup cold water and stir into cooking liquid. Cook until mixture bubbles and thickens. Can be served cold as an appetizer or salad, or hot as a vegetable.

Serves 6

◦§ SELMA SHARF, ROSLYN HEIGHTS HADASSAH, NEW YORK

Apple Spiced Brisket

5-pound first cut beef brisket
1 teaspoon salt
2-1/2 cups apple juice
1/3 cup honey
1 teaspoon ground cinnamon

1 teaspoon ground ginger
1 teaspoon ground nutmeg
1 small apple, peeled, cored, and
    coarsely chopped
2 tablespoons raisins

1. Preheat oven to 450 degrees.

2. Line 2-inch-deep roasting pan with heavy duty aluminum foil, leaving 1-1/2 inch collar around edges. Prick brisket with fork on both sides and sprinkle with salt. Place in prepared pan and cook, uncovered, about 1 hour. Degrease pan.

3. Combine apple juice, honey, cinnamon, ginger, and nutmeg and pour over roast. Cover pan and collar with foil, and fold edges to seal tightly. Reduce oven temperature to 350 degrees. Cook 1-1/2 to 2 hours, or until tender.

4. Remove brisket to heated serving platter; keep warm in low oven. Pour meat juices into saucepan; add apple and raisins. Bring to a boil. Reduce heat and simmer 3 minutes, or until apple is tender. Slice brisket thinly against the grain, and spoon apple-raisin sauce over slices.

Serves 8 to 10

◦§ ROSE WASSERMAN, DIX HILLS HADASSAH, NEW YORK

CHICKEN MARRAKESH, recipe right.

Chicken Marrakesh

4 whole chickens (2-1/2 pounds each), each cut into eighths
12 large cloves garlic, finely minced
3 tablespoons dried thyme
1 tablespoon ground cumin
2 teaspoons ground ginger
1 teaspoon salt
1 cup red wine vinegar
1 cup best quality olive oil

8 teaspoons green peppercorns, soaked in water and drained
2 cups whole pitted black olives
3 cups dried apricots
2 cups dried small figs
1/2 cup packed brown sugar
2 cups large pecan pieces
Grated zest of 4 lemons
1 cup good red wine

1. The day before, combine the chicken, garlic, thyme, cumin, ginger, salt, wine vinegar, oil, peppercorns, olives, apricots, and figs in 2 large bowls, dividing the ingredients equally; marinate covered in the refrigerator overnight. Mix several times during the day. Remove the bowls from the refrigerator 1 hour before cooking.

2. Preheat oven to 350 degrees.

3. Arrange chicken in single layer in 2 heavy, shallow baking pans. Spoon marinade over both pans. Sprinkle with brown sugar, pecans, and lemon zest. Pour wine between pieces in both pans.

4. Cover the pans with aluminum foil and bake 20 minutes. Remove foil and bake, basting frequently with the pan juices, 50 minutes.

5. Using a fork and slotted spoon, transfer the chicken, olives, dried fruit, and pecans to a large serving platter. Drizzle with a few large spoonfuls of the pan juices.

Serves about 10 to 12

 ROSELLE–CRANFORD HADASSAH, NEW JERSEY

Salonika Chicken with Prunes

TIP
This dish is better when cooked in advance and reheated before serving, giving the flavors a chance to marry.

1/4 cup olive oil

3-pound chicken, cut in serving pieces

Salt and freshly ground pepper to taste

2 medium onions, diced

3 cloves garlic, minced

8-ounce can tomato purée

1/2 teaspoon ground cinnamon

1 small bunch parsley

1/4 teaspoon cayenne

25 pitted prunes

Greek olives (optional)

1/2 cup red wine

1 cup chicken stock, or as needed

1. Preheat oven to 350 degrees.

2. Heat 3 tablespoons olive oil in large heavy frying pan. Season chicken with salt and pepper and fry until browned. Transfer to large pot.

3. Sauté onions and garlic in remaining 1 tablespoon oil until transparent. Add tomato purée, the cinnamon, parsley, cayenne, prunes, and olives if desired. Simmer until thick, then add red wine. Pour over chicken and add the stock.

4. Bake about 1 hour, until chicken is very tender.

Serves 4 to 6

◄§ YVONNE WAYNIK, FAIRFIELD HADASSAH, CONNECTICUT

Naomi's Tzimmes

TIP
You can add prunes, but watch them because they tend to stick on the bottom and can burn. The meat is usually served separately, though bits are left in the tzimmes.

3- to 4-pound brisket with some bone, or short ribs

1 large onion, cut in wedges

3 pounds carrots, cut in 1-inch slices

2 pounds new potatoes, cut in 1-inch chunks

3/4 cup sugar

Salt and freshly ground pepper to taste

KNEIDLACH

5 eggs

Half an onion, minced

1/4 cup chopped unrendered schmaltz

4-1/2 to 5 cups matza meal

1-1/2 teaspoons salt

1/3 teaspoon freshly ground pepper

1. Put brisket and onion in large pot. Add about 10 cups water and simmer, partly covered, until meat is tender, about 3 hours. Make sure water covers the meat; if not, add more.

2. When meat is almost done, add carrots, potatoes, sugar, salt, and pepper. Continue cooking until vegetables are almost done (if meat is done first, remove it).

3. Make kneidlach. Beat eggs in mixing bowl. Add onion, schmaltz and 2-3/4 cups water, then add enough matza meal so dough comes together but is not sticky. Add salt and pepper.

4. Bring liquid to a boil and drop in kneidlach from a large spoon. Lower heat so liquid simmers and cook until kneidlach are done, about 30 minutes. Meanwhile, cut meat into serving-size pieces and return to pot.

5. If tzimmes is watery, mix some matza meal with water and stir it in; let simmer a few minutes. If still watery, add some more. The tzimmes should be fairly thick.

Serves 8

•⊱ Naomi Chernin, Roslyn Heights Hadassah, New York

Tzimmes/Kugel

2 medium carrots, coarsely diced

1 medium sweet potato or yam, coarsely diced

1 large baking apple, seeded and coarsely diced

1/2 cup granulated sugar

1/2 cup packed light brown sugar

1/2 cup (1 stick) unsalted margarine, melted

1/2 cup matza meal

1/2 cup pitted prunes (optional), or raisins

2 tablespoons sweet wine or orange juice

1/2 teaspoon salt

1/2 teaspoon ground cinnamon

1. Preheat oven to 375 degrees. Grease 11 x 7 inch baking pan.

2. By hand or in food processor in two batches, chop and mix all ingredients. Put in prepared pan and bake 45 minutes, or until brown and bubbly.

Serves 6 to 8

•⊱ East Windsor Hadassah, Cranbury, New Jersey

TIPS

Before you drop all of the kloese into the boiling water, test one. If it falls apart, add more matza meal.

Leftovers are delicious fried.

Aunt Jen's Matza Kloese

2 sheets matza	1 teaspoon salt
2 tablespoons schmaltz	1/8 teaspoon freshly ground pepper
1/4 cup chopped onion	1/4 teaspoon ground ginger
2 to 4 eggs, lightly beaten	1/8 teaspoon freshly grated nutmeg
1 teaspoon chopped parsley	1/2 cup matza meal, or as needed

1. Soak matza in cold water a few minutes. Drain and squeeze dry.

2. Heat schmaltz in a skillet and fry onion until golden. Add matza and stir until mixture leaves the skillet clean. Remove from heat. Add eggs, parsley, salt, and seasonings. Add matza meal to make a soft dough. Remove to a bowl and let stand several hours. Meanwhile, bring a pot of water to a boil.

3. Shape into balls the size of marbles. Drop into boiling water and cook 15 minutes. Serve with brisket, red cabbage, or any dish with gravy.

Serves 4 to 6

➵ DORIS DREYFUSS, HARSTDALE HADASSAH, NEW YORK

Liver Kneidlach

1-3/4 cups matza meal	1/4 cup rendered chicken fat or
1/2 pound beef or calf's liver	vegetable oil
1 teaspoon oil	1 teaspoon salt
1 onion, sliced	1/4 teaspoon freshly ground black
3 eggs, lightly beaten	pepper

1. Pour 1-1/2 cups boiling water over matza meal. Stir to mix and set aside to cool. Kasher liver according to rabbinic specifications.

2. Heat oil in skillet over medium heat. Add onion and sauté about 10 minutes, until golden.

3. In meat grinder or food processor, process cooked liver and sautéed onions until almost smooth; add to matza meal with the eggs, chicken fat, the salt, and pepper. Stir to mix thoroughly.

4. Bring large pot of salted water to a rolling boil. Shape liver mixture into balls the size of walnuts and drop into boiling water. Cook, covered, 20 to 25 minutes.

Makes about 8

➵ PORTLAND HADASSAH, OREGON

Potato Latkes

3 pounds Idaho potatoes
2 medium onions, quartered
1/2 cup matza meal
4 eggs, lightly beaten

Salt and freshly ground pepper to taste
Vegetable oil for frying
Applesauce and sour cream
 for serving

1. Fit work bowl of food processor with grating disk. Cut potatoes into pieces to fit feed tube; grate potatoes and onions, using medium pressure. Remove to colander, squeeze dry, and place in mixing bowl.

2. Add matza meal and eggs, and stir to combine. Add salt and pepper. Mixture should be firm but moist.

3. Heat 1/4-inch vegetable oil in skillet until very hot. Form some potato mixture into patties and add to the hot oil. The size of the patties really doesn't matter. Cook as many as will fit in the pan in one layer at a time.

4. When latkes are golden on bottom, turn them over and brown other side. Remove to paper towels and keep warm in a 200-degree oven while you cook the rest. Serve hot with applesauce or sour cream.

Makes about 16

◆§ FLORENCE BARKAN AND SUSAN GRODNICK, ROSLYN HEIGHTS HADASSAH, NEW YORK

POTATO LATKES, recipe above.

Potato Knishes

4-1/2 cups mashed potatoes

3 eggs, lightly beaten

1/2 cup matza meal

1 tablespoon salt, divided

1/4 teaspoon freshly ground pepper

3 large onions, cut up

4 tablespoons oil

1. Preheat oven to 400 degrees. Lightly oil 13 x 9 inch baking pan.

2. Combine mashed potatoes, beaten eggs, matza meal, 2 teaspoons salt, and the pepper. Mix well.

3. Brown onions in oil and add remaining teaspoon salt. Flatten small pancakes with your hands out of the potato mixture. Cover with brown onions. Press another pancake on top.

4. Roll pancakes in matza meal and bake until brown, about 20 to 30 minutes.

Serves 6 to 8

ROCHESTER HADASSAH, NEW YORK

Nana Fannie's Romanian Eggplant Casserole

2 medium eggplants

4 eggs, lightly beaten

1-1/2 cups matza meal

Oil for frying

4 lemons, very thinly sliced

1 cup maple syrup

1/2 cup honey

1/2 cup coarsely chopped nuts (optional)

1. Slice eggplants very thin. Dip in beaten eggs, then dredge in matza meal. Chill several hours.

2. Heat oil and fry eggplant slices in hot oil until golden. Drain well on paper towels or brown paper bags. Preheat oven to 325 degrees.

3. In shallow baking dish, alternate layers of eggplant with layers of lemon slices. Top row should be lemons.

4. Heat maple syrup and honey to boiling. Pour over casserole and place in oven for about 2 hours, until syrup thickens. Sprinkle with nuts, if desired.

Serves about 8 as a side dish

SYLVIA DOFT, HEWLETT HADASSAH, NEW YORK

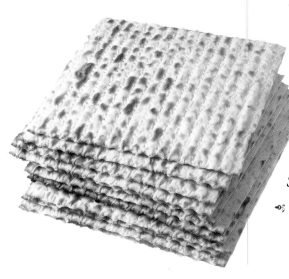

Israeli Mushroom Ragout

1/4 cup olive oil	1/2 teaspoon salt
1 medium onion, chopped	1/2 teaspoon paprika
1 pound mushrooms, quartered	1/4 teaspoon freshly ground pepper
1 teaspoon dried thyme	Pinch of cayenne
1 teaspoon dried cumin seeds	2 tablespoons chopped fresh parsley

1. Heat oil over medium heat in large skillet. Add onion and sauté about 7 minutes, until tender.

2. Add mushrooms, thyme, cumin, salt, paprika, and pepper. Sauté, stirring often, 15 to 20 minutes, or until mushrooms are well coated with spices and any liquid has evaporated.

3. Add cayenne, taste and adjust seasoning. Sprinkle with parsley.

Serves 6 to 8

◄ LYLAH HADASSAH, PINELLAS COUNTY, FLORIDA

Fried Matza

2 eggs	2 sheets matza
1/2 cup milk or water	3 tablespoons shortening
1/4 teaspoon salt	Sugar, cinnamon, applesauce, or
Dash of ground cinnamon	honey for serving

1. In a large bowl, beat eggs. Add milk or water, salt, and cinnamon.

2. Break matza into this mixture. Stir well, until soaked.

3. In large skillet, melt shortening over medium heat; add matza mixture. Cook, covered, over moderate heat about 10 minutes, until browned on underside.

4. Turn and brown other side about 3 minutes.

5. Serve hot, plain, or with sprinkling of sugar, cinnamon, applesauce, or honey.

Serves 2

◄ PORTLAND HADASSAH, OREGON

Sophie's Matza Brie à la Mode

4 sheets matza
2 eggs, lightly beaten
1/4 cup sugar
Zest and juice of 1 lemon
Pinch of cinnamon
1/2 teaspoon Passover vanilla
1/3 cup raisins

3 MacIntosh apples, peeled and
   grated or sliced paper thin
Oil for frying
Cottage cheese, vanilla ice
   cream, or whipped cream for
   serving

1. Break matza in small pieces. Put some in strainer to soften under running water; press out water with your hands. Repeat with a few strainerfuls of matzas.

2. Place matza in a mixing bowl. Add eggs, sugar, lemon zest and juice, the cinnamon, vanilla, raisins, and apples. Combine well.

3. Heat oil in large frying pan. Pour in batter to form thick pancake, shaping to fit contour of pan. Fry lightly until golden, but not overly so. Turn out onto a plate and return to pan to brown other side.

4. Serve topped with cottage cheese for lunch, or vanilla ice cream or whipped cream with tea and coffee.

Serves 6

◄§ SHEILA M. LINTON, SHATIL GROUP HADASSAH, NEW YORK, NEW YORK

Filled Matza Meal Pancakes

TIP
These pancakes are delicious served with something sweet like applesauce, or spicy like ratatouille, a seasoned mixture of eggplant and other vegetables.

5 medium russet potatoes,
   cooked in skins
1 cup matza meal
3 eggs, lightly beaten
2 teaspoons salt
1/4 teaspoon freshly ground
   pepper

1/2 pound cooked beef,
   chopped fine
1/2 pound kashered beef
   liver, chopped fine
Seasoning to taste
Matza cake meal
Oil for frying

1. Peel and mash hot potatoes. Add matza meal, eggs, salt, and pepper. Mix well into a soft dough. Cover and set aside.

2. Combine cooked beef with chopped liver and season to taste.

3. Turn dough out onto a board lightly dusted with matza cake meal and roll into one large ball. Divide in 10 equal pieces.

4. Working with one piece of dough at a time, roll into 2-1/2 to 3-inch rounds. Place spoonful of chopped meat mixture on lower half of circle. Brush edges lightly with water and fold dough over filling. Press edges together firmly to seal.

5. Heat oil in large skillet over medium-high heat. Cook pancakes a few at a time, until golden on both sides. Drain on paper towels.

Serves about 6

ᐟ§ ROCHESTER HADASSAH, NEW YORK

Cheese Blintzes

FILLING	CRÈPES
1-1/2 cups dry cottage cheese	3 eggs
2 eggs, lightly beaten	2/3 cup matza cake meal
1 teaspoon unsalted butter, melted	1/2 teaspoon salt
1 teaspoon sugar	
Salt to taste	

1. Make filling: In medium bowl mix cottage cheese with beaten eggs, melted butter, sugar, and salt; set aside.

2. Make crèpes: Beat 2 eggs with 1-1/2 cups water in a large bowl. Stir in cake meal and salt until smooth and well blended.

3. Grease and heat a small skillet. Pour a small amount of batter into skillet and swirl pan to coat. Cook on both sides until golden. Repeat until all batter is used.

4. Dividing equally, spoon filling onto each blintz and roll up.

5. Either cook filled blintzes in a little melted butter in a hot skillet, or bake at 350 degrees about 20 minutes, until heated through.

Makes about 2 dozen

ᐟ§ HATIKVAH HADASSAH, MIAMI, FLORIDA

Kishka

2 cups matza meal

2 carrots, grated

2 stalks celery, finely chopped

1 large onion, finely chopped

1/2 cup oil

1 egg, lightly beaten

1 teaspoon sugar

1 teaspoon salt

Freshly ground pepper to taste

Garlic powder to taste

TIP

You can easily make this in a processor and it can be baked and frozen until needed.

1. Preheat oven to 375 degrees. Grease 2 sheets of aluminum foil.

2. Combine all ingredients and stir to mix thoroughly. Divide in half; shape each half into log about 3 inches wide. Wrap tightly in prepared foil and place on baking sheet. Bake about 1 hour, or 45 minutes if to be used in cholent.

Serves 8

◄ ORA HADASSAH, DELRAY BEACH, FLORIDA

Passover Derma

3 cups crushed egg matza

1 large onion, chopped

1/2 cup grated carrots

1/2 cup finely chopped celery

1 cup (2 sticks) unsalted
    margarine, melted

2 eggs, lightly beaten

2 cloves garlic, crushed

1 teaspoon salt

1/4 teaspoon freshly ground
    pepper

1/2 teaspoon parve chicken-
    flavor bouillon powder

TIP

To measure the broken matza,
3 sheets crumbled matza = 2 cups.

1. Preheat oven to 350 degrees. Combine all ingredients in large bowl and stir to mix thoroughly.

2. Place aluminum foil on a cookie sheet and grease lightly. Spoon mixture onto center of foil and shape into a log about 14 inches long. Bring foil up and over mixture and pinch edges together to seal. Fold and pinch ends.

3. Bake about 45 minutes, or until cooked through. Unwrap and slice into 1-1/2-inch-thick slices.

Makes 8 to 10 slices

◄ SYLVIA RICH, ORA HADASSAH, DELRAY BEACH, FLORIDA

Cucumber Salad

15 small cucumbers (Kirbies), peeled and thinly sliced
2 onions, thinly sliced

1/2 cup fresh lemon juice
1 teaspoon salt

1. In a large bowl combine cucumber and onion slices. Add lemon juice and salt; stir to mix thoroughly.
2. Refrigerate in sealed container for 2 days, stirring twice a day.

Serves 12

◦§ RUTH ABRAMOWITZ, MONTCLAIR HADASSAH, NEW JERSEY

TIP

For a change, use sliced uncooked zucchini in place of cucumbers.

Layered Vegetable Loaf

Two (10-ounce) packages frozen spinach, thawed and drained
3 eggs
Salt to taste
Hefty 1/4 teaspoon freshly grated nutmeg

Milk or whipping cream as needed
Two (10-ounce) packages frozen cauliflower
3 cups sliced raw carrots (about 1 pound)

1. Butter 9 x 5 inch loaf pan well, line with wax paper, and butter wax paper well. Preheat oven to 300 degrees.
2. Purée spinach in blender or processor with 1 egg, about 3/4 teaspoon salt, and the nutmeg, adding 2 to 4 tablespoons milk, or as much as needed to make the mixture smooth and moist but not runny.
3. Cook cauliflower until tender; drain. Purée with 1 egg, about 1 teaspoon salt, and 3 to 6 tablespoons milk or cream, or as needed.
4. Cook carrots until tender; drain. Purée with 1 egg, about 3/4 teaspoon salt, and 2 to 4 tablespoons milk or cream, or as needed.
5. Pour spinach mixture into prepared pan, then layer in the cauliflower, then the carrot. Cover the top with buttered wax paper and set pan in a shallow pan of water. Bake 1 hour and 15 minutes, or until loaf no longer jiggles (this may take up to 30 minutes longer).
6. Remove from oven and wait 15 minutes. Lift off wax paper and run a knife around the sides. Put serving plate on top, invert the loaf, and carefully strip off the wax paper.

Serves about 8

◦§ SPRINGFIELD HADASSAH, ILLINOIS

TIP

Serve hot or cold; it's absolutely delicious both ways.

Sweet and Sour Beets

4 cups sliced, cooked, or canned
   beets, drained, 3/4 cup liquid
   reserved
3/4 cup raisins
1 tablespoon potato starch

1/4 cup sugar
3 tablespoons unsalted margarine
1/3 cup fresh lemon juice
Scallion, chopped, for garnish

1. Combine reserved beet liquid with raisins in saucepan. Bring to a boil, reduce heat, and simmer, covered, 5 minutes.

2. Blend potato starch with 2 tablespoons beet liquid and stir into raisin mixture. Add sugar and margarine. If serving cold, omit margarine. Cook over low heat, stirring constantly, until margarine is melted and sugar is dissolved. Add lemon juice and beets and simmer until heated through.

3. Scatter chopped scallion over top.

Serves 6 to 8

◆ *WEPAWAUG HADASSAH, ORANGE, CONNECTICUT*

Eingemachts
(Beet Preserves)

3 pounds winter beets
Sugar, as needed
1 or 2 lemons, sliced thin

1 cup chopped walnuts
1/2 teaspoon ground ginger

1. Cut or process beets into matchstick strips, and soak overnight in cold water.

2. Drain beets, reserving water. Put in heavy kettle, adding enough cooking water to barely cover beets, and bring to a boil. Add sugar in equal proportion to the beets.

3. Bring to a slow rolling boil, stirring until mixture jells. During last 5 minutes of cooking, add sliced lemons and chopped nuts.

4. Remove from stove and add ginger. Put in hot, sterile jars.

Serves about 12

◆ *ROSLYN OSTROW, BROWARD REGION HADASSAH, FLORIDA*

SWEET AND SOUR BEETS, recipe above, right.

Confectioners' Sugar

1 cup less 1-1/2 teaspoons granulated sugar

1-1/2 teaspoons potato starch

Pulverize sugar in blender or food processor. Sift it together with potato starch.

Makes 1 cup

◆ WEPAWAUG HADASSAH, ORANGE, CONNECTICUT

TIP

Because it is made with cornstarch, regular confectioners' sugar is not Kosher for Passover.

Honey Sponge Cake

6 eggs, separated, at room temperature
1/2 cup sugar
1/2 cup honey

Zest and juice of half a lemon
1/2 cup matza cake meal
3 tablespoons potato starch
1 tablespoon ground cinnamon

1. Heat oven to 325 degrees. Have handy an ungreased 10-inch tube pan.

2. Beat egg whites in large bowl until stiff. Continue beating while adding sugar very slowly. When whites are shiny, set aside.

3. Beat egg yolks with honey and lemon zest and juice. Fold in cake meal, potato starch, and cinnamon. Fold yolk mixture into whites, until all is incorporated. Pour into ungreased pan and bake 55 to 60 minutes. Invert on cake rack and let cool completely before removing from pan.

Serves about 14

◆ CLAIRE KORN, ROSLYN HEIGHTS HADASSAH, NEW YORK

Chocolate Pudding Cake

TIPS

To convert any recipe for Passover, use 2 tablespoons matza cake meal with 6 tablespoons potato starch for 1/2 cup flour.

To make chocolate curls or shavings, microwave the chocolate chunk on the lowest possible power for 10 seconds. Let stand a few seconds, then scrape across the surface with a vegetable peeler. If hard shards break instead of curling, microwave another 10 seconds, and so on until correct temperature is reached. The pressure of the peeler and the angle will determine whether you get curls or shavings.

CRUST
1/2 cup (1 stick) unsalted butter
2 ounces semisweet chocolate
1-1/3 cups matza meal
1/3 cup sugar

FILLING
9 ounces semisweet chocolate, coarsely chopped
11 ounces (8-ounce plus 3-ounce packages) cream cheese, softened

2/3 cup sugar
6 eggs, at room temperature
1 tablespoon Passover vanilla
1/3 cup whipping cream

TOPPING
1-1/2 cups whipping cream
1/4 cup Passover confectioners' sugar
1/2 teaspoon Passover vanilla
Chocolate curls or shavings

1. Make crust: Preheat oven to 375 degrees. Melt butter and chocolate in double boiler over gently simmering water. Stir until smooth. Mix in matza meal and sugar. Press mixture into bottom and halfway up sides of 9-inch springform pan. Bake until firm, about 8 to 10 minutes. Cool to room temperature and refrigerate until chilled.

2. Make filling: Melt chocolate in double boiler over gently simmering water, stirring until smooth; cool slightly. Beat cream cheese with sugar until light and fluffy. Beat in eggs 1 at a time, beating well after each addition. Blend in vanilla. Beat in chocolate and cream and pour into crust. Bake 30 to 35 minutes until outside is firm and lightly browned but center is still soft when pan is shaken. Refrigerate until well chilled, or up to 24 hours.

3. For topping, beat cream, confectioners' sugar, and vanilla to soft peaks. To serve, run a knife along the edge of pan and remove cake from springform. Set on platter. Spread whipped cream evenly over top. Garnish with chocolate curls. Serve chilled.

Serves 8 to 10

◄§ SPRINGFIELD HADASSAH, ILLINOIS

Metz Chocolate Cake

8 ounces semisweet or dark
  chocolate
1/3 cup milk
1/2 teaspoon Passover vanilla
2/3 cup plus 1 tablespoon sugar
3/4 cup potato starch
1/2 cup blanched almonds
6 eggs, separated, at room
  temperature

ROYAL ICING
3 ounces dark chocolate, chopped
3/4 cup Passover confectioners'
  sugar
1 egg white
1 tablespoon warm water

1. Preheat oven to 350 degrees. Butter 9-inch springform pan.

2. Melt chocolate in milk, stirring constantly, over low heat. When chocolate is completely melted, remove from heat and stir in vanilla, 2/3 cup sugar, and the potato starch. Mix lightly.

3. Grind almonds with 1 tablespoon sugar until fine. Add to egg yolks, then add egg yolk mixture to chocolate mixture.

4. Beat egg whites until stiff. Stir one quarter of egg whites into chocolate mixture to loosen. Add this to the remaining egg whites and fold together as gently as possible.

5. Pour mixture into prepared springform pan. Bake about 45 minutes. The center of the cake should be slightly soft. Let cool completely before turning it out.

6. Make royal icing: Melt the chocolate in top of double boiler over barely simmering water and let cool slightly. With wooden spoon, beat Passover confectioners' sugar with the egg white; beat into chocolate. Beat in warm water.

7. Set cake over a rack with waxed paper underneath to catch drippings. Pour the warm icing over cake and spread it with a spatula. You must work quickly because the icing will set very quickly.

Serves 8

◆§ LAURIE LINDRUP, GRAND RAPIDS HADASSAH, MICHIGAN

Chocolate Wine Cake

4 eggs, separated, at room
temperature
1/2 cup sugar
1/2 cup finely ground almonds
or walnuts

1/2 cup unsweetened cocoa powder
1/2 cup matza meal, sifted
1/2 cup raisins
1/4 cup sweet wine
Juice of 1 orange

1. Preheat oven to 250 degrees. Lightly grease 9 x 5 inch loaf pan.

2. Beat the yolks and sugar in bowl of electric mixer until lemon colored and thick. Add almonds, cocoa powder, matza meal, raisins, wine, and orange juice, mixing thoroughly.

3. Beat egg whites in another clean bowl with clean beaters until stiff. Lightly fold into yolk mixture just until combined. Pour into prepared pan. Bake 50 to 60 minutes, until a toothpick comes out clean when inserted in center of cake.

Serves 8

◦§ EUNICE ZARETT, HUNTINGTON HADASSAH, NEW YORK

Banana Nut Wine Cake

3/4 cup matza cake meal
1/4 cup potato starch
8 eggs, separated, at room
temperature
1-1/2 cups sugar, divided

Zest and juice of 1 orange
1 ripe banana, mashed
1/4 cup sweet red wine
1 cup ground nuts

1. Preheat oven to 350 degrees. Sift cake meal with potato starch; set aside. Have handy an ungreased 10-inch tube pan.

2. Beat egg yolks with 1 cup sugar until light lemon color and thick, 3 to 5 minutes. Add orange zest and juice, the banana, wine, and nuts.

3. In a clean mixing bowl with clean beaters beat egg whites until stiff. Gradually beat in remaining 1/2 cup sugar until whites are shiny. Fold into yolk mixture. Gently fold in cake meal mixture just until incorporated.

4. Pour into pan. Bake 1 hour, or until tester inserted in center comes out clean. Invert on wire rack. Let cool completely before removing from pan.

Serves 12

◦§ RENEE BRODSKY, DEBORAH-ZAHAVA HADASSAH, CHICAGO, ILLINOIS

Savarin with Strawberries

CAKE

6 eggs, separated, at room
   temperature
1 cup sugar, divided
1/2 cup matza cake meal
1/4 cup potato starch
1 teaspoon Passover vanilla or
   lemon juice
1/4 cup (1/2 stick) unsalted
   margarine, melted

WINE SAUCE

1/2 cup sugar
Juice of 1 lemon
1/2 cup sweet wine

FILLING

1 pint fresh strawberries, washed
   and hulled
1/2 cup apricot preserves
2 tablespoons lemon juice

1. Preheat oven to 350 degrees. Grease well a 10-inch tube pan and line bottom with baking parchment.

2. In a large bowl, beat egg whites until foamy; slowly beat in 1/2 cup sugar, 1 tablespoon at a time, until stiff but not dry. In another large bowl, beat egg yolks well; gradually beat in remaining 1/2 cup sugar until thick and lemon colored.

3. Combine cake meal with potato starch.

4. Fold egg-yolk mixture into egg whites, then gradually fold in dry ingredients. Add vanilla or lemon juice. Drizzle melted margarine very slowly into mixture; continue folding until blended.

5. Pour batter into prepared pan and bake about 40 minutes, until cake springs back when lightly touched. Let cool in pan.

6. Make wine sauce: Combine sugar and lemon juice with 1/4 cup water in small saucepan. Bring to a boil over medium heat; reduce heat and simmer 1 to 2 minutes. Stir in wine, remove from heat (makes approximately 1 cup).

7. When cake is completely cool, slide a knife around the edges of the pan to loosen; remove the cake onto a platter and baste with wine sauce. Fill the center of the cake with berries and their juice. Bring the apricot preserves and lemon juice to a boil; cook 1 minute. Let cool. Brush this carefully over the top and sides of the cake. Chill.

Serves 12 to 14

BINGHAMTON HADASSAH, NEW YORK

Egyptian–Sephardic Style Orange Cake

2 thin-skinned juice oranges
1-1/2 cups (1/2 pound) blanched
*   almonds*
1 cup sugar

6 eggs, separated, at room
*   temperature*
Passover confectioners' sugar

TIP
Double the recipe and make 2 layers. Spread strawberry jam and sliced banana as a filling.

1. Preheat oven to 350 degrees. Coat 10-inch springform pan (or regular layer-cake pan) with margarine and then with matza meal, shaking out excess meal.

2. Scrub oranges well and place in pot with a few inches of water. Cook over medium heat, covered, about 1 hour, until oranges are soft and easily pierced with a fork. Remove from water and let cool.

3. Cut open oranges and remove seeds. In food processor or by hand, finely mince orange zest and pulp.

4. Grind almonds in blender or processor with 1/2 cup sugar to the consistency of coarse flour. Transfer to large bowl, adding remaining sugar and the minced orange. Beat egg yolks lightly and fold into orange-nut mixture. Beat egg whites until stiff and fold in. Pour into prepared pan and bake about 1 hour, until lightly browned and cake feels firm (but not too hard) to the touch. Put on wire rack to let cool.

5. When cake is cool, run a knife around sides. Release the spring but let cake cool completely before removing from pan bottom. Remove and dust decoratively with Passover confectioners' sugar.

Serves 8 to 10

◦§ CHRIS GROSSMAN, CLIFTON PARK HADASSAH, NEW YORK

The Special Wheat

The year was 1938. Grandfather had a large grist mill in Durham, Pennsylvania, and his flour was always in demand. In late summer, Grandfather traveled to New York City to get his order for the special flour for the celebration of Passover. The rabbis were Grandfather's special customers and they ordered the special wheat. The dickering went back and forth at full speed, punctuated with bursts of laughter and numerous cups of coffee.

Dad planted the wheat in late fall. By winter, snows covered the ground, enriching the soil and plants. With warm spring rains the wheat grew tall and green. By June it developed full heads. We all prayed for perfect weather, because the beautiful performance could end in minutes if harsh winds or hailstones flattened the crop.

The rabbis had waited for grandfather's call. With satchels packed, they were ready for the train trip to Durham. First they came to the mill to see if Grandfather had fumigated the mills properly. In the evening, Mother drove them to Easton to stay in the homes of Orthodox families.

Very early the next morning the rabbis went out to the wheat fields. As they waited for the dew to dry they constantly prayed. When the moisture dried off it was time to start cutting. The rabbis yelled and waved, "Come on, hurry! No rain must touch our wheat!"

What a grand sight! Dad slowly drove the combine up and down the fields, row after row, the rabbis walking right behind, their heads bowed, continuously blessing the wheat and thanking God for the bountiful harvest. As hot as it was, the rabbis never took off their long heavy black wool coats. They had prayer shawls around their shoulders and big black hats on their heads. They didn't seem to mind the heat.

When the day's work was finished the wheat was taken to the mill. The rabbis took turns resting or praying over the wheat; it was never out of their sight, day or night. The next morning the rabbis blessed the wheat as it was milled. The flour was put in bags. These bags of special flour were loaded onto a train and the rabbis rode in the boxcar with the flour. A special bakery in New York made the flour into matza for the Passover celebration.

My family felt so privileged to grow the wheat and grind it into flour for the Jewish people. We felt great pride for having a crop grown in our valley for such a special occasion.

Lorretta R. Deysher, Middleburg, Pennsylvania

Brandied Chocolate Orange Tort

Matza cake meal for dusting
4 eggs, separated, at room
    temperature
1/2 cup sugar, divided
3/4 cup golden raisins or dried
    cherries, chopped
1/4 cup matza cake meal
4 ounces (3/4 cup) toasted
    almonds, ground

4 ounces semisweet chocolate,
    grated
6 tablespoons fresh orange juice
2 tablespoons brandy, or
    additional orange juice
1 tablespoon grated orange zest
Pinch of salt
Shaved semisweet chocolate

1. Preheat oven to 350. Grease bottom of 8-inch springform pan and dust with some matza cake meal, shaking off excess.

2. Beat yolks with 1/4 cup sugar until ribbons form when beaters are lifted, about 5 minutes. Combine raisins and the 1/4 cup cake meal. Fold raisin mixture, ground almonds, grated chocolate, orange juice, brandy, and orange zest into yolk mixture.

3. With clean dry beaters, beat egg whites with salt until soft peaks form. Gradually add remaining 1/4 cup sugar and beat until stiff but not dry. Fold whites into yolk mixture.

4. Turn into prepared pan. Bake until a toothpick inserted in center comes out clean, 55 to 65 minutes. Let cake cool completely in pan.

5. Remove sides of springform and garnish cake with shaved chocolate.

Serves 8 to 10

◄§ RICKY KAPLAN, LARGO, FLORIDA

The fig is the first tree to be mentioned in the Bible. When Adam and Eve had eaten the forbidden fruit, "The eyes of them both were opened, and they knew that they were naked; and they sewed fig leaves together and made themselves aprons." There is also a biblical reference to figs as a symbol of harmony:

"But they shall sit every man under his vine and under his fig tree and none shall make them afraid" (Micah 4:4).

Figs have been popular in the Middle East for at least five thousand years. The miracle is that so lush a honeyed fruit can thrive on hardscrabble ground. But thrive they do on the rocky slopes of Greece and sandy shores of North Africa. Even before domestication, figs grew along the banks of the Jordan River and around the Dead Sea.

There are over 700 varieties of figs, the Smyrna from western Turkey being the best known, although we also dote on California's fresh mission figs (so named because they were introduced by the Spanish mission fathers).

Pecan Macaroon Chocolate Fig Tart

FILLING
12 ounces dried Calimyrna figs
 or dried apricots, chopped
1 cup water
6 tablespoons sugar
1 tablespoon peeled and chopped
 fresh gingerroot
1 tablespoon fresh lemon juice
1 packed teaspoon grated
 lemon zest

CRUST
Matza cake meal
2 cups (8 ounces) pecans, toasted
 and cooled
3/4 cup sugar
1/4 teaspoon ground ginger
1/8 teaspoon salt
1 egg

4 ounces semisweet chocolate,
 chopped, plus additional
 chocolate and pecan halves
 for garnish

1. Make filling: Combine filling ingredients with 1 cup water in heavy saucepan. Stir until sugar dissolves and mixture boils. Reduce heat, cover, and cook until fruit is tender, about 35 minutes. Uncover and simmer 5 minutes more, stirring occasionally, until liquid is absorbed and filling is thick.

2. Transfer to food processor. With metal blade, pulse 5 times until mixture holds together. Transfer to bowl and let cool (this can be done 3 days ahead and refrigerated).

3. Make crust: Preheat oven to 350 degrees. Trace removable bottom of a 9- or 10-inch springform pan on wax paper and set aside. Line pan with heavy-duty foil. Grease foil and dust with cake meal.

4. Combine 2 cups pecans, the sugar, ground ginger, and salt in food processor and process until nuts are finely ground. Add egg and process until moist clump forms. Using moistened fingertips, press 1 cup dough over bottom and up sides of prepared pan (crust will be thin. If you like a thicker bottom crust, use all the mixture on the bottom and drizzle the chocolate directly onto the filling. Alternately, double the amount and use half on top). Bake crust until puffed and dry-looking, about 14 minutes. Transfer pan to rack; press bottom of crust lightly to flatten. Let cool and keep oven on.

5. Stir chocolate in top of double boiler set over simmering water until melted. Spread most of it out over bottom crust, leaving enough for final drizzle and dip. Spoon 1-3/4 cups filling over chocolate; keep remainder for another use.

Spicy and vibrant, ginger is a tantalizing treat prized in cuisines around the world. A reviver and a comforter, it has been found effective in helping sweat out a fever, soothing an upset stomach or motion sickness, and lowering cholesterol.

According to old herbal tracts, ginger thins the blood even better than garlic or onion—or aspirin. It's an anticoagulant, is said to relieve the pain, swelling and morning stiffness of arthritis, and to prevent and cure colds. And some swear by it for migraines.

Ginger is a natural for lowfat cooking, as it is one of the few spices that needs no oil to carry its racy flavor. Select an unblemished root, firm and heavy. A shiny look is not an indicator of freshness, since appearance can vary with country of origin. It is best wrapped in a paper towel to absorb moisture that might encourage mildew, then sealed in a plastic bag in the crisper.

Dried and ground, the flavor is very different and not an appropriate substitute for fresh. But it is delicious in its own right in savory dishes, and a sprightly addition to sweet ones.

6. Press remaining dough over traced wax circle, filling outline completely. Using paper as aid, turn dough circle over and onto tart, aligning carefully. Peel off paper. Pinch top dough to edge of crust to seal.

7. Bake tart until top is golden and dry-looking, about 30 minutes. Cool completely in pan on rack.

8. Wrap in foil and store 1 day at room temperature or refrigerate for 5 days. Push up pan bottom to release tart. Peel off foil. If desired, dip spoon into melted chocolate and drizzle in zigzag pattern over tart. Dip pecan halves halfway into melted chocolate and arrange around edge. Chill until chocolate sets, about 30 minutes. Serve cold or at room temperature.

Serves 10 to 12

➔ *Sheila Mott, DuPage/Will Hadassah, Naperville, Illinois*

Bimuelos (Matza Fritters)

6 sheets matza
6 eggs, lightly beaten
1/3 cup sugar
3 tablespoons matza meal
Vegetable oil for frying
Finely chopped nuts

SYRUP
2 cups sugar
Juice of half a lemon

1. Break matza into small pieces and soak in cold water; drain thoroughly. Add beaten eggs, the sugar, and matza meal. Beat well.

2. Heat 2 inches oil in deep skillet to 375 degrees. Drop batter by tablespoons into oil. Cook each side until golden; drain on paper towels.

3. Make syrup: Heat sugar with 2 cups water until sugar is dissolved. Stir in lemon juice and then turn off heat. Drop bimuelos in syrup. Remove with slotted spoon and roll in chopped nuts.

Makes approximately 3 dozen

➔ *Dora Levy, Rochester Hadassah, New York*

Chremsel

3 sheets matza

1 cup sugar

1/4 cup golden raisins

1/4 cup blanched almonds

1/4 cup (1/2 stick) unsalted
   margarine, melted

4 eggs, separated, at room
   temperature

1/4 teaspoon salt

1/4 teaspoon ground cinnamon

Oil for frying

Honey

Lemon Sauce (recipe follows)

1. Soak matza in water, then press out water. Put matza in bowl. Add sugar, raisins, almonds, margarine, egg yolks, salt, and cinnamon.

2. Beat egg whites until stiff and fold into matza mixture.

3. Heat oil in medium skillet. Drop mixture into pan by tablespoons to form a kind of pancake. Brown on both sides but don't fry too hard. Remove from pan to paper towels to drain.

4. Spread with honey while still warm, or serve with Lemon Sauce.

Serves 6

Lemon Sauce

Juice of 1 lemon

Juice of 1 orange

2 tablespoons potato starch

1/2 cup sugar

1 teaspoon grated lemon zest

1 teaspoon grated orange zest

3 eggs, separated, at room
   temperature

1. Add water to lemon and orange juices to make 1-1/4 cups. Place in double boiler and add potato starch, sugar, lemon and orange zests, and 3 egg yolks.

2. Bring mixture to a boil, stirring until it thickens. Remove from heat and let cool completely, covered with wax paper.

3. Beat egg whites well and fold into thickened sauce. Spoon over Chremsel.

Makes about 2 cups

◄ ILSA NATHAN, BIRMINGHAM HADASSAH, ALABAMA

Mandelbrot

1 cup (2 sticks) unsalted margarine,
   at room temperature
2 cups sugar
6 eggs
2-3/4 cups matza cake meal

3/4 cup potato starch
1 teaspoon ground cinnamon
1/2 teaspoon salt
1 cup chocolate morsels
1 cup chopped walnuts

1. Heat oven to 350 degrees. Grease 2 large cookie sheets.

2. Beat margarine and sugar in large bowl until light and fluffy. Add eggs, 1 at a time, beating after each addition. Fold in cake meal, potato starch, cinnamon, and salt. Stir in chocolate morsels and nuts. Chill 30 minutes.

3. Divide mixture into 4 equal portions; shape each into a 3/4-inch-wide log. Place 2 logs about 2 inches apart on each cookie sheet.

4. Bake about 35 minutes, or until golden. Slice when still warm. For added crispness, reduce oven to 300 degrees. Arrange cookies cut-side down on cookie sheets and bake until lightly golden, 15 to 20 minutes. Let cool completely.

Makes about 3 dozen

◆§ *Pauline Schwartz, Roslyn Heights Hadassah, New York*

Almond Macaroons

2 egg whites, at room temperature
1/4 cup sugar
1 teaspoon Passover vanilla

1/8 teaspoon salt
1-1/2 cups sweetened coconut
1/2 cup finely chopped almonds

1. Preheat oven to 300 degrees. Line cookie sheets with wax paper and lightly oil paper. Beat egg whites until foamy; blend in sugar, vanilla, and salt. Beat until stiff. Fold in coconut and almonds.

2. Drop by teaspoonfuls 1 inch apart onto prepared sheets. Bake 25 minutes, until golden and crunchy. Cool on sheets 1 minute. Slide wax paper onto wire rack and let cool 5 minutes. Remove cookies from wax paper and store loosely covered.

Makes about 4 dozen

◆§ *Shirley Rosen, Rutland Hadassah, Vermont*

Pecan Macaroons

6 egg whites

1 cup sugar

2 cups finely ground toasted
   pecans

1 teaspoon Passover vanilla

2 cups pecan halves, toasted

1. Preheat oven to 200 degrees. Grease cookie sheets.

2. Beat egg whites until stiff peaks form. Gradually add sugar by tablespoonfuls, beating until very stiff and dry. Fold in ground nuts and vanilla.

3. Drop by heaping teaspoonfuls onto prepared cookie sheets. Place pecan half on top of each cookie.

4. Bake until set, 15 minutes, than increase oven temperature to 300 degrees and bake 15 minutes more, or until cookies are baked through.

Makes 8 to 10 dozen

➳ Mrs. Lee Kiefer, Oklahoma City Hadassah, Oklahoma

Chocolate Macaroons

4 egg whites

1 cup sugar

12 ounces semisweet chocolate,
   melted

1 tablespoon fresh orange juice

1 teaspoon grated orange zest

Pinch of salt

2 cups chopped nuts or 4 cups
   coconut

1. Preheat oven to 325 degrees. Line cookie sheets with baking parchment.

2. Beat egg whites until stiff. Gradually beat in sugar. Beat in melted chocolate, orange juice, orange zest, and salt. Fold in nuts or coconut.

3. Drop by teaspoonfuls onto prepared sheets; bake 20 minutes.

Makes 6 to 8 dozen

➳ Mollie Franks, San Diego Hadassah, California

No Bake Chocolate-Nut Farfel Cookies

1 pound semisweet chocolate   *1 cup toasted walnuts, chopped*

1/4 cup sugar   *1-1/2 cups toasted matza farfel*

1. Line a cookie sheet with aluminum foil. Melt chocolate in top of double boiler.

2. Stir sugar into chocolate. Stir in toasted walnuts and matza farfel and mix thoroughly. Drop by tablespoonfuls onto prepared cookie sheet and refrigerate until firm.

Makes about 2-1/2 pounds

•§ HANNAH LEVINE HADASSAH, LEOMINSTER, MASSACHUSETTS

Meringues

2 egg whites   *1 teaspoon grated lemon zest*

2/3 cup sugar   *1 cup mini chocolate morsels*

1 teaspoon apple cider vinegar   *1 cup chopped walnuts*

1/2 teaspoon Passover vanilla

TIP

These are traditionally served at Passover, when flourless desserts are the rule. The meringue can be very sensitive to humidity, so it's best not to make them on a damp day.

1. Preheat oven to 350 degrees. Cover 2 large cookie sheets with baking parchment.

2. Beat egg whites until stiff. Slowly add sugar and apple cider vinegar. Add vanilla and lemon zest. Carefully fold in chocolate morsels and walnuts.

3. Drop by teaspoonfuls onto prepared cookie sheets.

4. Bake 10 minutes. Shut off oven and leave cookies for 5 hours without opening oven. If prepared in the evening, leave overnight.

Makes about 5-1/2 dozen

•§ ROSE GOLDMAN, SHELANU HADASSAH, NEW YORK, NEW YORK

Babanatza

Half of an 8-ounce box matza
  farfel
4 eggs, lightly beaten
1/2 cup raisins
1/2 cup sugar

1/2 cup chopped nuts plus
  additional nuts for topping
  (optional)
1 tablespoon ground cinnamon
3/4 cup honey, divided

1. Preheat oven to 325 degrees. Grease 13 x 9 inch baking pan.

2. Soak matza farfel in water until soft. Squeeze dry.

3. Place drained matza in large mixing bowl and stir in eggs, raisins, sugar, chopped nuts, cinnamon, and 1/2 cup honey. Pour into prepared pan and sprinkle additional nuts on top. Bake about 1 hour.

4. Pour 1/4 cup honey over top while still warm. Cut into 2 inch squares and serve warm or cold.

Serves 12

➺ Ann Ofengender, Indianapolis Hadassah, Indiana

Lemon Squares

1/2 cup (1 stick) unsalted butter
3/4 cup cake meal
1-1/2 cups sugar, divided
2 eggs

2 tablespoons potato starch
3 tablespoons fresh lemon juice
Passover confectioners' sugar
  (optional)

1. Preheat oven to 325 degrees. Line 8-inch square pan with foil, leaving 1 inch extended over sides. Grease bottom and sides of foil.

2. Combine butter, cake meal, and 1/2 cup sugar. Press into prepared pan. Bake 20 minutes and remove from oven.

3. Beat eggs, remaining cup sugar, the potato starch, and lemon juice and pour over crust. Return to oven and bake 20 to 25 minutes.

4. Let cool and cut into squares.

5. If desired, sprinkle with Passover confectioners' sugar.

Makes 16 squares

➺ Ellen Raboy, Shira Hadassah, Port Chester, New York

TIP
Recipe may be doubled and baked in a 13 x 9 inch pan.

Matza Meal Pie Crust

1 sheet matza	1 egg
1/3 cup matza meal	2 tablespoons sugar
1 tablespoon oil	Pinch of salt

1. Preheat oven to 375 degrees. Grease 9-inch pie pan.

2. Soak matza in hot water; squeeze as dry as possible. Combine soaked matza with matza meal and oil. Mix in egg, sugar, and salt until well blended

3. Press mixture on bottom and up sides of prepared pan and bake 15 to 20 minutes. Let cool before filling.

Makes one 9-inch pie crust

◄§ PORTLAND HADASSAH, OREGON

Nut Pie Crust

1/2 cup finely chopped nuts	1/4 teaspoon salt
1/2 cup matza meal	1/4 cup oil
2 tablespoons sugar	1 egg white

1. Preheat oven to 375 degrees. Lightly grease 9-inch pie pan.

2. Mix nuts with matza meal, sugar, and salt. Beat oil with egg white until combined; stir into nut mixture. Press firmly against bottom and sides of prepared pan. Bake 15 minutes.

Makes one 9-inch pie crust

◄§ RANA LEVY, TAMPA HADASSAH, FLORIDA

Crystallized Orange Nuts

1/4 cup orange juice
1 cup sugar

2 cups pecan halves

1. Butter large cookie sheet with sides.

2. Combine orange juice and sugar in 2-quart glass baking dish. Mix well. Stir in pecans. Cover with plastic wrap, leaving a corner open to vent. Microwave on medium 6 minutes. Stir and continue cooking 4 to 6 minutes longer or until syrup crystallizes.

3. Immediately spread and separate glazed nuts on prepared cookie sheet to let cool.

Makes about 2 cups

⌐§ SYRACUSE HADASSAH, NEW YORK

Matza Brickle

4 sheets matza
1 cup (2 sticks) salted butter
1 cup packed dark brown sugar

12 ounces (2 cups) chocolate morsels
1 cup coarsely ground walnuts
or almonds, or sliced almonds

1. Preheat oven to 450 degrees.

2. Line large cookie sheet with sides with heavy-duty aluminum foil.

3. Lay out matza as close as possible in 1 layer in pan, breaking pieces to fit. Melt butter with brown sugar in saucepan, stirring frequently, until it bubbles. Pour over matza; spread to coat. Put in oven for a minute or two.

4. Sprinkle chocolate morsels over top and return to oven 1 minute, or until morsels are soft.

5. Remove from oven and with spatula spread chocolate to cover the matza. Sprinkle with nuts.

6. Freeze 20 minutes, or until hard. Crack, put in plastic zipper bags, and store in freezer.

Serves about 12

⌐§ BEYRL LIEFER, WESTPORT HADASSAH, CONNECTICUT

MAIMOUNA

Maimouna is a celebration held by Maghrebi Jews at the end of the last day of Passover, which according to tradition is the anniversary of the death of Maimonides' father, Maimon ben Joseph.

These Jews—from Northwest Africa, comprising the coastlands and the Atlas Mountains of Morocco, Algeria, and Tunisia—set their tables with food and drink having symbolic significance according to local tradition. A live fish swimming in a bowl is usually placed on the table as a symbol of fertility. The menu includes lettuce leaves dipped in honey, buttermilk, and pancakes spread with butter and honey. It continues with a "lucky dip," a bowl of flour in which golden objects are placed—in some places it contains five eggs and five beans and dates. On this night people eat no meat—only dairy foods and wafers made of fried dough resembling pancakes known as muflita.

On the day following the holiday, the actual day of Maimouna, modern Israelis of Moroccan heritage celebrate with picnics and a large gathering in Jerusalem.

Imberlach

2 pounds honey
1 cup plus 2 tablespoons wine
1 pound matza farfel

1 tablespoon ground ginger
1 cup broken walnuts
1/4 chopped hazelnuts

1. Bring honey and wine to a boil. Add farfel, ginger, and nuts and boil 5 minutes, stirring constantly.

2. Spread on wet board to 1/2-inch thickness and pat down with your hands, which have been moistened with wine. Refrigerate 1 hour, then cut into squares.

Makes about 2-1/2 pounds

◁ Eunice Zarett, Huntington Hadassah, New York

Nont

1 cup honey
1/2 cup sugar
2 pounds walnuts, coarsely
    chopped

Juice of 1 lemon
1 tablespoon matza meal

1. Combine honey with sugar in a large saucepan. Bring to a boil over medium heat; add nuts. Lower heat and cook, stirring, 5 minutes; add lemon juice. Stir almost constantly until mixture gets as brown as you like, then add matza meal and stir another five minutes.

2. Wet bread board. With rolling pin, roll hot mixture flat and thin. Smooth on a little cold water, let cool 15 to 20 minutes. Cut into diamond shapes or as desired.

Makes about 2-1/2 pounds

◁ Rose Silverman, Huntington Hadassah, New York

PURIM AND SHAVUOT

Introduction by Susan R. Friedland

When I was a girl, waybackwhen, my sister dressed me as a piece of hamantaschen for the annual Purim festival at our synagogue. While all the other girls went as Queen Esther and got to wear makeup and pretty dresses and carry wands, like Cinderella (who was everyone's model for Queen Esther), I was trapped in a tight cocoon, from head to toe, of brown wrapping paper. With a hole for my head, and a large piece of cardboard at my shoulders, my sister created an informal triangle held together with Scotch tape and straight pins and I was forced to take tiny little steps and walk like a parody of a Japanese woman. My sister thought mohn would be easier to re-create than prune and so she set to work making small black dots across my paper-wrapped shoulders. The getup was unique and I think I won a prize. And perhaps that's why I've always liked Purim and hamantaschen (though I am partial to prune).

Purim inaugurates a happy season in Jewish life. It is itself a giddy and joyous celebration of good over evil. Esther, the queen of Persia, and Mordechai, her uncle, pulled a fast one on Haman, the anti-Semitic prime minister to King Ahasureus, Esther's husband, and saved the Jews of Persia. Haman, in the name of the king, had proclaimed a civil decree to kill all the Jews. No one knew Esther was Jewish until she revealed the truth to Ahasureus in a plea to save her people from Haman's order of extinction.

Horrified about what had been going on behind his back, Ahasureus ordered that Haman and his 10 sons be hanged on the gallows that had been intended for Mordechai. Legend further has it that Mordechai wrote letters to all the Jews telling them to celebrate on the fourteenth day of Adar because they had been saved. He instructed them to send treats to each other and gifts to the poor. Purim means "lottery" and it is said to be celebrated on the fourteenth of Adar because Haman drew number 14 from the lottery—the day he planned to start the extermination of the Jews.

The story is told in the Megillah—the Scroll of Esther, where there is no mention of God, perhaps because the holiday is celebrated with so much silliness. Scholars are doubtful about the historical accuracy of the Purim legend and think it may have originated in an ancient pagan festival that was appropriated by the Jews. But the fourteenth of Adar, which falls

Susan R. Friedland is the author of Shabbat Shalom *and* The Passover Table. *She is the Director of Cookbook Publishing and Executive Editor at HarperCollins Publishers.*

FRUIT TABBOULEH, recipe page 192.

near the vernal equinox, is the Jewish Mardi Gras, an exuberant holiday, no matter what its origins.

Apart from listening to the Megillah and sounding the grogger every time Haman's name is mentioned, two inviolable Purim traditions are *mishloach manot* or *shalach manot* (sending portions)—the giving of food to friends—and *mattanot le-evyonim*—the mitzvah of giving to the poor, which goes beyond the general mitzvah of tzedakah.

The home ritual associated with Purim is the seudah, or feast. Generally a late and lavish lunch, it is an observation of the "feasting and gladness" instruction in the book of Esther (9:22). Though there is no kiddush, no challahs, the Purim seudah is second only to the Passover Seder in importance as a special meal and it is the only meal at which alcohol consumption is encouraged to increase the elation. In Sephardic communities, vegetarian meals are served to commemorate Queen Esther's diet when she lived in the palace and did not want to violate the laws of kashrut. In addition to a good meal, the seudah should include all kinds of merriment: A purimspeil is essential, the sillier the better.

Though there is no special food, the eating of hamantaschen, which was brought to this country by Jews from Germany and Eastern Europe, is an essential part of the celebration. Legend has it that Haman wore a tricornered hat, and that is how we get the traditional hamantaschen shape. It is hard to know why such a delicious pastry was named for a man so hated by the Jews. The pastries are stuffed with various fillings, including lekvar, or prune jam, and poppy seeds, or mohn. The poppy seeds are said to be a reminder that Queen Esther fasted for three days, eating only seeds when she broke her fast at night, praying to God to repeal the decree. Other Purim treats include Haman's Ears, a pastry dough deep fried in oil that is traditional in Sephardic communities. These confections, called Fazeulos, Figeolas, Mafis, or Orecchi di Ammon, depending on the community that makes them, are pinched in the middle to resemble a butterfly, which is meant to evoke the shape of Haman's ear.

Purim is also the signal to start thinking about Passover, whose central meaning is liberation. The most hopeful time of year, spring bursts forth as did the Jews out of Egypt. The food is a real challenge as so much is forbidden. But creative Jewish cooks have come up with a wonderful assortment of traditional and contemporary foods that keep us focused on the sacrifices of forty years of wandering, and still taste good!

Shavuot celebrates the receiving of the Torah. Fifty days after the Exodus from Egypt, the revelation at Sinai and the receiving of the Ten

Commandments occurred. According to traditional doctrine, all the Torah was revealed at Sinai, both the written and the oral. Scholars and theologians debate what happened at Sinai, but for observant Jews, Sinai is central to their beliefs. Before Sinai, the Bible describes Shavuot as an agricultural festival, a feast of the summer wheat harvest as well as a feast of the first fruits. It was the start of the agricultural cycle that ends with Sukkot, the final harvest of the year. Apart from decorating our homes with flowers, plants, and fruits, it is traditional to eat dairy food for Shavuot.

One explanation for this is that when the Israelites received the laws of kashrut at Sinai, they realized that their pots and dishes weren't kosher, so they discarded them and ate only uncooked dairy foods. Another explanation traces the custom to the verse in Song of Songs (4:11): "The knowledge of the Torah is like milk and honey under the tongue." Whatever the explanation, Shavuot is a feast of cheese blintzes, cheese kreplach, cheesecake, lokshen kugel with cheese, and borscht with sour cream.

RIGHT: Shavuot (Pentacost). *Moritz Daniel Oppenheim, 1880. Oil on canvas. The Jewish Museum, New York, New York. Gift of The Oscar and Regina Gruss Charitable and Educational Foundation.*

PURIM

TIP

Nahit is a traditional Purim salad or appetizer. Cooked hana dal may also be seasoned with spices of your choice—allspice, cumin, or garlic, onion powder, or spicy paprika—placed on a baking sheet and toasted in a 375 degree oven until crisp.

Hana Nahit

2 cups dried hana dal (chickpeas), soaked overnight and
  cooked, or 2 cans (15 ounces
  each) garbanzo beans
1/4 cup nonfat mayonnaise
1 clove garlic, minced
1 tablespoon finely chopped
  scallion
1 tablespoon finely chopped
  shallot
2 tablespoons finely chopped
  flat-leaf parsley
1 tablespoon capers, rinsed and
  drained
Freshly ground pepper to taste
Fresh lemon juice to taste

1. Place cooked chickpeas in colander to drain. Rinse and drain again. If using canned chickpeas, rinse well and drain. Combine remaining ingredients in a bowl. Taste and adjust seasonings.

2. Stir in drained chickpeas. Adjust seasonings, and refrigerate.

Makes about 4 cups

◄§ SHELANU HADASSAH, NEW YORK, NEW YORK

Falafel

1 pound dry nahit (chickpeas)
6 cloves garlic
3/4 cup dry bread crumbs
1 teaspoon ground cumin
1-1/2 teaspoons salt
1/8 teaspoon freshly ground
  black pepper

1. Soak nahit overnight in cold water to cover.

2. Drain thoroughly.

3. Place with garlic in bowl of food processor and process until finely ground. Add bread crumbs, cumin, salt, and pepper. Mix thoroughly and form into 1-inch balls.

4. Preheat 3-inches oil until hot. Fry falafel balls until golden.

Makes about 18

◄§ JUNE COHEN, ROCHESTER HADASSAH, NEW YORK

Tahini Salad Dressing

1/4 cup tahini (sesame seed paste)
1/4 cup fresh lemon juice

1 tablespoon chopped parsley
1 clove garlic, chopped fine
1 to 1-1/2 teaspoons salt

Beat tahini in medium bowl with lemon juice, parsley, garlic, and salt. Beat in 1/4 cup water. If too thick, adjust consistency by adding extra lemon juice and/or water.

Makes about 3/4 cup

↪ JUNE COHEN, ROCHESTER HADASSAH, NEW YORK

Honey Poppy Seed Dressing

1/3 cup honey
1/2 cup oil
1 teaspoon grated onion
3 tablespoons white wine vinegar
2 tablespoons fresh lemon juice

1/2 teaspoon dry mustard
1/2 teaspoon all-purpose seasoning
1 teaspoon poppy seeds

Microwave honey 3 seconds in 2-cup measuring cup. Transfer to blender or covered jar and add remaining ingredients except poppy seeds. Blend or shake well, then add poppy seeds. Enjoy over vegetable or chicken salad, or even a fruit salad.

Makes 1-1/2 cups

↪ MILWAUKEE HADASSAH, WISCONSIN

Hummus

2 tablespoons tahini (sesame seed paste)

2 cloves garlic, minced

1/2 teaspoon salt

1/4 teaspoon freshly ground pepper

1/2 cup vegetable oil, divided

19-ounce can chickpeas, drained and rinsed, liquid reserved

1/4 cup fresh lemon juice

2 tablespoons chopped parsley

In blender or food processor, purée tahini, garlic, salt, pepper, and 1/4 cup oil until smooth. Add chickpeas, lemon juice, and remaining oil. Process until smooth, adding a bit of reserved chickpea liquid if needed to thin. Stir in parsley.

Makes 2 cups

◆ MOLLY SCHNEIDER, NAOMI-HANNAH YASSKY HADASSAH, BROOKLYN, NEW YORK

Caraway Seed Bread

2 (1/4-ounce) packages active dry yeast

2-1/2 cups warm water

1/4 cup (4 tablespoons) shortening, softened

2 tablespoons sugar

4 teaspoons salt

6 cups all-purpose or bread flour, divided

1/4 cup caraway seeds

Melted unsalted margarine

Kosher salt

1. Sprinkle yeast into warm water in large mixing bowl and stir to dissolve. Add shortening, sugar, and salt. Stir in 3 cups flour and beat on high 2 minutes; add caraway seeds. Add 3 more cups flour; cover and let stand 30 minutes. Beat flour into batter.

2. Meanwhile, preheat oven to 375 degrees. Grease two 9 x 5 inch loaf pans or four 1-pound coffee cans.

3. Fill pans or cans with dough and punch down with floured hands. Cover and let stand 30 minutes.

4. Bake until golden, about 40 minutes to 1 hour. Remove from cans or pans immediately. Brush tops with margarine and sprinkle with kosher salt.

Makes 2 large or 4 small loaves

◆ BEK HURWICH, BIRMINGHAM HADASSAH, ALABAMA

FALAFEL, recipe page 186; PITA, recipe page 191; HUMMUS, recipe above right.

Pita
(Middle Eastern Flat Bread)

1 (1/4-ounce) package active
   dry yeast
1 teaspoon sugar

1-1/4 cups warm water
4 cups all-purpose flour
1/2 teaspoon salt

1. Dissolve yeast and sugar in water. Sift flour and salt and add yeast mixture.

2. Mix and knead dough lightly for about 1 minute. Divide into 20 equal pieces. Roll each piece into a ball, then roll out, one at a time, into a very thin circle. Set aside on trays. Cover lightly and allow to rise about 30 minutes.

3. Roll dough very thin once more and let rise 30 minutes. Meanwhile, heat oven to 500 degrees.

4. Bake 2 to 3 minutes, until puffed and golden.

Makes 20

◆§ Carol Goldberg, Rochester Hadassah, New York

Persian Soup

2 to 3 cups plain yogurt
1 cup cold water or milk
1/2 cup sour cream
1/2 cup raisins (or any other
   dried fruit)
1 egg, hard cooked and chopped
1 cucumber, peeled, seeded, and
   chopped, plus thin unpeeled
   slices for garnish

1 tablespoon fresh lemon juice
1 teaspoon salt
1 teaspoon freshly ground pepper
1 tablespoon finely chopped
   parsley
1 tablespoon finely chopped
   dill
4 ice cubes

1. Put ingredients in large bowl; mix well. Refrigerate, covered, 2 hours or overnight.

2. Spoon into individual serving bowls or cups and garnish with parsley and/or dill. Float an ice cube in each serving.

Serves 4

◆§ Aliza Shevrin, Ann Arbor Hadassah, Michigan

Persian Soup, recipe right.

Cheese and Onion Kreplach

TIP
These may be refrigerated uncooked in a single layer in a buttered baking pan until needed, then baked at 350 degrees until browned.

DOUGH	FILLING
3 eggs, lightly beaten	8-ounce package cream cheese, at room temperature
1/2 teaspoon salt	2 tablespoons chopped onion
2 to 2-1/4 cups all-purpose flour	2 tablespoons chopped parsley
	2 tablespoons bread crumbs
	Butter or unsalted margarine for frying (optional)

1. Make dough: Combine 2 beaten eggs with 1/2 cup water. Add salt and enough flour to form a soft ball. On lightly floured board knead dough until smooth and elastic. Cover and let stand 10 minutes.

2. Make filling: Combine cream cheese and remaining beaten egg until well blended. Add onion, parsley, and crumbs and mix well.

3. Divide dough in half. On floured board, roll each half 1/8-inch thick; cut into 3-inch squares. Spoon rounded teaspoon filling on each square. Lightly dampen edges, fold dough to form a triangle, and press edges to seal.

4. Bring large pot of salted water to a boil. Cook kreplach a few at a time 3 to 4 minutes, or until they float; drain. Fry in butter or margarine until lightly browned.

Makes about 2 dozen

◦ᔤ SARA GELFOND, WEST ORANGE HADASSAH, NEW JERSEY

Fruit Tabbouleh

TIP
Apply dressing sparingly; this recipe makes more than enough extra to lightly dress a fruit salad also.

	DRESSING
1 cup bulgur wheat	1/4 cup plain lowfat or nonfat yogurt
1/4 cup almonds, coarsely chopped	1/4 cup fresh lemon juice
1 cup seedless red grapes, cut into halves	2 tablespoons olive oil
1 cup blueberries	2 tablespoons mango or peach chutney
1 cup fresh pineapple chunks	2 teaspoons finely grated gingerroot
3 tablespoons finely chopped fresh mint, plus mint leaves for garnish	1 teaspoon honey Dijon mustard (optional)
	1/4 to 1/2 teaspoon salt

Bulgur is a quick-cooking form of whole wheat that has been cleaned, parboiled, dried, ground into particles, and sifted into different sizes. Biblical references indicate it was prepared by the ancient Hebrews some 4,000 years ago, and modern nutritionists discovered what the ancients only guessed at: It has a rich supply of B vitamins and Vitamin E and calcium, phosphorous, and iron. It has a tender, chewy texture, a pleasant nutty aroma and taste, excellent shelf life, and requires minimal cooking.

A delicious nutritious staple of Middle Eastern cooking, tabbouleh (also called burghul) is a dish of bulgur wheat usually mixed with chopped tomatoes, onions, mint, olive oil, lots of lemon juice, and parsley, parsley, parsley. This recipe takes it to another level in its use of fruit.

1. In medium saucepan, bring 1 cup water to a boil and stir in bulgur. Remove from heat; cover and let stand 30 minutes. Uncover and fluff with a fork. Transfer to a medium bowl.

2. Place almonds in small dry skillet and cook over medium heat, stirring, about 4 minutes, or until golden. Set aside.

3. In a small bowl, combine ingredients for dressing. Measure about 1/3 cup of dressing and stir into bulgur; add grapes, blueberries, pineapple, and chopped mint. Cover and refrigerate about 2 hours. Remove from refrigerator 30 minutes before serving. Stir in almonds and garnish with mint leaves.

Serves 6

➵ *Faye Fischman, Pittsburgh Hadassah, Pennsylvania*

Semak Mah Taheen
(Fish with Sesame)

3 to 4 pounds fish fillets	Dressing
2 tablespoons unsalted butter, melted	*3 tablespoons tahini (sesame seed paste)*
1 to 2 cloves garlic, crushed	*3 tablespoons fresh lemon juice*
Juice of 2 lemons	*1/2 teaspoon garlic salt*
Salt and freshly ground pepper to taste	*3 sprigs parsley, finely chopped*

1. Preheat oven to 400 degrees. Lightly butter 13 x 9 inch baking pan.

2. Brush fish with melted butter. Cut across skin and insert crushed garlic in cut areas. Pour juice from 2 lemons over fish, and season with salt and pepper.

3. Bake, skin side down, 50 minutes, until fish is easily pierced with a fork but is still moist.

4. Mix tahini with 3 tablespoons water until smooth. Add 3 tablespoons lemon juice and the garlic salt, and mix well. Pour over fish and garnish with parsley.

Serves 6

➵ *Rachel E. Fremaff, Fair Lawn Hadassah. New Jersey*

PISTACHIO CHICKEN WITH HONEY-MUSTARD
SAUCE, recipe above, right.

Pistachio Chicken with Honey-Mustard Sauce

1/3 cup all-purpose flour	1/4 cup unsalted margarine,
1 cup finely chopped salted	melted
pistachios	2 eggs, lightly beaten
4 boneless, skinless chicken breast	1/2 cup Dijon mustard
halves	3 tablespoons honey

1. Preheat oven to 350 degrees. Grease 13 x 9 inch baking dish. Place flour and pistachios in separate plastic bags.

2. Dip chicken breasts in melted margarine to coat; place 1 at a time in bag with flour, shaking to coat. Shake off excess flour. Dip each breast in egg and shake off excess egg. Dip in bag with chopped pistachios and shake to coat.

3. Place chicken breasts in prepared baking dish and bake about 30 minutes.

4. Mix honey and mustard and spoon some over each chicken breasts.

Serves 4

❧ FAIR LAWN HADASSAH, NEW JERSEY

Cashew Chicken

3 fryers, cut up	1/4 cup soy sauce
1 small onion, sliced	1 tablespoon wine vinegar
1 heaping tablespoon parve	1 large can (29 ounces) sliced
chicken-style bouillon powder	peaches, drained, liquid reserved
1/2 cup honey	12 ounces salted cashew nuts

1. Preheat oven to 350 degrees. Put chicken pieces, onion, bouillon powder, and 1/2 cup water in large broiler pan and bake 30 minutes.

2. Combine honey, soy sauce, wine vinegar, and peach juice and pour over chicken. Arrange peach slices over chicken and bake 30 minutes longer, basting from time to time. Sprinkle with cashews and bake 30 minutes more.

Serves 10 to 12

❧ SUNNY BRODSKY, SPRINGFIELD HADASSAH, MASSACHUSETTS

Poppy Seed Chiffon Cake

3/4 cup poppy seeds

6 eggs, separated, at room
   temperature

2 teaspoons vanilla extract

1/2 cup oil

1/2 teaspoon baking soda

2 cups all-purpose flour

1 teaspoon salt

2 teaspoons baking powder

1-1/2 cups sugar, divided

1/2 teaspoon cream of tartar

1. Soak poppy seeds in 1 cup warm water overnight; do not drain.

2. Preheat oven to 350 degrees. Have on hand an ungreased 10-inch tube pan. Beat egg yolks and vanilla extract, the oil, and baking soda until smooth and well blended.

3. In a separate bowl, sift flour with salt, baking powder, and 3/4 cup sugar; add to poppy seed mixture and beat 6 minutes. In another bowl with clean beaters, beat egg whites until stiff. Gradually add remaining 3/4 cup sugar and the cream of tarter. Fold batter thoroughly into beaten egg whites.

4. Pour into tube pan and bake 1 hour 15 minutes.

5. Invert pan until cake is cooled completely. Run a thin knife blade around rim to loosen cake, then remove from pan.

Serves about 12

◄§ BARBARA ANNANG (FROM BERNADINE GOLDMAN), LOS ALAMOS HADASSAH,
NEW MEXICO

BELOW: ESTHER SCROLL AND CASE. *Case: Maker, Baruch Dornheim. Germany, late 19th to early 20th century. Silver, repoussé, partly gilt; and ink and watercolor on parchment. HUC Skirball Cultural Center, Museum Collection.*

Purims Katan

~

According to the Book of Esther, Purim is the feast instituted by Mordechai to celebrate the deliverance of the Jews from Haman's plot to kill them. The Talmud instructs that one must recite a thanksgiving benediction on returning to the place where one was once miraculously saved.

In observance of this custom Jewish communities or families celebrate the anniversary of their escape from destruction by reciting special prayers and with a ritual similar to that of Purim. These special Purims are called Purim Katan (minor Purim) or Purim followed by the name of the community or special event. The traditions of enjoying a special meal and giving charity to the poor were also applied to these special Purims:

- Purim of Samuel Ha-Nagid, 1039 Spain. Saved from death plot of conspirators.

- Purim Mo'ed Katan, 1200 Italy. Jews permitted to practice Judaism after having been forced to convert to Islam.

- Purim Martinez, 1339 Castille. Escape from annihilation following accusations by Jew-baiter Gonazalez Martinez, the king's adviser.

- Purim Verona, 1607 Verona. Granted permission to lock ghetto gates from inside instead of outside.

- Purim Fettmilch, 1616 Frankfurt am Main. Expelled Jews readmitted to town and Jew-baiter Fettmilch executed.

- Vorhang Purim (Curtain Purim), 1622 Prague. Beadle of synagogue saved from hanging for keeping stolen curtains.

- Purim Medzibezh, 1648-49 Poland. Saved from annihilation by Chmielnicki's band.

- Purim Cavaillion, 1677 Provence. Saved from blood libel accusation.

- Plum Jam Purim, 1731 Jungbunzlau. David Brandeis and family saved from accusation of having killed gentiles by poisoning plum jam.

- Purim Baghdad, 1733 Baghdad. Relieved from Persian oppression.

- Purim Takka (Window Purim), 1741 Hebron. Saved from annihilation by miraculous find of ransom money on the windowsill of the synagogue.

- Purim Mstislavl, 1744 Russia. Saved from slaughter by Cossaks.

- Purim de los borrachones (Purim of the Drunken), 1806 Bulgaria. Saved from annihilation following accusation that the ruler had been poisoned by his Jewish physician.

- Purim Hitler, 1943 Casablanca. Escape from riot and Nazi occupation.

In the days of Jacob, almonds were reckoned among the best fruits of the land. The rod of Aaron was an almond twig, and the fruit of the almond was one of the subjects used to decorate the golden candlesticks in the Temple.

Almonds yield nearly half their weight in a bland oil, which is used for allaying heartburn, softening and relaxing solids, in bronchial diseases, and for tickling coughs. The Hebrew name for almonds, shakad, signifies "to watch for," fitting for a tree whose beautiful flowers, appearing in Eretz Yisrael in January, herald the wakening of creation.

Baklava

2 cups walnuts
1 cup almonds
3 slices toasted bread
1/3 cup sesame seeds
1/4 cup sugar
1 teaspoon ground cinnamon
One (16-ounce) package phyllo
  leaves
Oil or melted unsalted margarine
  as needed

SYRUP
3 cups sugar
1/2 cup honey
1/2 teaspoon fresh lemon juice

1. Preheat oven to 350 degrees. Brush 13 x 9 inch pan with oil.

2. Grind nuts in processor with toasted bread and sesame seeds; add sugar and cinnamon. Mix well.

3. Take phyllo leaves from package and lay out on table. Cover with damp towel so they will not dry out.

4. Layer 2 phyllo sheets in prepared pan and brush with oil. Layer on another 2 sheets; brush again with oil and sprinkle with some of the nut mixture. Continue layering in this manner until pan is filled to within 4 sheets of the top.

5. Take 2 of the last 4 sheets, lay them on top, and brush with oil. Then lay on the last 2 sheets and brush with oil. Trim any excess phyllo from sides. Without cutting all the way through, cut lengthwise into strips 1-1/2 inches wide, then diagonally to make diamond shapes.

6. Spray lightly with water before baking—it will keep the phyllo from curling. Bake 30 minutes, or until golden.

7. Make syrup: Combine sugar with 3 cups water. Bring to a boil and cook 15 minutes, until slightly thick, adding honey and lemon juice while still boiling. Remove from heat.

8. Remove baklava from oven and pour hot syrup evenly over. Let cool in pan on wire rack overnight, then cut through into diamonds.

Serves about 12

◄ CORA LEVY, ROCHESTER HADASSAH, NEW YORK

BAKLAVA, recipe above, right.

Classic Hamantaschen with Chocolate, Honey Hazelnut, or Prune Apricot Fillings

DOUGH

3 cups all-purpose flour

1 tablespoon baking powder

3/4 cup (1-1/2 sticks)
  lightly salted butter or
  margarine, softened

2/3 cup sugar

3 eggs, plus 1 egg beaten with
  1 tablespoon water

1 teaspoon vanilla extract

CHOCOLATE FILLING (recipe follows)

HONEY HAZELNUT FILLING
  (recipe follows)

PRUNE APRICOT FILLING (recipe follows)

1. Whisk to stir flour with baking powder. Cream butter or margarine with sugar. Beat flour mixture into this creamed mixture; beat in 3 eggs and the vanilla extract. Refrigerate, wrapped, at least 2 hours.

2. Preheat oven to 350 degrees. Grease cookie sheets or line with baking parchment.

3. Roll out pastry to 1/8-inch thickness; cut in 3-inch circles. Place 1 teaspoon filling in center of each circle. Lightly moisten edges and fold edges of dough up to center in triangle shape; pinch corners but do not close tops completely. Brush with egg-water mixture (you don't have to do this unless you want a nice shine) and place on prepared sheets.

4. Bake 20 minutes, until golden. Let cool 1 to 2 minutes on sheet, then remove to wire racks.

Makes about 4 dozen

Chocolate Filling

1/2 cup unsweetened cocoa
  powder

1/3 cup sugar

1/4 cup milk

1-1/2 teaspoons vanilla extract

1 cup chopped nuts

Mix together all ingredients.

Makes about 2 cups

Honey Hazelnut Filling

3/4 cup honey

1 cup chopped hazelnuts

1/3 cup breadcrumbs

1 teaspoon grated orange zest

Combine all ingredients and stir constantly over low heat until ingredients come together.

Makes about 2 cups

Prune Apricot Filling

1/2 pound pitted prunes, cut up

1/4 cup chopped nuts

1/4 cup raisins

1/4 cup sugar

2 tablespoons cut-up dried apricots

1 teaspoon ground cinnamon

1/2 teaspoon fresh lemon juice

Mix together all ingredients.

Makes about 2 cups

◦§ WENDY ELLIMAN, JERUSALEM, ISRAEL

Hamantaschen Cheese Dough

1 cup (2 sticks) unsalted butter, softened

8-ounce package cream cheese, softened

2 cups all-purpose flour

1/4 cup confectioners' sugar

1. Cream butter with cream cheese. Add flour and confectioners' sugar. Wrap and refrigerate 4 hours or overnight.

2. Preheat oven to 400 degrees. Grease cookie sheets.

3. Roll out dough 1/8-inch thick. Cut in 3-inch circles, and fill. Bring edges up to form triangle. Place on prepared sheets and bake 12 to 15 minutes.

Makes: about 3 dozen

◦§ NORTH BOUNDARY HADASSAH, CHICAGO, ILLINOIS

Hamantaschen

DOUGH

4 cups sifted all-purpose flour

1/2 cup sugar

2 teaspoons baking powder

1 teaspoon grated orange zest

1/2 teaspoon salt

4 eggs

1/2 cup oil

1/4 cup fresh orange juice

FILLING

1 pound prunes, finely chopped

1/2 cup crushed pineapple,
  thoroughly drained

2 tablespoons apricot jam

1/2 cup granulated sugar

1 teaspoon ground cinnamon

1 teaspoon grated orange zest

1/4 cup finely chopped nuts

1. Preheat oven to 350 degrees. Sift flour with sugar, baking powder, orange zest, and salt. Make well in center of dry ingredients and break eggs into the well.

2. Add oil and mix well. Add orange juice, stirring until all is absorbed. Knead until smooth and satiny.

3. Mix ingredients for filling.

4. Roll out dough on well-floured surface to 1/8-inch thickness. Cut into 2-1/2-inch rounds. Place small amount of filling on each round. Bring up edges of dough in triangular shape. Pinch together over filling, but do not close completely. Place on ungreased baking sheet and bake about 30 minutes, until nicely browned.

Makes about 5 or 6 dozen

◄§ BONNIE LIPTON, HADASSAH NATIONAL PRESIDENT

Left: HAMENTASCHEN, recipe above, right.

RIGHT: GROGGER. *Moshe Zabari. Jerusalem, 1996. Silver; carnelian beads; and lapis beads. HUC Skirball Cultural Center, Museum Collection. Museum Purchase with funds provided by Susanne and Paul Kester.*

Taraleekos
(Sephardic Sesame Cookies)

3 eggs

1 cup sugar

1/2 cup oil

1 teaspoon vanilla extract

3 cups all-purpose flour

1 teaspoon baking powder

1/2 teaspoon salt

2 egg whites, lightly beaten

1/2 cup sesame seeds

1. Preheat oven to 350 degrees. Grease cookie sheet.

2. Beat eggs, sugar, oil, and vanilla extract until smooth. Combine flour, baking powder, and salt. Add to egg mixture; mixing first with large spoon, then with hands until workable. Refrigerate 4 hours or overnight.

3. Roll out an eighth of dough to thickness of little finger. Cut into 5-inch-long pieces. Shape like donut, pinching ends together. Brush tops with egg white, and sprinkle with sesame seeds. Repeat with remaining dough. Put on prepared cookie sheet and bake 15 to 20 minutes.

Makes 5 dozen

◄§ SARAH CASSORLA, ROCHESTER HADASSAH, NEW YORK

Mohn Kichels

1/4 pound (1 stick) unsalted
    margarine, melted

1/2 cup sugar

1 egg, lightly beaten

1/4 cup poppy seeds, a bit less

1-1/2 cups all-purpose flour

1 teaspoon baking powder

Pinch of salt

1. Preheat oven to 350 degrees. Grease baking sheet.

2. Combine margarine with sugar; add egg. Fold in poppy seeds. Combine flour with baking powder and salt and work into margarine mixture.

3. Make walnut size balls and flatten with bottom of small glass dipped in flour.

4. Bake 12 to 15 minutes.

Makes about 1-1/2 dozen

◄§ ESTHER GOLDMAN, FRAMINGHAM HADASSAH, MASSACHUSETTS

Pepper is the berry of a tropical climbing vine. If the berries are picked before they are mature and placed to dry in the sun, they wrinkle and turn very dark; this is black pepper. But if they are left to finish ripening, they are soaked and the outer skins rubbed off, leaving only the pale seed; this is dried to give white pepper. Once ground, pepper goes stale very quickly, so it is best to buy peppercorns and grind them as needed. It is also best to add pepper at the end of cooking or it will lose its kick.

Peppered Onion Kichlach

2-1/2 cups all-purpose flour
1 teaspoon baking powder
3/4 teaspoon salt
1/4 teaspoon freshly ground black pepper, plus additional for sprinkling

2 eggs, lightly beaten
1/4 cup oil
1 large onion, grated
2 tablespoons poppy seeds

1. Preheat oven to 375 degrees. Grease cookie sheet.

2. Combine flour, baking powder, salt, and 1/4 teaspoon pepper in large mixing bowl. Stir in beaten eggs, the oil, 1/4 cup water, and the grated onion until a soft dough forms.

3. Turn dough out onto lightly floured surface. With 2-1/2 -inch cookie cutter, cut into circles. Place on prepared sheet. Sprinkle with poppy seeds or pepper.

4. Bake 15 minutes, or until golden. Remove to wire rack; let cool.

Makes 1-1/2 to 2 dozen

Ethel Rowland, Roslyn Heights Hadassah, New York

Poppy Seed Onion Cookies

3 cups all-purpose flour
2 teaspoons baking powder
1 teaspoon salt
2 eggs, lightly beaten

1/2 cup oil
2 medium onions, grated
1/3 cup poppy seeds

1. Preheat oven to 350 degrees. Grease cookie sheet.

2. Sift flour with baking powder and salt. Beat in eggs and oil, grated onions, and poppy seeds. Mix until a soft dough forms.

3. Turn out onto lightly floured board and knead gently. Roll out to 1/4-inch thickness. Prick with fork. Cut into 3-inch squares and place on prepared cookie sheet.

4. Bake about 15 minutes, until golden.

Makes 1-1/2 to 2 dozen

Marion Pakula, Huntington Hadassah, New York

Almond Lace Wafers

3/4 cup unblanched almonds
1/2 cup (1 stick) unsalted butter,
   softened
1/2 cup sugar

1 tablespoon all-purpose flour
1 tablespoon heavy cream
1 tablespoon milk
Pinch of salt

1. Preheat oven to 350 degrees. Grease 2 cookie sheets generously and coat with flour.

2. Work almonds through nut grater, or process in food processor, and measure 3/4 cup. Combine almonds in saucepan with butter, sugar, flour, cream, milk, and salt, and cook over low heat, stirring constantly, until butter melts. Drop mixture by teaspoonfuls 5 or 6 at a time on prepared cookie sheets.

3. Bake 8 or 9 minutes, or until cookies turn a light caramel color with centers still bubbling. Let cool 1 minute, then transfer top-side down to paper towels. Roll immediately over handle of wooden spoon and place on wire racks to cool. Regrease and flour cookie sheets before each batch.

Makes 2 dozen

ৰু PORTLAND HADASSAH, OREGON

Peanut Butter Cookies

1/2 cup (1 stick) unsalted butter,
   softened
1/2 cup peanut butter
1/2 cup granulated sugar
1/2 cup packed brown sugar

1 egg
1-1/4 cups all-purpose flour
1/2 teaspoon baking powder
3/4 teaspoon baking soda
1/4 teaspoon salt

1. Preheat oven to 375 degrees. Grease cookie sheet.

2. Mix thoroughly butter, peanut butter, granulated sugar, brown sugar, and egg. In separate bowl stir together flour, baking powder, baking soda, and salt and blend into sugar mixture. Chill about 30 minutes.

3. Roll dough into balls the size of walnuts. Place 3 inches apart on prepared cookie sheet. With floured fork, press balls down in a criss-cross pattern. Bake 10 to 12 minutes, until set but not hard.

Makes about 3 dozen

ৰু NAOMI STRACHMAN, SHATIL HADASSAH, NEW YORK, NEW YORK

Sugar-Free Chocolate Nut Noodles

Two 3-ounce sugar-free chocolate
bars, broken in pieces

3/4 cup chow mein noodles
1/2 cup unsalted peanuts

1. Place sheet of wax paper on cookie sheet or use small paper candy cups.

2. Place broken candy bars in saucepan over low heat, and stir with wooden spoon until chocolate is melted. Stir in noodles and peanuts until thoroughly combined.

3. Spoon by teaspoons onto wax paper or into paper candy cups. Refrigerate at least 2 hours.

Makes 24 pieces

◆§ SYBIL KAPLAN, OVERLAND PARK HADASSAH, KANSAS

Maple Nut Balls

1/2 pound (2 sticks) unsalted
butter or margarine, softened
1/4 cup granulated sugar
4 teaspoons maple extract

2 cups ground nuts
2 cups all-purpose flour
Confectioners' sugar

1. Preheat oven to 300 degrees. Grease baking sheet.

2. Beat butter or margarine with granulated sugar and maple extract. Stir in nuts and flour. Roll into small balls. Put on prepared baking sheet and bake 45 minutes (do not let cookies brown). Roll in confectioners' sugar. Freezes well.

Makes about 6 dozen

◆§ DIANE SILVERMAN, CLIFTON PARK HADASSAH, NEW YORK

Spiced Nuts

1 egg white

1 teaspoon cold water

1 pound shelled walnuts or pecans

1/2 cup sugar

1/2 teaspoon cinnamon, or
more to taste

1/4 teaspoon salt

1. Preheat oven to 225 degrees. Have at hand an ungreased cookie sheet.

2. Beat egg white with water until frothy. Add nuts and stir to coat with egg white. In a separate bowl mix sugar, cinnamon, and salt. Pour over nuts and mix well.

3. Spread nuts in a single layer on cookie sheet. Bake 1 hour, stirring occasionally.

Makes 1 pound

➤ Faye Kidder, Rebecca Stein, Clifton Park Hadassah, New York

Rum Balls

1 cup firmly packed brown sugar

1/2 cup (1 stick) unsalted
butter or margarine

1 egg, lightly beaten

1 cup chopped pitted dates

1 teaspoon vanilla extract

1 tablespoon rum or brandy

2 cups toasted rice cereal

1/2 cup chopped nuts

Shredded coconut or additional
chopped nuts

1. Set aside wax paper lined cookie sheet.

2. Combine brown sugar, butter or margarine, the egg, and dates in saucepan, and cook over low heat until thick. Remove from heat. Add vanilla extract, rum or brandy, the rice cereal, and nuts. Mix together, then let cool slightly.

3. Oil hands lightly and shape mixture into 1-inch balls. Roll in shredded coconut or additional chopped nuts. Place on cookie sheet and refrigerate 2 hours. Store in cookie tin. Freezes well.

Makes 3 to 4 dozen

➤ Hadassah Israel

POPPY SEEDS

The tiny dried seeds of the opium poppy, native to the ancient Middle East, are sweet and mild, with a nutlike flavor and a faint nutty aroma. Popular in breads, cakes, and hamantaschen, they contain 44 to 50 percent fixed oil, the principal components of which are linoleic and oleic acids. No, they are not narcotic; the fluid that becomes opium is present in the bud only before the seeds are fully formed.

Poppy Seed Candy

1 pound poppy seeds	2 cups chopped nuts
2 cups honey	1/2 teaspoon powdered ginger
1/2 cup sugar	

1. Have the poppy seeds ground for you when you buy them. If this is not possible, grind them in a food chopper or pound with mortar and pestle.

2. Cook honey and sugar until syrupy. Toss in poppy seeds and cook until mixture is thick, about 20 minutes, stirring frequently.

3. Drop a little mixture on wet surface; if it doesn't run it is thick enough. Stir in nuts and ginger. Moisten hands. Pat out mixture onto wet board to thickness of about 1/2 inch. Let cool 5 minutes, then cut into diamonds or squares with a sharp knife. If knife sticks, dip into hot water. Cool completely and lift from board with spatula.

Makes about 4 dozen

◄§ PORTLAND HADASSAH, OREGON

Susam
(Sephardic Sesame Seed Candy)

1 pound sesame seeds	1 cup honey
1/2 cup all-purpose flour	1/4 cup fresh lemon juice
3/4 cup sugar	2 cups sliced almonds, toasted

1. Combine sesame seeds and flour in large skillet and toast until golden brown. Boil sugar, honey, 3/4 cup water, and lemon juice in large saucepan 20 to 30 minutes, until thick. Add sesame seeds and almonds to syrup. Simmer about 10 minutes, stirring with wooden spoon. Let cool.

2. Spread sesame mixture to about 1/2-inch thickness on wet wooden board. Allow to cool until firm enough to cut into diamond shaped pieces.

Makes 50 pieces

◄§ SARAH CASSORLA, ROCHESTER HADASSAH, NEW YORK

SHAVUOT

TIP
The white and brown sugars can be adjusted down.

Mom's Kugel

1 pound medium egg noodles, cooked **al dente**

7 eggs, lightly beaten

1/2 pound (2 sticks) unsalted butter, melted

1-1/2 cups granulated sugar

1 teaspoon vanilla extract

8-ounce can crushed pineapple, drained

1 cup raisins

1/2 cup packed brown sugar

1 teaspoon ground cinnamon

1. Preheat oven to 350 degrees. Grease 13 x 9 inch pan.

2. Combine noodles with eggs, melted butter, granulated sugar, vanilla extract, crushed pineapple, and raisins. Place in prepared pan. Combine brown sugar with cinnamon and sprinkle over top.

3. Bake about 45 minutes, until kugel is golden and bubbly.

Serves 12

➤ RHODA YASSKY, FAIR LAWN HADASSAH, NEW JERSEY

Cherry Noodle Kugel

8-ounce package broad egg noodles

8-ounce package cream cheese, at room temperature

1 cup sour cream

1/4 cup sugar plus 2 tablespoons

16-ounce can cherry pie filling

3/4 teaspoon ground cinnamon, divided

1/2 cup chopped walnuts

1. Preheat oven to 350 degrees. Grease 8 x 8 inch baking pan. Cook noodles according to package directions; drain well.

2. Beat cream cheese with sour cream and 1/4 cup sugar until smooth and well blended. Toss with noodles. Mix cherry pie filling with 1/2 teaspoon cinnamon.

3. Place half the noodle mixture in prepared baking dish. Spread with cherry mixture. Top with remaining noodles.

4. Sprinkle with walnuts and remaining 2 tablespoons sugar mixed with remaining 1/4 teaspoon cinnamon. Bake 30 minutes, until golden and bubbly.

Serves 6 to 8

⊸ DOROTHY WERTHEIMER, WEST ORANGE HADASSAH, NEW JERSEY

Wine Noodle Kugel

2 cups uncooked fine noodles	3 tablespoons melted unsalted
3 eggs, separated, at room	butter or margarine
temperature	Zest and juice of 1 lemon
1/4 cup packed brown sugar	1/2 cup chopped nuts or raisins
1 cup dry white wine	(optional)

1. Preheat oven to 350 degrees. Grease 2-quart heat-resistant glass baking pan.

2. Cook noodles according to package directions and drain.

3. Beat egg whites until stiff but not dry; set aside. Beat egg yolks with brown sugar until thick and creamy. Add wine, melted butter, lemon zest, and juice, and chopped nuts or raisins if desired.

4. Fold in beaten egg whites and stir mixture into cooked noodles.

5. Spoon into prepared pan. Bake 30 to 40 minutes, or until set and golden.

Serves 8 to 10

⊸ ZELDA LEVINSON, SYRACUSE HADASSAH, NEW YORK

Pineapple–Ricotta Kugel

12 ounces medium noodles

8 ounces ricotta cheese

8-ounce package cream cheese

4 tablespoons (1/2 stick) unsalted
butter, melted

1/4 cup sour cream

1/2 cup sugar

5 eggs, lightly beaten

3/4 cup drained crushed pineapple

1/2 cup golden raisins, plumped in
hot water and drained

2 teaspoons vanilla extract

1 teaspoon ground cinnamon

1-1/2 cups milk, scalded

TOPPING

1/2 cup corn-flake crumbs,
coarsely crushed

1/4 cup sugar

1 teaspoon ground cinnamon

1. Preheat oven to 350 degrees. Butter 13 x 9 inch heat-resistant glass baking pan.

2. Cook noodles according to package directions. Drain.

3. Beat ricotta cheese with cream cheese, melted butter, and sour cream; stir in sugar, eggs, pineapple, raisins, vanilla extract, and cinnamon. Combine with noodles and pour into prepared pan. Pour scalded milk over mixture.

4. Mix topping ingredients and sprinkle over noodles. Bake about 1 hour, or until cooked through and golden.

Serves 8

◄ JUNE ZFANEY, NORTH BOUNDARY HADASSAH, CHICAGO, ILLINOIS

PINEAPPLE-RICOTTA KUGEL, recipe above, right.

Blintzes

3 cups all-purpose flour

6 tablespoons sugar

1 teaspoon salt

4 eggs

4 tablespoons unsalted butter,
   melted

3 cups milk

FILLING

1-1/2 pounds cottage cheese

15-ounce container ricotta cheese

2 eggs

4 tablespoons sugar

1 teaspoon vanilla extract

1 teaspoon lemon extract

1 teaspoon salt

Additional unsalted butter
   for frying

Sour cream for serving

1. Make batter: Mix flour, sugar, and salt and set aside. Beat eggs until frothy; beat in melted butter and milk. Combine egg mixture with dry ingredients and beat till smooth.

2. Heat 6- or 7-inch skillet. Grease lightly with butter. Skillet is hot enough when drops of water sprinkled on surface dance in small beads.

3. Pour batter into pan and swirl pan to completely cover bottom; immediately pour excess back into bowl. Cook over medium heat about 1 minute, until lightly browned. Turn out onto towel browned side up. Repeat with remaining batter.

4. Make filling: Combine ingredients; mix well. Spoon 1-1/2 tablespoons filling onto center of each crêpe. Fold in 1 inch of opposite sides and roll up from unfolded sides.

5. Heat skillet; melt butter. Fry blintzes a few at a time, about 4 to 5 minutes, turning to brown second side. Serve with sour cream. Can be frozen before browning.

Makes about 3 dozen

WENDY HONIGMAN, JACKSONVILLE HADASSAH, FLORIDA

Sour Cream Batter for Blintzes

1 egg

1/4 cup milk

3/4 cup sour cream

1/8 teaspoon salt

1 cup sifted all-purpose flour

Unsalted butter for frying

1. Preheat oven to 450 degrees. Butter 13 x 9 inch baking dish.

TIP

This batter makes a rich pancake that is more suitable for sweet fillings.

2. Beat egg with milk, sour cream, and salt. Stir in the flour, mixing until smooth.

3. Heat some butter in 7-inch skillet. Pour in about 2 tablespoons batter, tilting pan to spread evenly. Fry until browned and turn to brown other side. Invert pan to remove crèpe. Continue with remaining batter.

4. Place heaping tablespoon of your choice of filling on each crèpe. Tuck in opposite sides and roll up. Arrange in a prepared baking dish and bake 10 minutes.

Serves about 16

◄§ PORTLAND HADASSAH, OREGON

Blueberry or Other Berry Fillings for Blintzes

1-1/2 cups blueberries or other berries	1 teaspoon cornstarch
3 tablespoons sugar	1/8 teaspoon freshly ground nutmeg

Toss all ingredients together carefully, so as to crush as few berries as possible.

Makes enough for about 16 blintzes

◄§ PORTLAND HADASSAH, OREGON

Apple Filling for Blintzes

1 egg white	1/2 teaspoon ground cinnamon
1-1/2 cups finely chopped apples	3 tablespoons brown sugar
1/4 cup sugar	3 tablespoons unsalted butter

1. Preheat oven to 400 degrees. Butter 13 x 9 inch baking pan.

2. Beat egg white until it begins to stiffen. Folk in apples, sugar, and cinnamon. Fill pancakes and arrange in prepared pan. Sprinkle with brown sugar and dot with butter. Bake 20 minutes.

Makes enough for about 18 blintzes

◄§ PORTLAND HADASSAH, OREGON

Egg and Onion Filling for Blintzes

1/2 cup (1 stick) unsalted butter, softened, divided

4 medium onions, coarsely chopped

5 hard cooked eggs, chopped

1/4 teaspoon salt

1/4 teaspoon freshly ground pepper (optional)

1/8 teaspoon sugar

1. In large skillet, heat 1/4 cup butter over medium heat; add onions and sauté until golden, about 10 minutes. Remove from heat.

2. Stir in chopped cooked eggs, remaining 1/4 cup butter, the salt, pepper, and sugar. Let cool and use as a blintz filling.

Makes about 2 cups

❧ WILLIAMSPORT HADASSAH, PENNSYLVANIA

Cheese Blintz Loaf

FILLING

Two (8-ounce) packages cream cheese, softened

1 pound farmer cheese

2 eggs, lightly beaten

Pinch of salt

4 tablespoons sugar

1 tablespoon fresh lemon juice

BATTER

1/2 cup (1 stick) unsalted butter, softened

1/4 cup sugar

2 eggs, lightly beaten

3/4 cup milk

1-1/4 cups all-purpose flour

1 teaspoon baking powder

Pinch of salt

1. Preheat oven to 350 degrees. Grease 9 x 5 inch loaf pan. Mix all filling ingredients and set aside.

2. Make batter: Cream butter with sugar, then add eggs, milk, flour, baking powder, and salt. Pour half of batter into prepared pan. Spread filling over batter and cover with remaining batter. Bake 45 minutes.

Serves 6

❧ ROS BLOOMSTON, BIRMINGHAM HADASSAH, ALABAMA

BLINTZES, recipe page 214; BLUEBERRY OR OTHER BERRY FILLINGS FOR BLINTZES, recipe page 215.

Banana Blintz Loaf

1/4 cup (1/2 stick) unsalted margarine, melted

3-ounce package cream cheese

1 pound cottage cheese

3 eggs, lightly beaten

1/2 teaspoon fresh lemon juice

1/2 teaspoon vanilla extract

1/2 cup whole-wheat pastry flour

1/2 teaspoon baking powder

1 teaspoon ground cinnamon

4 very ripe bananas, mashed

1/4 cup honey (optional)

1. Preheat oven to 325 degrees. Grease 8 x 8 inch baking pan.

2. Combine margarine, cream cheese, cottage cheese, and eggs in blender or food processor. Blend until smooth. Add lemon juice, vanilla extract, whole-wheat flour, baking powder, and cinnamon; blend.

3. Add bananas and, if desired, honey. Blend until thoroughly mixed. Pour into prepared baking pan and bake 40 or 50 minutes, until nicely browned and set.

Serves 6 to 8

➺ MARCY BECKER, TAMAR HADASSAH, WILMETTE, ILLINOIS

Blintze Soufflé

1-1/2 cups sour cream

1/2 cup fresh orange juice

4 eggs

1/4 cup (1/2 stick) unsalted butter, melted

2 tablespoons sugar

1 teaspoon vanilla extract

12 frozen blintzes

1/2 teaspoon ground cinnamon (optional)

1. Preheat oven to 350 degrees. Grease shallow casserole.

2. Place sour cream, orange juice, eggs, melted butter, sugar, and vanilla extract into blender. Blend until smooth and thoroughly mixed.

3. Place blintzes in bottom of prepared casserole. Pour sour cream mixture over the top. Sprinkle with cinnamon, if desired. Bake about 45 minutes, or until set and golden.

Serves 6

➺ CHARLES YASSKY, CHAVEROT HADASSAH, ROCKLAND COUNTY, NEW YORK

Palacsinta
(Hungarian Crèpes)

CRÈPES	FILLING
4 eggs	1 pound farmer cheese
1/2 cup milk, divided	2 heaping tablespoons sour cream
2 tablespoons sugar	2 tablespoons sugar
1/2 teaspoon grated lemon zest	1 tablespoon unsalted butter or
Dash of salt	margarine, melted
1 cup plus 2 tablespoons	Vanilla extract
all-purpose flour	Grated lemon zest
Unsalted butter for frying	Confectioners' sugar

1. Make crèpes: Beat eggs, 1/4 cup milk, the sugar, lemon zest, and salt in medium bowl. Beat in flour until smooth. Stir in remaining 1/4 cup milk. (If batter is too thick, add more milk.)

2. With buttered paper towel, wipe a little butter around an 8- or 10-inch nonstick skillet. Heat pan; when pan is heated pour in some batter. Swirl to completely cover bottom and immediately pour excess back into bowl.

3. Cook over medium heat until crèpe is cooked through and sides are lightly browned. Invert pan over a towel or plate to remove crèpe. Repeat with remaining batter.

4. Make filling: In large bowl combine farmer cheese, sour cream, sugar, melted butter, vanilla extract, and lemon zest to taste.

5. Preheat oven to 350 degrees. Butter 13 x 9 inch heat-resistant glass baking pan. Spoon about 2 tablespoons filling in center of each crèpe; fold in edges to form a square. Place in prepared baking pan; bake, covered, about 20 minutes, or until heated through. Sift confectioners' sugar over the palacsinta.

Serves 6

◄§ ELIZABETH PALAGE, ROCHESTER HADASSAH, NEW YORK

TIP

These thin pancakes or crèpes are usually stacked 6 or 7 high, and layered with a filling. The stack is traditionally cut in wedges before serving.

Strawberry Pancake

2 tablespoons unsalted butter or
margarine

4 eggs, separated

1 cup milk

1 cup all-purpose flour

2 tablespoons sugar

1/2 teaspoon vanilla extract

1 pint fresh strawberries, hulled
and halved or quartered

1 tablespoon confectioners' sugar

1. Heat oven to 425 degrees. Place 1 tablespoon butter in each of 2 deep 9-inch pie plates. Put in oven. Beat egg whites until stiff. Beat eggs yolks with milk, flour, sugar and vanilla extract.

2. Fold egg whites into yolk mixture. Remove pie plates from oven and pour half of batter into each; arrange berries decoratively on top. Bake 20 minutes, or until golden. Sprinkle with confectioners' sugar.

Serves 4

◄§ CHAVEROT HADASSAH, SUFFERN, NEW YORK

Lemon Pancake

1/2 cup all-purpose flour

1/2 cup milk

2 eggs, lightly beaten

1/8 teaspoon freshly grated
nutmeg

2 tablespoons unsalted butter

1 tablespoon confectioners' sugar

Juice of half a small lemon

Maple syrup, honey, or jam

1. Preheat oven to 425 degrees. In mixing bowl, combine flour, milk, eggs, and nutmeg. Beat lightly, leaving batter a little lumpy.

2. Melt butter in 10-inch ovenproof skillet over medium-high heat. When very hot, pour in batter.

3. Bake 15 to 20 minutes, or until puffed and golden. Sprinkle with confectioners' sugar and lemon juice. Serve with maple syrup, honey, or jam.

Serves 2

◄§ RENEE FORREST, DELRAY BEACH HADASSAH, FLORIDA

TIP
Serve this with fresh blueberries or sweet, juicy figs when in season.

STRAWBERRY PANCAKE, recipe above, right.

Potato Cakes Cordon Bleu

3 small potatoes (3/4 pound)
1 egg
1/4 cup shredded Swiss cheese
1 small onion, grated

1 tablespoon all-purpose flour
1/4 teaspoon salt
1/8 teaspoon freshly ground pepper
2 tablespoons unsalted butter

1. Peel potatoes and grate into large bowl of cold water. Drain; rinse in cold water. Squeeze well.

2. Beat egg until frothy. Add potatoes, cheese, onion, flour, salt, and pepper; stir to blend.

3. Heat butter in large nonstick skillet over medium-high heat and drop potato mixture by tablespoons into hot butter. Cook on each side about 5 or 6 minutes, until well browned.

Serves 4

◆§ JAN ALLEN, BIRMINGHAM HADASSAH, ALABAMA

Hot Mushroom Turnovers

8-ounce package cream cheese, softened
1/2 cup (1 stick) unsalted butter, softened, plus 3 tablespoons
1-1/2 cups all-purpose flour, plus 2 tablespoons

1/2 pound mushrooms, minced
1 large onion, minced
1 teaspoon salt
1/4 teaspoon dried thyme
1/4 cup sour cream
1 egg, lightly beaten

1. Combine cream cheese, 1/2 cup butter, and 1-1/2 cups flour in small bowl and mix well to form a ball. Wrap in wax paper and refrigerate 1 hour.

2. Meanwhile, sauté mushrooms and onions in 3 tablespoons butter. Add salt, thyme, and 2 tablespoons flour and mix well. Add sour cream and stir.

3. Meanwhile, preheat oven to 450 degrees. Grease cookie sheets.

4. Remove half the dough from refrigerator and roll out on floured board 1/8-inch thick. Cut in circles with floured 3-inch cookie cutter. Place

1/2 teaspoon mushroom mixture on each circle. Brush edge of circle lightly with beaten egg, fold closed, and crimp edges with fork to seal. Repeat with remaining dough and filling and brush each top with beaten egg,

5. Place on prepared cookie sheets and bake 15 minutes, or until golden. Serve piping hot.

Makes about 60

•⤳ ST. PAUL HADASSAH, MINNESOTA

Cabbage Strudel

2-pound head cabbage	1 teaspoon ground cinnamon
2 teaspoons salt	1 teaspoon caraway seeds
4 tablespoons vegetable oil	8 phyllo leaves
1 medium onion, coarsely	6 tablespoons (3/4 stick) unsalted
chopped	butter, melted
Freshly ground pepper	1/2 cup fine breadcrumbs
1 tablespoon sugar	1 egg white, lightly beaten

1. Core cabbage and shred in food processor. Toss with salt and let stand 15 minutes.

2. Meanwhile, put 1 tablespoon oil in small heavy skillet and brown onion until golden.

3. Squeeze extra water out of cabbage. Add remaining 3 tablespoons oil to a large heavy skillet and brown cabbage slowly and carefully. Combine onion and cabbage; and sprinkle with pepper, sugar, cinnamon, and caraway seeds.

4. Preheat oven to 350 degrees. Grease 12 x 7 inch jelly-roll pan. Cover pastry board with a cloth. Lay 1 phyllo leaf at a time on the board and brush with melted butter. Sprinkle with 1 tablespoon bread crumbs and some pepper. Repeat until you have layered 4 leaves and topping.

5. Spoon out half the cabbage mixture 4 inches in from the edge along the longer side of the phyllo. Fold edge over filling and roll up jelly-roll fashion. Place seam side down on prepared pan. Repeat with remaining phyllo leaves and cabbage filling. Brush both rolls with melted butter, and brush with egg white. Bake 45 minutes, until golden.

Serves 8 to 12

•⤳ LEILA HIRSCH, DIX HILLS HADASSAH, NEW YORK

Arabian Squash Cheese Casserole

2 medium butternut squash

3 tablespoons unsalted butter, or oil

1 cup chopped onion

2 cloves garlic, minced

1 cup chopped green and red bell pepper

2 eggs, lightly beaten

1 cup buttermilk

1 cup feta cheese, crumbled

1 teaspoon salt

1. Preheat oven to 375 degrees. Grease 11 x 7 inch baking pan or casserole.

2. Cut squash in half lengthwise and scoop out seeds. Place face down on a cookie sheet and bake 30 minutes, or until soft. Scoop out cooked flesh and mash.

3. Melt butter in a large skillet over medium heat. Add onion and garlic and sauté about 5 minutes. Add bell pepper and cook 5 minutes more, until peppers are barely tender.

4. Beat eggs and buttermilk in large bowl. Stir in cooked squash, the bell pepper mixture, feta cheese, and salt. Spread mixture into prepared casserole. Bake, covered, about 25 minutes; remove cover and cook 10 minutes more, or until lightly browned on top.

Serves 6

ở *Hadassah Israel*

Carrot Burgers

2 large carrots, cut in chunks

1/2 cup walnuts

Half a small onion, cut in chunks

1 cup fresh bread crumbs

1 tablespoon chopped parsley

1 cup cottage cheese

1 egg, lightly beaten

1 tablespoon Worcestershire sauce

1 teaspoon salt

1 cup fine dry bread crumbs

Oil for frying

Hamburger buns and fixings

1. In food processor finely chop carrots, walnuts, onion, fresh bread crumbs, and parsley. In large bowl mix cottage cheese with beaten egg, Worcestershire sauce, and salt. Stir in carrot mixture thoroughly. Form into 6 burgers and roll in dry breadcrumbs.

2. Heat oil in large skillet over medium-high heat. Cook burgers until golden on both sides. Serve hot on hamburger buns with favorite fixings.

Serves 6

ở *East Windsor Hadassah, Cranbury, New Jersey*

TIP

Worcestershire sauce takes its name from the English town where is was first bottled. It usually contains garlic, soy sauce, tamarind, onions, molasses, lime, anchovies, vinegar, and various seasonings.

Verenickes with Cream Cheese

2 cups all-purpose flour
2 whole eggs
2 eggs, separated
3/4 teaspoon salt, divided

Two (8-ounce) packages
cream cheese, softened
2 tablespoons sour cream
Sour cream for serving

TIP
Let filled verenickes rest on a floured baking sheet while making others. The dough is soft and flour helps prevent it from sticking.

1. Make dough: Combine flour, whole eggs, egg yolks, 2 to 3 table-spoons water, and 1/2 teaspoon salt until dough forms. Divide in half.

2. Make filling: Beat cream cheese until smooth. Beat in 2 tablespoons sour cream, the egg whites, and remaining 1/4 teaspoon salt to combine.

3. Roll out dough 1/8-inch thick and cut into 3 inch rounds. Place 1 teaspoon cream cheese filling in center of each round. Moisten edges lightly with water, fold over edges, and seal. Repeat with remaining dough and filling.

4. Bring a large pot of salted water to a boil. Poach verenickes 15 minutes. Remove with slotted spoon. Serve with sour cream.

Makes 24

⋅❧ PORTLAND HADASSAH, OREGON

Shlishkal
(Potato Dumplings)

4 to 5 medium potatoes
1 egg, lightly beaten
1 teaspoon salt
1 to 1-1/2 cups all purpose flour

3 tablespoons unsalted butter,
melted
1/2 cup fine bread crumbs

1. Boil potatoes until just tender. Peel and let dry a few hours or overnight.

2. Grate potatoes. Add egg and salt and mix in 1 cup flour until dough is formed that can be rolled out. Add remaining 1/2 cup flour if necessary.

3. On floured board, roll out small piece of dough with your hands to form a long pencil. Cut off 1-inch pieces and set aside. Repeat with remaining dough. Meanwhile, bring large pot of salted water to a boil.

4. Drop into boiling water and boil 5 minutes. Drain and toss in pan with melted butter and fine bread crumbs.

Serves 4 to 6

⋅❧ HELEN WINSTEN, OAKLAND HADASSAH, CALIFORNIA

Cheese Bourekas

16-ounce package frozen phyllo
   dough
1 pound feta cheese
2 pounds pressed cheese or
   pot cheese

4 eggs
1 teaspoon salt, or to taste
Oil for brushing

TIP
To vary this recipe, one (10-ounce) box frozen chopped spinach, thawed and squeezed dry, may be added to the cheese mixture.

Oil generously 13 x 9 inch pan. Line with half the phyllo sheets, each oiled lightly. Spread cheese mixture over and top with remaining pastry sheets, each oiled lightly. Bake at 375 degrees 30 to 40 minutes, or until golden, and cut into 3-inch diamonds. Best when served warm.

1. Defrost phyllo sheets according to package directions. Put between 2 pieces of wax paper and cover with a lightly dampened towel.

2. Preheat oven to 425 degrees. Crumble feta into small pieces and blend well with pressed cheese, eggs, and salt.

3. Remove 2 phyllo sheets at a time, keeping remainder covered. Place on a flat surface and brush very lightly with oil. With narrow end facing you, cut lengthwise into 3 strips. Fold each in half lengthwise and brush lightly with oil again.

4. Put 1 tablespoon cheese mixture on bottom right-hand corner of strip. Fold over to left side in a triangular shape and continue folding right to left, left to right, as in folding a flag. Lightly oil top of finished triangle and put on baking sheet. Repeat with remaining phyllo and cheese mixture.

5. Bake 20 to 25 minutes, or until golden. Serve warm.

Serves about 18

DORA LEVY, ROCHESTER HADASSAH, NEW YORK

Florida Orange Julius

12-ounce container frozen
   orange-juice concentrate
1 cup whole milk
1 cup water

1 or 2 tablespoons sugar
2 teaspoons vanilla extract
Ice cubes to fill the blender

Combine all ingredients in blender and blend until smooth and frothy, or until you can no longer hear ice being chopped up.

Serves 4

YETTA STRACHMAN, HILLCREST-SABRA SCOPUS HADASSAH, BROWARD, FLORIDA

FLORIDA ORANGE JULIUS, recipe right.

Old-Fashioned Cheese Kuchen

1/3 cup raisins

1 cup all-purpose flour

1/2 teaspoon baking powder

1 cup sugar, divided

3 eggs, divided

3 tablespoons unsalted butter,
    melted

1-1/4 cups milk, divided

2 cups dry curd cottage cheese

1/4 cup cornstarch

2 teaspoons grated lemon zest

2 tablespoons fresh lemon juice

1/2 teaspoon vanilla extract

1/2 teaspoon grated nutmeg

1. Preheat oven to 375 degrees. Butter an 8 x 8 inch baking pan.

2. Cover raisins with hot water. Let stand 5 minutes to plump, then drain.

3. Sift flour, baking powder, and 1/4 cup sugar into mixing bowl.

4. Beat 1 egg lightly and combine with 1 tablespoon melted butter and 1/4 cup milk. Stir into flour mixture and blend well. Spread mixture into prepared baking pan.

5. In another bowl, beat cottage cheese with remaining cup milk, 3/4 cup sugar, 2 eggs, 2 tablespoons melted butter, the cornstarch, grated lemon zest, lemon juice, vanilla extract, raisins, and grated nutmeg until smooth and well blended. Pour over dough in pan.

6. Bake about 50 minutes, or until filling is set. Let cool in pan. Cut into squares.

Makes 16 two-inch squares

❧ ANNETTE FELDMAN, OAKLAND HADASSAH, CALIFORNIA

Randy's Favorite Cheesecake

CRUST

1 cup all purpose flour

1/4 cup sugar

1/4 teaspoon vanilla extract

1 egg yolk

1/4 cup (4 tablespoons)
    melted unsalted butter,
    plus additional as needed

BATTER

2-1/2 pounds cream cheese, softened

5 eggs

1-1/2 cups sugar

3 tablespoons fresh lemon juice

1 teaspoon vanilla extract

CURRANT JELLY-BERRY TOPPING
    (recipe follows)

SOUR CHERRY TOPPING
    (recipe follows)

1. Preheat oven to 375 degrees. Set rack on center shelf. Lightly butter sides of 9- or 10-inch springform pan.

2. To make crust, combine all ingredients and pat evenly over bottom of the pan. Using pie weights on wax paper, bake 15 minutes. Remove from oven, remove pie weights and wax paper, and lower oven temperature to 325 degrees.

3. Make batter: Gradually combine all ingredients in mixer until smooth. Pour into pan and bake 1 hour. Turn off heat and leave cake in oven *with door closed* 1 hour longer. Let cool, then top with fruit, or serve plain. This needs time to set; refrigerate several hours before serving.

Serves 10 to 12

Currant Jelly-Berry Topping

1 cup currant jelly
1 hefty teaspoon cornstarch

2 tablespoons water
4 cups ripe berries

Heat jelly. Put through sieve and bring to a simmer. Blend cornstarch with water and stir into jelly until clear. Let cool. Arrange fruit on top of cheesecake and brush with cooled jelly.

Sour Cherry Topping

16-ounce can pitted sour cherries, drained, liquid reserved
1/2 cup sugar

2 tablespoons cornstarch
1 teaspoon fresh lemon juice

Add water to cherry liquid to equal 3/4 cup. Combine sugar and cornstarch; blend in with cherry liquid. Simmer 5 minutes and add lemon juice and cherries. Let cool, then spread over cake.

◆§ *JAN MICHEL, LOS ANGELES HADASSAH, CALIFORNIA*

Chalatobouriko
(Custard Pastry)

FILLING

1 quart milk

2 tablespoons uncooked cream of
    rice cereal

2 tablespoons unsalted butter

8 eggs

1/2 cup sugar

1 teaspoon vanilla extract

PASTRY

1/2 pound phyllo dough

1/2 pound (2 sticks) unsalted
    butter or margarine, melted

SYRUP

1 cup sugar

1 tablespoon unsalted butter

1. Make filling: In large pan, combine milk, cream of rice, and butter, and cook slowly until mixture thickens. Remove from heat, cover, and let cool.

2. Beat eggs well, stir in sugar and vanilla extract until thoroughly blended. Slowly stir into cooled milk mixture, stirring constantly.

3. Preheat oven to 350 degrees. Line 13 x 9 inch pan with 1 layer of phyllo. Brush with melted butter. Repeat process using 10 to 12 sheets of phyllo. Pour in custard filling. Cover with 3 to 4 sheets of phyllo, brushing each layer with melted butter.

4. Sprinkle lightly with water and remaining melted butter. Bake about 1 hour, until golden and knife inserted in custard comes out clean.

5. Make syrup: In medium pan heat 1 cup sugar with 1 cup water and the butter until sugar dissolves. Cook for about 10 to 15 minutes, or until thick and syrupy.

6. Remove from oven and pour syrup over custard pastry.

Serves about 18

✑ EVELYN GAEL, HUNTINGTON HADASSAH, NEW YORK

Basbouza

2 cups uncooked farina	1/4 pound (1 stick) unsalted
1 cup sugar	butter, melted
3/4 cup grated coconut	
1/2 cup all-purpose flour	SYRUP
1 teaspoon baking powder	1 cup sugar
1/2 cup milk	Several drops of vanilla extract

1. Preheat oven to 350 degrees. Grease 13 x 9 inch pan.

2. Combine farina, sugar, grated coconut, flour, and baking powder in large mixing bowl. Stir in milk and melted butter until smooth and well blended. Spread in prepared pan. Bake about 30 minutes, or until set.

3. Meanwhile, make syrup: Stir sugar with 1 cup water and the vanilla extract in small pan over medium heat, until sugar is dissolved. Cook about 8 to 10 minutes, or until mixture is thick and syrupy.

4. Remove Basbouza from oven. While still hot, cut into small diamond shapes. Pour hot syrup over.

Makes about 2 dozen

◄§ LILLIAN SCHUAL, HUNTINGTON HADASSAH, NEW YORK

Sour Cream Cookie Twists

3 cups all-purpose flour	1/2 cup (1 stick) unsalted butter,
2 teaspoons baking powder	softened
Pinch of salt	1 cup sour cream
	Granulated sugar

1. Preheat oven to 400 degrees. Grease cookie sheet.

2. Sift flour, baking powder, and salt. Knead in butter and sour cream until smooth. Divide in thirds. Keep 2 parts refrigerated while working with the third.

3. Roll out dough on well sugared board to 1/8-inch thickness. Sprinkle sugar on top. Cut strips about 4 inches long and twist loosely. Put on prepared cookie sheet. Bake 12 to 14 minutes, until cookies have started to take on color. Repeat with remaining dough.

Makes about 7 dozen

◄§ MRS. MAURICE TOBIN, MANCHESTER HADASSAH, NEW HAMPSHIRE

Kolaches

1/2 pound farmer cheese
1 cup (2 sticks) unsalted butter, softened
2 cups all-purpose flour

Apricot or strawberry preserves
1/2 cup finely chopped nuts
Confectioners' sugar

1. Force cheese through sieve or food mill. Mix with butter and flour until blended. Wrap in wax paper and refrigerate overnight.

2. Preheat oven to 375 degrees.

3. Roll dough about 1/4-inch thick on well floured surface. Cut with 2-1/2 inch cookie cutter. Make a small depression in each and put 1/2 teaspoon preserves or single piece of fruit from preserves in center of each cookie. Sprinkle with a few nuts.

4. Bake 20 to 22 minutes, until delicately browned. Dust with confectioners' sugar when cool.

Makes 3-1/2 dozen

◆ PORTLAND HADASSAH, OREGON

Apricot Horns

1 pound (4 sticks) salted butter or margarine, softened
16-ounce container creamed cottage cheese
4 cups all-purpose flour

1-1/2 cups ground almonds
1-1/4 cups granulated sugar
2 egg whites, lightly beaten
Apricot jam
Confectioners' sugar

1. Blend together butter, cottage cheese, and flour. Shape into 1-inch balls, cover with plastic wrap, and refrigerate overnight.

2. Preheat oven to 375 degrees. Grease cookie sheets.

3. Combine nuts with sugar. Lightly flatten each ball into a 3-inch round. Place jam in center and roll up in horn shape. Brush tops with beaten egg white, then sprinkle with nut-sugar mixture.

4. Place on prepared cookie sheets and bake 20 to 22 minutes. When cool, dust with confectioners' sugar.

Makes 6 dozen

◆ PORTLAND HADASSAH, OREGON

Rice Custard Pudding

1/2 cup short grain rice
1/4 pound (1 stick) unsalted
   butter or margarine
3 eggs, lightly beaten

2 cups milk
1/2 cup sugar
1-1/2 teaspoons vanilla extract
1 pound apples, grated

TIP
Quarter fresh strawberries and sprinkle with sugar. Toss gently and let sit until berries have begun to release their juices, then serve over rice pudding. Or try the pudding with Apricot Sauce (recipe below, right).

1. Preheat oven to 350 degrees. Grease shallow 6-cup baking pan.

2. Cook rice according to package directions.

3. When rice is cooked, place in large mixing bowl. Gradually stir in melted butter, eggs, milk, sugar, and vanilla extract until thoroughly combined. Stir in grated apples.

4. Spoon or pour rice mixture into prepared pan. Place pan in larger pan of enough hot water to come halfway up sides of pan (a *bain marie*).

5. Bake 40 to 45 minutes, until knife inserted in center comes out clean.

6. Let cool, then refrigerate at least 3 hours. Serve with fruit sauce.

Serves 6

◆§ SANTA CRUZ HADASSAH, CALIFORNIA

Apricot Sauce

1/4 cup sugar
1 teaspoon fresh lemon juice

1/2 pound ripe apricots or 2 large
   ripe peaches, halved and pitted
2 tablespoons confectioners' sugar

1. Combine sugar and lemon juice in medium saucepan with 1 cup water. Bring to a boil and cook, stirring, until sugar is dissolved. Add apricots and reduce heat. Simmer until tender; remove from heat and let apricots cool in syrup.

2. Drain, reserving syrup. Purée apricots with confectioners' sugar in blender; add 1/4 cup reserved liquid and blend to incorporate. Strain through a fine sieve, adding reserved liquid if needed.

Makes about 1-1/4 cups

◆§ GILDA BARLAS WEISSBERGER, PARK SLOPE HADASSAH, BROOKLYN, NEW YORK

Simchas

SIMCHAS—LIFE'S CELEBRATIONS

Introduction by Joan Nathan

Joan Nathan is the author of seven cookbooks, including Jewish Cooking in America, which won The James Beard Award and the International Association of Culinary Professionals/Julia Child Cookbook of the Year Award. She hosts the nationally syndicated PBS television series, Jewish Cooking in America with Joan Nathan, based on the book. In her latest masterwork, The Foods of Israel Today, she takes us on a historical journey through the land to meet its people, and captures the spirit of Israel with a most remarkable blend of food and culture.

Page 234–235, left to right: POTATO-ONION BREAD, recipe page 242; MOTHER'S PICKLED SNAPPER, recipe page 239; and CHERRY CHOCOLATE CAKE, recipe page 254.

OPPOSITE: KETUBBAH. Ferrara, Italy, 1775. Ink, tempera, and gold paint on parchment. HUC Skirball Cultural Center, Museum Collection. Kirschstein Collection.

Nearly every life-cycle event in our family seems to revolve around food. After all, isn't that what a simcha is all about?

Twenty-seven years ago my first cookbook, *The Flavor of Jerusalem*, was about to come out. My soon-to-be-husband Allan and I had met in Jerusalem at the Western Wall, so naturally we wanted to celebrate our wedding with Israeli food.

In preparing for the wedding, my mother and I visited Providence's kosher caterer. We told him right away that we didn't want the usual. He suggested stuffed derma and potato knishes for hors d'oeuvres. My mother said no, she didn't want them. He served them anyway.

The wedding dinner wasn't a total defeat, though. On one of my trips to Israel I had tasted something exotic. It was called hummus and I wanted to share the garlicky, lemony taste of the dip with my friends at this important event. I still remember how much the guests loved it. It seems hard to believe now, but most had never tasted anything like it.

As at every Jewish function, we began our meal with a blessing over the wine and a *motzi*, a blessing over the bread. We had a giant challah twisted in the Ashkenazic tradition, but I really wanted to serve berches, the potato challah passed down in my German Jewish family. I like the symbolism that 10 fingers are involved in bread-making, and that there are 10 transformations from planting to final baking. I really wanted to make the bread myself, but because of *kashrut*, we had to settle for one from the bakery.

For the main course we decided on recipes from my book, an orange ginger chicken and rice. I can't remember the vegetable or the salad, but I do recall the dessert: the American Colony Chocolate Cake. It took a lot of coaxing to persuade the caterer not to make the cake overly sweet, and he finally gave in to my request for the chocolate almond torte interior. But then he covered it with an awful sugary white frosting to make sure the cake would not have to be refrigerated.

It's not just the food, but also the symbolism and ritual of Jewish life-cycle events that make the experience so rich and memorable. I have been to weddings where the bride and groom fasted for 24 hours before the service, a custom that dates to talmudic times. They fast to atone for their past sins before they start a new life together, the same reason we fast on Yom Kippur. Also, as on Yom Kippur, the bride and groom are dressed in white. The *kittel* for men—and nowadays for some women too—is a symbol of purity. It is worn when entering a new state of being such as marriage and, symbolic of a shroud, it is a reminder of our mortality as well.

Another tradition is the breaking of a dinner plate (wrapped in a napkin, of course) by the mothers of the bride and groom. They smash the plate to remind us that even in joyous times we must remember the destruction of the Temple. I knew that the wineglass my new husband stomped on also referred to the destruction of the Temple.

By the time my son David was born and I suffered through the joy and pain of his bris, I realized wine was symbolic and that no Jewish milestone is observed without it. That first sip the mohel dabbed on his lips not only sedated him, but also introduced him at a very early age to the celebratory role of wine in Judaism. At every simcha there is wine and a blessing is said over it.

Not only do we introduce the Sabbath by thanking God for the fruit of the vine, but we also end it with the Havdalah ceremony by pouring wine until it spills over the top of the cup. This reminds us of the overabundance of our good fortune at having the Sabbath, and symbolizes the hope that this luck will spill over into the new week.

The Havdalah ceremony usually begins with an introduction followed by blessings: over sweet spices, light, and wine. The blessing over the spices may be compensation for the loss of the additional soul that traditionally accompanies a Jew on the Sabbath, or maybe it is to carry the sweet sense of the day throughout the week. We bless the light to signify that work is now permitted, and to stress the departure of the Sabbath Queen. The blessing over the wine stems from the duty to recite Havdalah over wine, as in the Kiddush.

By the time the bat mitzvah of Daniela, my first daughter, came around, I understood the symbolism of food and was also better equipped to insist on my culinary preferences. By then I had written *The Jewish Holiday Kitchen* and our very patient rabbi, not knowing what he was in for, allowed me to cater the celebration. It was not easy. Everything had to be prepared in the synagogue kitchen and we had to hire a *mashgiach* to supervise. A local retired baker showed Daniela (and her sister Merissa and brother David at their bar and bat mitzvahs) how to six-braid challahs, which we prepared ahead and froze.

For hors d'oeuvres I picked the hit parade of Jewish dishes: Greek spanikopita, a seasoned spinach-feta cheese mixture wrapped in phyllo leaves, mini-bagels with cream cheese and smoked salmon, and hummus.

It is, of course, not only the joyous occasions that call for rituals that invest the event with meaning. Mixed with our simchas are the inevitable deaths, and like every family we have had our share. The meal after a funeral should consist of round foods, symbolic of the circle of life: chickpeas, bagels, eggs. The meals, prepared by friends of the mourners, become a sense of support, enabling the bereaved to truly mourn within the strength of community.

My children are almost grown now and I can concentrate on another round of simchas—hopefully they'll be weddings. And with each event comes the special foods handed down with their intricate histories, and the generations upon generations of people whose lives and stories are entwined, as the foods are, with the simchas and our lives.

Pickled Salmon

6 red salmon fillets
1 carrot, thinly sliced
1 parsley root, peeled and sliced
1 teaspoon salt
1/4 teaspoon freshly ground pepper

BRINE
1 cup cider vinegar
1 onion, sliced
1/2 cup packed brown sugar
1/2 cup raisins

2 bay leaves
1-inch piece gingerroot
1/2 teaspoon ground ginger
3 cloves garlic, halved
1 stick cinnamon
1/4 teaspoon ground allspice
  (optional)
1/4 teaspoon freshly grated
  nutmeg (optional)
Parsley sprigs and lemon slices

1. Place fish in saucepan with carrot, parsley root, salt, and pepper. Cover with water and bring to a boil. Skim, lower heat, and simmer about 10 to 15 minutes, until fish is tender but firm. Let cool. Transfer fish to a large bowl.

2. Combine ingredients for brine through nutmeg in another pan and bring to a boil. Let cool, and pour over fish. Cover tightly and refrigerate 24 hours.

3. Cut fish into thin slices as appetizer for 12, or thicker slices as a main course for 6. Garnish with parsley sprigs and lemon slices.

Serves 6 to 12

◆§ *Hadassah Israel*

Mother's
Pickled Snapper

1 teaspoon kosher salt	*1/4 teaspoon freshly ground*
2 pounds snapper fillets	*pepper*
2 tablespoons white vinegar	*1 lemon, sliced*
2 to 3 large onions, thinly sliced	*Juice of half a lemon*
1/2 cup packed brown sugar	*1 bay leaf*
2 tablespoons raisins (optional)	*Fresh dill for garnish*
1/2 teaspoon salt	

1. Salt fish and pour a little vinegar over it.

2. In a large, shallow pan, bring to a boil 3 cups water, the sliced onions, brown sugar, raisins, salt, and pepper, and simmer over low heat 15 minutes. Add fish.

3. Cook fish gently 5 minutes; add sliced lemon, lemon juice, and bay leaf. Cook about 10 minutes longer. Garnish with onion-raisin mixture and lemons and sprinkle with fresh dill. May be served hot or cold, but the longer it stays, the better the taste!

Serves 4

◆§ *Jean Patiky, Huntington Hadassah, New York*

Middle Eastern Appetizer Meatballs

1/2 pound lean ground beef

1/4 pound ground lamb

2 cloves garlic, minced

1/2 cup chopped onion

1 egg, lightly beaten

1/4 cup pine nuts, coarsely chopped

1/4 cup chopped fresh parsley

1 teaspoon salt

1/2 teaspoon dried thyme

1/2 teaspoon curry powder

1/4 teaspoon freshly ground pepper

1/2 teaspoon ground allspice or cinnamon

Oil for frying

Combine all ingredients until well blended. Form into 1-inch balls. Heat a little oil in skillet and cook meatballs, a few at a time, shaking pan, until browned on all sides.

◦ᣟ *Serves 12 as part of hors d'oeuvres*

DORIS MILLER, ANN ARBOR HADASSAH, MICHIGAN

TIP

The meatballs can be prepared and reheated on a cookie sheet in a 350-degree oven for 5 to 10 minutes.

Moroccan Cigars

2 tablespoons oil, divided, plus additional as needed

2 pounds beef stew meat, cut in chunks

1 large onion, chopped

1 tablespoon ground cumin

1 tablespoon paprika

1 tablespoon salt

2 teaspoons garlic powder

1 teaspoon turmeric

1/2 teaspoon freshly ground pepper

Warka dough (really thin dough used for Chinese egg rolls), or 16-ounce package wonton wrappers

Flour and water mixed to form a gooey, not watery, dough

Matbucha, for dipping (recipe follows)

1. Heat 1 tablespoon oil in large pot over medium-high heat. Add meat and brown in batches. Remove meat from pot and set aside.

2. Heat remaining tablespoon oil in same pot. Add onion and spices and cook until onion softens, about 5 minutes. Return meat to pot. Add water to cover. Cover pot and cook over medium-low heat about 1-1/2 hours, or until meat is soft, always making sure pot has water. Let cool.

TIP

This recipe is from a Moroccan family recipe and has been passed down through several generations. It takes a lot of time, but it's awesome.

3. Put meat mixture in food processor a little at a time and grind with a little oil each time. Mixture should be thick, not watery—about the consistency of mashed potatoes.

4. Warka dough usually comes in a circle. Cut in half. Form fingers (long strips) with ground meat. Enclose each finger in dough and roll it closed as if making an egg roll. Seal closed with flour-and-water mixture.

5. Deep-fry cigars. Serve with Matbucha for dipping.

Makes about 90

Matbucha

2 pounds red bell peppers
1 tablespoon olive oil
6 cloves garlic, minced
Ten (14.5 ounce) cans diced tomatoes, drained, liquid reserved
2 teaspoons salt

1/2 teaspoon freshly ground pepper
2 tablespoons paprika
1 tablespoon ground cumin
1/4 teaspoon harissa (Israeli hot sauce) (see TIP opposite)

1. Roast bell peppers: Preheat broiler. Halve, seed, and devein peppers. Arrange on foil-lined baking sheet cut side down and broil until the skin blackens, about 15 minutes. Transfer to a plastic bag. Seal, and let peppers steam at least 15 minutes. When cool, peel and finely chop.

2. Meanwhile, heat oil in large kettle over medium heat. Add garlic and sauté until you can smell the aroma. Add tomatoes and cook over medium heat about 1-1/2 hours, until tomatoes get really soft and juice has almost evaporated. If mixture starts to burn, add some reserved tomato juice, very little at a time.

3. Add salt, pepper, paprika, cumin, and harissa. Add bell peppers and cook 45 minutes longer.

4. Use as a dip for Moroccan cigars.

Makes 1 to 1-1/2 quarts

◄§ *DIANNE CASPI OHAYON, SHATIL GROUP HADASSAH, NEW YORK*

Potato-Onion Bread

1 pound white potatoes, peeled
  and cut up

1 cup milk

5 to 6 scallions, finely chopped
  (about 1/2 cup)

2 tablespoons unsalted butter

4 to 5 cups all-purpose or bread
  flour

2 teaspoons sugar

1 (1/4-ounce) package active
  dry yeast

2 teaspoons salt

1/4 teaspoon freshly ground black
  pepper

2 egg whites

1 egg yolk lightly beaten with
  1 teaspoon water

1. Cook potatoes in boiling water to cover until fork tender. Drain, reserving 1/4 cup cooking liquid.

2. Mash potatoes. Stir in reserved potato water, the milk, scallions, and butter. Heat over low heat until mixture just feels warm when tested on wrist. Transfer to large mixing bowl and beat until smooth.

3. In another large bowl, combine 1-1/2 cups flour, the sugar, yeast, salt, and pepper. Beat into potato mixture with electric mixer until blended. Beat in egg whites. Stir in 1-1/2 cups flour until thick. With wooden spoon stir in 1 cup flour to make soft dough, adding more flour if dough is too soft.

4. Turn out onto floured board. Knead until smooth and elastic, about 10 minutes, adding more flour as needed to prevent sticking. Shape dough into ball. Place in large greased bowl; turn to coat entire surface. Cover with clean towel and let rise in warm place until doubled in bulk, about 1 hour. Meanwhile, grease two 8 x 4 inch loaf pans.

5. Punch down dough; divide in half. Roll out one half on floured surface with floured rolling pin into 11 x 7 inch rectangle. Starting at narrow end, roll up tightly; pinch seam to seal and fold ends under. Place seam down in prepared pan. Repeat with remaining dough. Cover with towel, and let rise until doubled, about 1 hour. Meanwhile, preheat oven to 375 degrees.

6. Brush loaves with egg wash. Bake 35 to 40 minutes, or until golden and loaves sound hollow when tapped. Remove from pan and let cool on wire rack.

Makes 2 loaves

◆§ CHARLOTTE WIENER, SAN DIEGO HADASSAH, CALIFORNIA

Whole-Wheat Honey Challah

Six (1/4-ounce) packages active
   dry yeast
1 tablespoon plus 1 cup honey
4 cups warm water, divided
1 cup oil

5 eggs, plus 1 egg beaten
   for glaze
2 tablespoons salt
8 cups whole-wheat flour
12 cups all-purpose or bread flour

1. Dissolve yeast and 1 tablespoon honey in 2 cups warm water in large bowl. Let stand until bubbly, then beat in oil, 5 eggs, 1 cup honey, and remaining 2 cups warm water. Mix well. Gradually add dry ingredients and knead 5 to 10 minutes, until elastic but not sticky.

2. Divide dough in half, place in 2 oiled bowls and turn to grease tops. Cover with damp cloth and let rise in warm place 1 to 2 hours. Punch down and let rise 1 hour longer. Meanwhile, grease six 8 x 4 inch loaf pans.

3. Divide into 6 parts. Braid 6 loaves and put in prepared pans. Let rise, covered, 1 hour longer.

4. Meanwhile, preheat oven to 350 degrees. Brush each challah with beaten egg and bake 35 minutes to 1 hour, until brown.

Makes 6 loaves

◆ SHIRA HADASSAH, PORT CHESTER, NEW YORK

Bread-and-Butter Pickles

16 medium Kirby cucumbers
6 medium onions, thinly sliced
2 green bell peppers, chopped
2 cloves garlic, minced
1/3 cup salt
Cracked ice as needed

1-1/2 teaspoons turmeric
2 tablespoons mustard seed
5 cups sugar
1-1/2 teaspoons celery seed
3 cups cider vinegar

Thinly slice cucumbers into large bowl. Add onions, bell peppers, and garlic. Add salt. Cover with cracked ice. Mix well. Let stand 3 hours. Drain cucumbers well. Combine remaining ingredients and add cukes to mixture. Seal in hot, sterile jars.

Makes 8 pints (or 4 quarts)

◆ ELAINE COHEN, NORTH HILLS HADASSAH, PITTSBURGH, PENNSYLVANIA

Pickles should be slim. One 8-quart basket fills about 12 quart jars.

Quart-size canning jars and covers should be sterilized and ready.

DILL

Native to the Mediterranean area and Russia, dill has plumes of fine blue-green leaves and bright yellow flowers in flattish heads. Its reputation as a soothing herb is supported by the fact that both leaves and seeds contain a mild sedative. A century or so ago, dill water was used to calm restless babies.

In central and eastern Europe chopped dill leaves are often used as a garnish for boiled potatoes or sour-cream sauces.

KOSHER DILL PICKLES, recipe above, right.

Kosher Dill Pickles

For each quart:
About 5 to 7 Kirby pickles
(depending on size; about
3-1/2 inches long), washed
1 teaspoon pickling spices
1 flower or seed head of dill

1 small hot red pepper (or half a
large one)
1 clove garlic, crushed
1-1/2 tablespoons coarse salt
1-1/2 to 2 cups cold water

1. Soak pickles in cold water, then scrub. Soak about 1 hour in cold salted water.

2. Meanwhile, sterilize jars and covers.

3. Pack pickles in upright position into quart jars. Then fill each one with pickling spices, dill, hot pepper, and garlic. Dissolve coarse salt in the 1-1/2 to 2 cups cold water while placing other ingredients into jars. Fill jars with salt solution to about 1/2 inch from top. Seal tightly. Place jars in cool room. Ready as new dills in 4 days.

Makes multiples of 1 quart

◆ SYLVIA GERTZOG, ROCHESTER HADASSAH, NEW YORK

Cherry Chicken

3 fryers, cut up
2 cups chopped onions
1 cup port wine
12-ounce bottle chili sauce

3/4 cup packed brown sugar
3/4 cup white raisins
16-ounce can pitted sour cherries

1. Preheat broiler. Broil chicken until golden, then remove chicken and reduce oven temperature to 350 degrees.

2. Place chicken in large roasting pan or baking dish. Stir onions, port wine, 1 cup water, the chili sauce, brown sugar, and raisins in saucepan and heat gently. Pour over browned chicken.

3. Bake, covered with aluminum foil, 1 hour. Remove foil. Drain cherries and sprinkle over chicken. Bake, uncovered, 45 minutes.

Serves 12

◆ BERNICE POPKIN, HUNTINGTON HADASSAH, NEW YORK

Gingered Roast Turkey

STUFFING

3 cups cooked long grain rice

1 large onion, finely chopped

1 apple with skin, seeded and finely
    chopped

2 carrots, grated

2 tablespoons grated lemon zest

1/2 teaspoon salt

1/2 teaspoon freshly ground pepper

3 tablespoons unsalted margarine,
    melted

1/2 cup white wine

1/2 cup raisins (optional)

12-pound turkey

Salt

Freshly ground pepper to taste

Powdered ginger to taste

Paprika to taste

2 cloves garlic, crushed

One quarter of a lemon

Oil

SAUCE

4 tablespoons margarine

3 tablespoons orange marmalade

4 teaspoons orange liqueur

1. Preheat oven to 350 degrees. Set aside shallow roasting pan.

2. Combine stuffing ingredients through raisins. Dry turkey thoroughly inside and out. Sprinkle turkey cavity with salt and dry seasonings; rub with crushed garlic and the lemon quarter. Stuff cavity and neck loosely. Sew closed or fasten with skewers.

3. Sprinkle outer surface with dry seasonings; rub with crushed garlic and lemon. Brush with oil. Wrap in aluminum foil and place in pan breast side down. Roast 1-1/2 hours. Turn breast up to cook evenly and roast 1-1/2 hours more.

4. Meanwhile, make sauce. Melt margarine, stir in marmalade and liqueur.

5. Open foil to let turkey brown. Baste with sauce and roast 30 minutes longer, until internal temperature reaches 180 to 185 degrees.

Serves 12

◄§ HADASSAH ISRAEL

Aunt Janice's Brisket

8-pound brisket

2 cloves garlic, crushed

2 onions, coarsely chopped

Grinding of freshly ground pepper

1 teaspoon Worcestershire sauce

Two (1-ounce) packets onion-soup mix

12-ounce bottle chili sauce

12-ounce can beer

8 carrots

3 slices rye bread

1. Preheat oven to 350 degrees. Rub brisket with garlic and place on bed of chopped onions in roasting pan with tight-fitting lid.

2. Over brisket place in the following order: pepper, Worcestershire sauce, onion-soup mix, chili sauce, and beer. Lay carrots in pan around brisket. Tear bread into small pieces and tuck under brisket. Cover pan and place in oven.

3. After 45 minutes reduce oven temperature to 275 degrees. Cook another 2-1/2 to 3 hours, or until fork tender.

4. Remove from oven; allow to rest 10 minutes. Slice at an angle and place on platter with carrots.

Serves 16

◦§ *Tara Wolman, Springfield Hadassah, Massachusetts*

Judy's Brisket

MARINADE	1/4 cup cola soda
2 cloves garlic	3 tablespoons ketchup
1 medium onion, cut in quarters	1-1/2 teaspoons salt
2 tablespoons red wine vinegar	1 teaspoon freshly ground
1/4 cup dry red wine	pepper
1/2 cup oil	
1/4 cup honey	5- to 6-pound beef brisket

1. Make marinade: Process garlic and onion in food processor until onion is minced. Add remaining marinade ingredients and process until well blended.

2. Pour marinade over brisket; cover and let sit 1 to 2 hours at room temperature, or refrigerate overnight.

3. Preheat oven to 300 degrees. Cook brisket, covered, approximately 1 hour per pound, or until tender. When brisket is very tender, remove it from the oven and let cool, then refrigerate.

4. The brisket will slice better the next day. Remove hardened fat and discard. Slice brisket. To reheat, place the sliced brisket in the sauce; cover and warm in oven.

Serves 10

◦§ *Judi Steinberg, North Boundary Hadassah, Chicago, Illinois*

Fruited Acorn Squash

6 acorn squash

4 tablespoons soft unsalted margarine

Salt (optional)

4 apples, peeled, cored, and sliced

1/2 cup drained pineapple tidbits

2 oranges, peeled and cut in segments

1/2 cup dried cranberries (optional)

1/2 cup slivered almonds, toasted

1/3 cup packed brown sugar

1. Preheat oven to 375 degrees.

2. Cut squash in half crosswise (it is a more attractive cut) and remove seeds. If necessary, slice off bottom of squash to level. Spread soft margarine on insides and top. Sprinkle with salt. Arrange apple slices, pineapple tidbits, orange segments, and dried cranberries in the squash.

3. Sprinkle with almonds and brown sugar and dot with margarine.

4. Bake about 1 hour, or until squash is tender.

Serves 6

❧ ANNETTE FELDMAN, OAKLAND HADASSAH, CALIFORNIA

TIP

If another vegetable is on the menu, this recipe will serve 12.

Roasted Garlic

8 whole fresh heads garlic

6 tablespoons unsalted butter

1/4 cup plus 2 tablespoons dry
   white wine

1/4 cup plus 2 tablespoons parve
   chicken-flavor bouillon

Salt and freshly ground pepper
   to taste

1/2 pound farmer cheese

6 tablespoons sour cream

4 to 6 scallions, finely chopped

1. Preheat oven to 325 degrees. Remove outer layers of skin from garlic, leaving cloves and head intact. Select baking dish just large enough to hold clusters in one layer. Rub baking dish with butter and arrange heads close together. Dot each with butter; pour wine and bouillon over all and sprinkle with salt and pepper. Cover pan securely with foil and bake 45 minutes. Uncover and bake 15 minutes longer.

2. Blend farmer cheese with sour cream. Stir in scallions and season with salt and pepper. To eat, break off one clove at a time and press out the flesh. Top with a bit of sauce.

Serves 8 to 16 or more

❧ RITA SCHIFFREN, LENOX HILL HADASSAH, NEW YORK, NEW YORK

FRUITED ACORN SQUASH, recipe above, right.

Moroccan Couscous

2 tablespoons olive oil

1 pound lamb shoulder, cut in
 1-1/2 inch cubes

3-1/2 to 4-pound chicken, cut in
 12 pieces

2 large onions, sliced

2 cloves garlic, crushed

4 large carrots, cut in 1-inch
 chunks

1 teaspoon salt, plus additional as
 needed

1/4 teaspoon freshly ground
 pepper

1 stick cinnamon

1 tablespoon grated gingerroot

1 tablespoon turmeric

2 cups defatted chicken broth or
 water, or as needed

1/2 pound couscous

4 medium zucchini, sliced in
 1-inch rounds

20-ounce can chickpeas, drained
 and rinsed

1/4 cup flour

2 tomatoes, cut in chunks

1 cup raisins

14-ounce can artichoke hearts,
 drained and halved

4 tablespoons unsalted margarine

1/4 cup slivered almonds, toasted

1. In Dutch oven, heat oil over medium high heat. Add lamb; cook 8 to 10 minutes, or until browned. Remove lamb and set aside. Add chicken pieces to pan and cook about 10 minutes, until browned on all sides. Remove chicken and set aside. Add onion and garlic to pan; sauté until golden.

2. Return lamb and chicken to pan. Add carrots, salt, pepper, cinnamon stick, gingerroot, turmeric, and enough broth to cover. Bring to a boil, lower heat, and simmer 30 minutes.

3. Meanwhile, soak couscous in cold water 30 minutes, drain and rinse. Line colander or strainer with cheesecloth. Place couscous in strainer and place strainer over simmering meat. Cover tightly and simmer 20 minutes.

4. Add zucchini and chickpeas to meat. Stir couscous with fork. Cover and simmer 15 minutes more.

5. In small bowl combine flour with 1/4 cup cold water. Add to meat; stirring constantly until mixture thickens.

6. Add tomatoes, raisins, and artichoke hearts, and cook 5 minutes more.

7. Toss cooked couscous with margarine and salt to taste. Make a bed of couscous on large serving platter. Arrange meat and vegetables in center. Pour some thickened broth over. Sprinkle with almonds.

Serves 8

◄§ CHARLOTTE SULTAN, SAN DIEGO HADASSAH, CALIFORNIA

Meva Potatoes

3 tablespoons clarified butter or 3 tablespoons shortening	1/2 teaspoon cumin seeds
1/3 cup each cashews, peanuts, and almonds	5 medium potatoes, peeled and diced
	1 teaspoon ground coriander
2/3 cup raisins	1/2 teaspoon ground cumin
5 tablespoons vegetable oil	1/4 teaspoon turmeric powder
1/2 teaspoon mustard seeds	Pinch of ground ginger
	Ground red pepper and salt, to taste

1. Heat clarified butter. Sauté nuts and set aside. Sauté raisins and set aside.

2. Heat oil in skillet and fry mustard and cumin seeds until they pop. Put diced potatoes in the pan and mix well. Cover and cook on medium low heat, stirring occasionally.

3. After 10 or 15 minutes add all the spices and stir well. Continue to stir occasionally until tender and cooked. Stir in nuts and raisins. Serve warm.

Serves 4 to 6

Rita Ajmera, Clifton Park Hadassah, New York

Outrageous Kugel

16-ounce package wide egg noodles	4 eggs, lightly beaten
	1 cup sour cream
1/2 cup (1 stick) unsalted butter, melted, divided	3/4 cup applesauce
	2/3 cup sugar
1 cup chopped walnuts	1 teaspoon ground cinnamon
3/4 cup packed brown sugar	1 teaspoon salt

1. Preheat oven to 350 degrees. Grease 10-inch bundt pan. Cook egg noodles according to package directions. Drain thoroughly.

2. Meanwhile, pour 1/4 cup melted butter into bottom of pan. Sprinkle on walnuts and brown sugar.

3. In large bowl, combine drained noodles with eggs, sour cream, applesauce, sugar, remaining 1/4 cup melted butter, the cinnamon, and salt. Pour into pan on top of nut mixture.

4. Bake about 1 hour. Let cool completely before turning out of pan.

Serves 12 to 16

Shara Wass, Hatikvah Hadassah, Miami, Florida

Fabulous Rice Pudding

1/2 cup raisins	3/4 cup sugar
1/2 cup uncooked short-grain rice	4 eggs
	2 cups heavy cream
2 cups light cream	2 tablespoons vanilla extract
2 cups milk	Dash of freshly grated nutmeg

1. Soak raisins in 1/2 cup cold water.

2. Mix rice, light cream, milk and sugar in top of double boiler. Cover and cook over simmering water about 1 to 1-1/2 hours, stirring occasionally.

3. Beat eggs in large bowl. Slowly add rice mixture to eggs, beating constantly and vigorously. Return mixture to top of double boiler and continue cooking until mixture coats spoon. Refrigerate until cold.

4. In large bowl with electric mixer, beat heavy cream until soft peaks form. Fold cream gently into cold rice with drained raisins and vanilla extract. Spoon into serving bowls, sprinkle with nutmeg, and chill.

Serves 6 to 8

BETH SCHNITMAN, TAMAR HADASSAH, WILMETTE, ILLINOIS

Mae's Rice and Noodle Pudding

TIP
Try making this with short-grain rice; it cooks up tender but firm.

1 cup uncooked rice	1 cup (1/2 pound) cottage cheese
1 pound medium egg noodles	1 cup sugar
2 cups milk	1 cup golden raisins
3.4-ounce box instant vanilla pudding	1/2 cup (1 stick) unsalted butter, softened
6 eggs, lightly beaten	Cinnamon-sugar
1 cup sour cream	

1. Preheat oven to 350 degrees. Grease two 13 x 9 inch baking pans.

2. Bring 4 quarts water to a boil. Stir in rice and cook 7 minutes. Stir in noodles and cook 5 minutes longer. Strain under hot water, then let drain about 15 minutes. Place in large bowl.

There is nothing ordinary about the seductively aromatic vanilla bean. The long thin pod is the fruit of the luminous celadon-colored vanilla planifolia which, of over 20,000 orchid varieties, is the only one that bears anything edible. Because of the extremely labor-intensive, time-consuming process by which it's obtained, pure vanilla is relatively expensive. It begins with the blossoms, which open only one day a year and then only for a few hours.

Because this particular orchid has only one natural pollinator, the Melipona bee, which cannot possibly handle the task in time by itself, the flower must be hand pollinated, otherwise no vanilla bean. It takes six weeks to reach full size and after that eight to nine months to mature and three to six months to cure. After months of drying in the sun by day and sweating in blankets at night, the beans ferment, shrinking by 400 percent and turning their characteristic dark brown. Vanilla extract is made by macerating chopped beans in an alcohol-water solution in order to extract the flavor, and aged for several months. Imitation vanilla is entirely artificial, and can't compare with the real thing.

3. Heat milk and stir in vanilla pudding. Cook, stirring, until mixture just begins to thicken. Stir into noodle-rice mixture.

4. In a separate bowl, combine eggs, sour cream, cottage cheese, sugar, and raisins. Add to noodle-rice mixture and mix well. Place in colander over a bowl to drain, reserving drained liquid.

5. Spread half of noodle-rice mixture into each prepared pan, then pour strained liquid equally over each and dot tops with butter. Sprinkle with cinnamon-sugar and bake 1 hour.

Serves 14 to 16

◆ *MAE SHAKIN, EMMA LAZARUS HADASSAH, DOBBS FERRY, NEW YORK*

Flourless Chocolate Cake

9 ounces semisweet chocolate	4 eggs
1 ounce unsweetened chocolate	1-1/2 tablespoon vanilla extract
1/2 cup confectioners' sugar, plus	2 tablespoons coffee liqueur
additional for dusting	1-1/2 cups whipping cream
1-1/2 teaspoons cornstarch	

1. Preheat oven to 350 degrees. Butter and flour 10-inch springform pan and line bottom with wax paper. Melt chocolates in top of double boiler over simmering water. When melted, remove from heat and let cool.

2. With a whisk, mix 1/2 cup confectioners' sugar with cornstarch in medium bowl. In another bowl, beat eggs with vanilla extract and coffee liqueur. Add sugar mixture and beat until thick, foamy, and tripled in volume.

3. Blend a little egg mixture into cooled chocolate. Mix well, then fold in remaining egg mixture.

4. Whip cream and lightly fold into chocolate. Pour into prepared pan. Bake 1 hour, or until tester comes out clean. Turn oven off, leaving door partially open, and let cake cool in oven. Turn out cake and carefully peel off wax paper. Sprinkle with confectioners' sugar.

Serves 12 to 16

◆ *DONA DICK, DEBORAH-ZAHAVA HADASSAH, CHICAGO, ILLINOIS*

Cherry Chocolate Cake

2 cups all-purpose flour	1/2 cup cooking oil
3/4 cup sugar	2 teaspoons vanilla extract
1 teaspoon baking soda	21-ounce can cherry-pie filling
1 teaspoon ground cinnamon	1 cup semisweet chocolate pieces
1/8 teaspoon salt	1 cup walnuts, chopped
2 eggs, beaten	Confectioners' sugar

1. Preheat oven to 350 degrees. Grease and flour 10-inch tube pan.

2. In a large mixing bowl, stir together flour, sugar, baking soda, cinnamon and salt. In another bowl, combine eggs, oil and vanilla extract; add to flour mixture. Mix well. Stir in cherry-pie filling, chocolate pieces and walnuts. Turn into prepared pan.

3. Bake 1 hour. Let cool in pan on wire rack 15 minutes. Remove from pan and let cool. Sift confectioners' sugar over top.

Serves about 18

❧ BEVERLY SILVERMAN, TAMAR HADASSAH, WILMETTE, ILLINOIS

Oneg Shabbat Kiddush Cake

1 cup (2 sticks) unsalted margarine	2 teaspoons baking powder
	Pinch of ground nutmeg
2 cups sugar	3/4 cup sweet sherry
6 eggs	3/4 cup finely chopped walnuts
3 cups all-purpose flour	or pecans

1. Preheat oven to 350 degrees. Grease and flour 10-inch Bundt pan. Cream margarine with sugar until light and fluffy. Add eggs one at a time, beating well after each addition.

2. Combine flour, baking powder, and nutmeg and add to creamed mixture alternately with sherry. Mix well after each addition. Blend in chopped nuts.

3. Pour batter into prepared pan. Bake 50 to 60 minutes. Let cake cool in pan 15 to 30 minutes before turning out onto cooling rack.

Serves 10 to 12

❧ PHYLLIS RINGEL, GREAT NECK HADASSAH, NEW YORK

Grandmother's Coffee Cake
(Kugelhopf)

3 cups sifted all-purpose flour
2 teaspoons baking powder
1 teaspoon baking soda
1/2 teaspoon salt
3/4 cup (1-1/2 sticks) unsalted
    butter, at room temperature
1-1/2 cups granulated sugar
Grated zest of 1 orange
3 eggs
1 cup sour cream
3/4 cup golden raisins

FILLING
1/2 cup packed brown sugar
1/3 cup sifted all-purpose flour
Grated zest of 1 large orange
1/4 cup (1/2 stick) unsalted
    butter, at room temperature
2 teaspoons ground cinnamon

GLAZE
1 cup confectioners' sugar
1 tablespoon orange liqueur
3 tablespoons fresh orange juice

1. Preheat oven to 350 degrees. Grease a 10-inch Bundt pan.

2. Sift flour with baking powder, baking soda, and salt. In another bowl, beat butter with granulated sugar and orange zest until combined; beat in eggs one at a time, beating well after each addition.

3. Add flour mixture alternately with sour cream to butter mixture and beat until smooth and creamy.

4. Pour two thirds of batter into prepared pan. Combine filling ingredients and sprinkle over batter in pan. Add raisins to remaining batter and pour over filling. Bake 50 minutes.

5. Remove cake from oven to wire rack and let cool 10 minutes, then turn out onto serving plate. Blend confectioners' sugar with liqueur and orange juice until smooth, and spread over warm cake.

Serves 12 to 15

◄ HADASSAH ISRAEL

Apple Banana Cake

2 cups all-purpose flour
2 tablespoons baking soda
1 teaspoon cinnamon
1/2 teaspoon salt
1/2 cup oil
2 eggs
1-1/2 cups sugar
1 teaspoon vanilla extract
2 medium bananas, mashed
4 cups peeled, cored, and
 chopped apples

1 cup chopped nuts
1/2 cup raisins (optional)
1/2 cup diced peaches or apricots

FROSTING
8 ounces confectioners' sugar
1/2 stick (4 tablespoons) unsalted
 margarine
4 ounces cream cheese
1-1/2 teaspoons vanilla extract

1. Preheat oven to 350 degrees. Grease and flour 13 x 9 inch baking pan.

2. Sift flour, baking soda, cinnamon, and salt and set aside. Beat oil, eggs, sugar, and vanilla extract. Stir in flour mixture and bananas and beat 3 minutes at medium speed.

3. Gently stir in apples, nuts, raisins, and peaches. Pour mixture into prepared pan. Bake 45 to 55 minutes. Allow to cool on wire rack.

4. Thoroughly combine frosting ingredients and spread on cake when cool.

Serves 20

◆ ESTHER BROWN, NORTH HILLS HADASSAH, PITTSBURGH, PENNSYLVANIA

Baklava Cake

1 cup milk
1-1/2 cups (3 sticks) unsalted
 butter, at room temperature
2 eggs, lightly beaten
4 cups all-purpose flour
4 teaspoons baking powder
1/4 teaspoon salt
1 cup chopped walnuts

2 tablespoons sugar
1/2 teaspoon ground cinnamon

SYRUP
1 cup sugar
3/4 cup honey
2 teaspoons fresh lemon juice

1. Preheat oven to 375 degrees. Grease 13 x 9 inch baking pan.

2. Heat milk until warm. Add butter and stir until butter is melted. Let cool, then transfer to large bowl. Stir in beaten eggs.

3. Sift flour with baking powder and salt; add to egg mixture, and beat well.

4. Mix nuts, 2 tablespoons sugar, and the cinnamon. Add to batter and spread in prepared pan. Bake 25 minutes, until a wooden toothpick inserted in the center comes out clean. Do not overbake. Cut into diamond shapes while still hot.

5. Boil 1 cup sugar, the honey, 3/4 cup water, and the lemon juice 5 minutes. Let cool and pour over cake.

Serves 20

◆§ RUTH ZANVILLE, SAN DIEGO HADASSAH, CALIFORNIA

Nut Torte

9 eggs, separated, at room temperature	8 teaspoons sugar
4 cups ground hazelnuts	1 tablespoon cornstarch
1-1/4 cups sugar	2 cups not too dry but not too sweet white wine
	Juice of half a lemon
WINE CREAM	3-ounce package kosher gelatin
4 eggs, separated, at room temperature	1/2 cup warm water

1. Preheat oven to 350 degrees for 30 minutes. Grease 10-inch springform pan. Beat 9 egg whites until stiff but not dry. Combine egg yolks, hazelnuts, and sugar, and fold in the beaten whites.

2. Put into prepared pan and bake 40 to 45 minutes. Turn the oven off, open the door, and let the cake cool in the oven 15 minutes.

3. Make the Wine Cream: In top of double boiler over simmering water, stir 4 egg yolks, the sugar, cornstarch, wine, and lemon juice. Keep stirring carefully until the mixture starts to thicken a bit. Beat egg whites and fold into the yolk mixture. Add gelatin and mix well. Refrigerate.

4. Remove sides of springform. Cut cake horizontally through the middle. Cover bottom half with whipped cream or Wine Cream and cover with the top half. Or leave the torte whole and serve it with either cream in a pretty bowl.

Serves 12 to 14

◆§ LOTTE STERN, ZAHAVA HADASSAH, NORTHBROOK, ILLINOIS

NUT TORTE: photo page 258.

Holle Grasch

At our Orthodox synagogue in Gerolzhoifen, a small town in northern Bavaria, we had a tradition that I'm afraid will be lost. Holle Grasch was a naming ceremony for every newborn. The name came from the Hebrew cholen, meaning the sick one, and grasch, German slang stemming from greisch-geschrien—crying, the thought being that the mother, the sick one, would cry out the name of the baby from her bed.

All the children of the town were invited. The newborn was in the bassinet and the children stood around in a little circle. The rabbi asked, "What shall the name of the baby be?" and we children picked up the bassinet and in unison called the name of the baby. This was done three times. The children received large fancy bags filled with sweets, and our parents were then served coffee and cake. My mother used to make a nut torte (see recipe page 257).

Lotte Stern, Zahava Hadassah, Northbrook, Illinois

HOLLE GRASCH. *Alis Guggenheim. 1950. Oil on canvas. The Israel Museum. Gift of Siegmund Weiner and Eva Weiner-Karo, Lucerne, Switzerland.*

Ruthe's Rugelach

DOUGH
5-1/2 cups all-purpose flour
1 pound (4 sticks) unsalted butter,
    at room temperature
1 cup sour cream
3/4 cup sugar
Pinch of salt

FILLING
1 cup sugar combined with 2
    tablespoons ground cinnamon
1/2 cup chopped walnuts
1/4 cup raisins

1. Put flour, butter, sour cream, 3/4 cup sugar, and the salt in a bowl and work it with your hands until they come clean, adding a little flour if needed. Divide dough into 4 equal sections. Wrap in plastic, and refrigerate at least 2 hours or overnight.

2. Preheat oven to 350 degrees Lightly butter cookie sheets or line with baking parchment.

3. On lightly floured surface, roll out one section of dough into a circle about 1/8-inch thick. Cut into 12 wedges and sprinkle with 1/4 cup sugar-cinnamon mixture, 2 tablespoons chopped nuts, and 1 tablespoon raisins. Roll up each wedge from wide end and put on prepared cookie sheets points down, about an inch apart. Repeat with remaining dough and filling. Bake about 20 minutes, or until rugelach start to show some color. Let cool on wire rack.

Makes about 4 pounds dough, 4 dozen cookies

•≥ HENRIETTA GOLDMAN, JACKSONVILLE HADASSAH, FLORIDA

Oneg Shabbat Potato Chip Cookies

1-1/2 cups (3 sticks) unsalted
    margarine, at room
    temperature
1-1/2 cups sugar
2 eggs

2 teaspoons vanilla extract
2-1/2 cups all-purpose flour
1-1/2 cups finely crushed unsalted
    potato chips
1-1/2 cups finely chopped pecans

Preheat oven to 375 degrees. Cream margarine with sugar, eggs, and vanilla extract. Add flour (dough should be soft; do not add extra flour), potato chips, and nuts and mix well. Drop by teaspoons an inch apart onto ungreased cookie sheets. Bake 8 to 10 minutes, until edges are light brown.

Makes 3 to 4 dozen

•≥ BARBARA BRANDE, BIRMINGHAM HADASSAH, ALABAMA

TIP
This is a very crisp, light cookie that freezes well but will lose its crispness if not protected from humidity.

RUTHE'S RUGELACH, recipe above, right.

Index